Windows® 2000 Professional For Dummies®

W9-BLI-456

Network Hints

- Don't write down your password or share it with somebody else.
- Choose a password that's easy for you to remember but hard for someone else to guess: The name of your neighbor's dog, for example, or the color of your best friend's car.
- Use the password-protected screen saver when you leave your cubicle to gossip.
- Double-click the My Network Places icon to access files and folders on other computers.
- Always log off before turning off your computer. (Ask your Network Administrator if you're supposed to turn your computer off at all; some computers stay on 24 hours.)

Helpful Hints

- Don't turn off your computer without giving Windows 2000 Professional fair warning. First, click on the Start button and then choose Shut Down from the menu. When Windows asks what you want the computer to do, select Shut down. Finally, when Windows 2000 says it's all right to turn off your computer, go ahead and turn it off.
- Don't know what a certain button does in a program? Rest your mouse pointer over the button for a few seconds; a helpful box often pops up to explain the button's purpose.
- If you're baffled, try pressing F1, that "function key" in the upper-left corner of your keyboard. A "help" window appears, bringing hints on your current program.
- To quickly organize the windows on the Desktop, click on the taskbar's clock with your right mouse button. When a menu appears, click on one of the tile options, and all your open windows will be neatly tiled across your screen.
- To keep icons organized in neat rows across your Desktop or in windows, click on the icon's background. When the menu pops up, choose Auto Arrange from the Arrange Icons menu.

Handling Files within a Program

To Do This . . .	Do This . . .
Start a new file	Press Alt, F, N.
Open an existing file	Press Alt, F, O.
Save a file	Press Alt, F, S.
Save a file under a new name	Press Alt, F, A.
Print a file	Press Alt, F, P.

Cut and Paste Stuff

To Do This . . .	Press These Keys . . .
Copy highlighted stuff to the Clipboard	Ctrl+C or Ctrl+Insert.
Cut highlighted stuff to the Clipboard	Ctrl+X or Shift+Delete.
Paste stuff from the Clipboard to the current window	Ctrl+V or Shift+Insert.
Copy an entire screen to the Clipboard	PrintScreen
Copy the current window to the Clipboard	Alt+PrintScreen.

For Dummies: Bestselling Book Series for Beginners

Windows® 2000 Professional For Dummies®

Organizing a Pile of Windows

To Do This . . .	Do This . . .
See a list of all windows	Look at the icons on the taskbar.
Move from one window to another window	Press Alt+Tab+Tab or click on the window's name on the taskbar.
Tile the windows across the screen	Click on an empty part of the taskbar with the *right* mouse button and then click on Tile Windows Horizontally or Tile Windows Vertically.
Cascade the windows across the screen	Click on an empty part of the taskbar with the *right* mouse button and then click on Cascade Windows.
Shrink a window into a taskbar button	Click on the window, press Alt+spacebar, and press N.
Shrink all the windows	Click the Desktop icon on the Quick Launch bar.

My Computer and Windows Explorer

To Do This . . .	Do This . . .
Copy a file to another location on the *same* disk drive	Hold down Ctrl and drag it there.
Copy a file to a *different* disk drive	Drag it there.
Move a file to another location on the *same* disk drive	Drag it there.
Move a file to a *different* disk drive	Hold down Shift and drag it there.
Remember how to copy or move files	Hold down the *right* mouse button while dragging and then choose Copy or Move from the menu.
Select several files	Hold down Ctrl and click on the filenames.
Look at a different directory	Double-click on that directory's icon.

For Dummies: Bestselling Book Series for Beginners

Windows® 2000 Professional

FOR

DUMMIES®

Windows® 2000 Professional FOR DUMMIES®

by Andy Rathbone and Sharon Crawford

Hungry Minds™

Best-Selling Books • Digital Downloads • e-Books • Answer Networks • e-Newsletters • Branded Web Sites • e-Learning

New York, NY ◆ Cleveland, OH ◆ Indianapolis, IN

Windows® 2000 Professional For Dummies®

Published by
Hungry Minds, Inc.
909 Third Avenue
New York, NY 10022
www.hungryminds.com
www.dummies.com

Library of Congress Catalog Card No.: 99-66324

ISBN: 0-7645-0641-2

Printed in the United States of America

10 9 8 7

1B/RT/QW/QR/IN

Distributed in the United States by Hungry Minds, Inc.

Distributed by CDG Books Canada Inc. for Canada; by Transworld Publishers Limited in the United Kingdom; by IDG Norge Books for Norway; by IDG Sweden Books for Sweden; by IDG Books Australia Publishing Corporation Pty. Ltd. for Australia and New Zealand; by TransQuest Publishers Pte Ltd. for Singapore, Malaysia, Thailand, Indonesia, and Hong Kong; by Gotop Information Inc. for Taiwan; by ICG Muse, Inc. for Japan; by Intersoft for South Africa; by Eyrolles for France; by International Thomson Publishing for Germany, Austria and Switzerland; by Distribuidora Cuspide for Argentina; by LR International for Brazil; by Galileo Libros for Chile; by Ediciones ZETA S.C.R. Ltda. for Peru; by WS Computer Publishing Corporation, Inc., for the Philippines; by Contemporanea de Ediciones for Venezuela; by Express Computer Distributors for the Caribbean and West Indies; by Micronesia Media Distributor, Inc. for Micronesia; by Chips Computadoras S.A. de C.V. for Mexico; by Editorial Norma de Panama S.A. for Panama; by American Bookshops for Finland.

For general information on Hungry Minds' products and services please contact our Customer Care Department within the U.S. at 800-762-2974, outside the U.S. at 317-572-3993 or fax 317-572-4002.

For sales inquiries and reseller information, including discounts, premium and bulk quantity sales, and foreign-language translations, please contact our Customer Care Department at 800-434-3422, fax 317-572-4002, or write to Hungry Minds, Inc., Attn: Customer Care Department, 10475 Crosspoint Boulevard, Indianapolis, IN 46256.

For information on licensing foreign or domestic rights, please contact our Sub-Rights Customer Care Department at 212-884-5000.

For information on using Hungry Minds' products and services in the classroom or for ordering examination copies, please contact our Educational Sales Department at 800-434-2086 or fax 317-572-4005.

For press review copies, author interviews, or other publicity information, please contact our Public Relations Department at 317-572-3168 or fax 317-572-4168.

For authorization to photocopy items for corporate, personal, or educational use, please contact Copyright Clearance Center, 222 Rosewood Drive, Danvers, MA 01923, or fax 978-750-4470.

Hungry Minds is a trademark of Hungry Minds, Inc.

About the Authors

Andy Rathbone started geeking around with computers in 1985 when he bought a boxy CP/M Keypro 2X with lime-green letters. Like other budding nerds, he soon began playing with null-modem adapters, dialing up computer bulletin boards, and working part-time at Radio Shack.

Andy began combining his two interests, words and computers, by selling articles to a local computer magazine. During the next few years, Andy started ghostwriting computer books for more famous computer authors, as well as writing several hundred articles about computers for technoid publications like *Supercomputing Review, CompuServe Magazine, ID Systems, DataPro,* and *Shareware.*

In 1992, Andy and *DOS For Dummies* author/legend Dan Gookin teamed up to write *PCs For Dummies,* which was runner-up in the Computer Press Association's 1993 awards. Andy subsequently wrote the first edition of *Windows For Dummies* as well as *Windows 95 For Dummies* and *Windows 98 For Dummies.* He has also written *MP3 For Dummies* and *Upgrading and Fixing PCs For Dummies.*

Andy lives with his most excellent wife, Tina, and their cat in San Diego, California. When not writing, he fiddles with his MIDI synthesizer and tries to keep the cat off both keyboards.

Like Andy, **Sharon Crawford** came to computers in a roundabout way. In the early '80s, she was an electrician repairing subway cars in New York City. Though it seems astonishing that anyone would want to leave such a glamour job, she did.

After moving home to California, she went back to school to study the finer points of electronics and in 1988, armed with a degree and some ingenious lies, she landed her first technical writing job.

After a couple of years, Sharon was fortunate enough to get a job in the technical department of a computer book publishing house. After a few months, she convinced a gullible acquisitions editor to give her a shot at a book. Since then, Sharon and her husband Charlie Russel have collaborated on many books including *NT and UNIX Intranet Secrets* (IDG Books Worldwide, Inc.), *Windows 2000 Server Administrator's Companion* (Microsoft Press), and *Upgrading to Windows 98* (Sybex).

Sharon and Charlie live in a nice house on a hill with many cats and one dog. They have given up on trying to keep cats off any of the keyboards.

Publisher's Acknowledgments

We're proud of this book; please send us your comments through our Online Registration Form located at www.dummies.com.

Some of the people who helped bring this book to market include the following:

Acquisitions, Editorial, and Media Development

Associate Project Editor: Darren Meiss

Acquisitions Editor: Steven H. Hayes

Technical Editor: Jim McCarter

Associate Permissions Editor: Carmen Krikorian

Media Development Coordinator: Megan Roney

Editorial Manager: Rev Mengle

Media Development Manager: Heather Heath Dismore

Editorial Assistant: Jamila Pree

Production

Project Coordinator: Regina Snyder

Layout and Graphics: Amy M. Adrian, Brian Drumm, Angela F. Hunckler, Kate Jenkins, Barry Offringa, Tracy Oliver, Jill Piscitelli, Brent Savage, Janet Seib, Michael A. Sullivan, Doug Rollison, Brian Torwelle, Mary Jo Weis, Dan Whetstine

Proofreaders: Laura Albert, Vickie Broyles, John Greenough, Joanne Keaton, Marianne Santy, Rebecca Senninger

Indexer: Sharon Hilgenberg

General and Administrative

Hungry Minds Technology Publishing Group: Richard Swadley, Vice President and Executive Group Publisher; Bob Ipsen, Vice President and Group Publisher; Joseph Wikert, Vice President and Publisher; Barry Pruett, Vice President and Publisher; Mary Bednarek, Editorial Director; Mary C. Corder, Editorial Director; Andy Cummings, Editorial Director

Hungry Minds Manufacturing: Ivor Parker, Vice President, Manufacturing

Hungry Minds Marketing: John Helmus, Assistant Vice President, Director of Marketing

Hungry Minds Production for Branded Press: Debbie Stailey, Production Director

Hungry Minds Sales: Michael Violano, Vice President, International Sales and Sub Rights

Contents at a Glance

Cartoons at a Glance

By Rich Tennant

page 71

page 351

page 313

page 205

page 331

page 7

Cartoon Information:
Fax: 978-546-7747
E-Mail: richtennant@the5thwave.com
World Wide Web: www.the5thwave.com

Table of Contents

Chapter 3: Windows 2000 Stuff Everybody Thinks You Already Know 37

Chapter 4: Network Things Administrators Think You Already Know 59

Introduction

Welcome to *Windows 2000 Professional For Dummies*! Of course, you're no dummy. You're just one of the millions who *feel* like a dummy when sitting in front of a computer. This book looks similar to earlier *Windows For Dummies* books you may have seen through the years, but it's been completely revamped to describe Windows 2000 Professional, the "business" version of Microsoft Windows. If you're moving up to Windows 2000 Professional from Windows NT 4 or Windows 98 or Windows 95, you'll find plenty of similarities, thank goodness.

Regardless of your Windows heritage, the basic premise of the book boils down to this: Some people want to be Windows wizards. They love interacting with dialog boxes. In their free moments, they randomly press keys on their keyboards, hoping to stumble onto a hidden, undocumented feature. They memorize long strings of computer commands while they're organizing their socks-and-underwear drawer.

And you? Well, you're light-years ahead of most computer nerds. You can make conversation with a neighbor without mumbling about the latest "Flash ROM Upgrades," for example. But when it comes to Windows and computers, the fascination just isn't there. You just want to get your work done, go home, feed the dog, walk the cat, and relax for a while. You have no intention of changing, and nothing's wrong with that.

That's where this book comes in handy. You'll pick up a few chunks of useful computing information while reading it. You certainly won't become a Windows 2000 wizard, but you'll know enough to get by quickly, cleanly, and with a minimum of pain so you can move on to the more pleasant things in life.

About This Book

Don't try to read this book in one sitting; you don't need to. Instead, treat this book like a dictionary or small encyclopedia. Turn to the page with the information you need, and say, "Ah, so that's what that's supposed to mean." Then put down the book and move on.

Don't bother trying to remember all the Windows buzzwords, like *NetBEUI* or *domain controller*. Leave that stuff for the computer geeks. In fact, if anything technical comes up in a chapter, a road sign warns you well in advance. That way, you can either slow down to read it or speed on around it.

You won't find any fancy computer jargon in this book. Instead, you find subjects like these, discussed in plain old English:

- Preparing yourself to brave the cold, corporate world of Windows 2000
- Figuring out what to do when the network turns into a "not work"
- Starting programs by clicking on little buttons
- Making sure that your favorite old programs still run under the new Windows 2000
- Finding common-language translations for those awfully technical networking terms

There's nothing to memorize and nothing to learn. Just turn to the right page, read the brief explanation, and get back to work. Unlike other books, this one enables you to bypass any technical hoopla and yet still get your work done.

How to Use This Book

Something in Windows 2000 will eventually leave you scratching your head. No other program brings so many buttons, bars, or babble to the screen. When something in Windows 2000 has you stumped, use this book as a reference. Look for the troublesome topic in this book's table of contents or index. The table of contents lists chapter and section titles and page numbers. The index lists topics and page numbers. Page through the table of contents or index to the spot that deals with that particular bit of computer obscurity, read only what you have to, close the book, and apply what you've read.

There's no learning involved. There's no remembering, either, unless you want to remember something so you don't have to grab the book the next time the same situation comes up.

If you're feeling spunky and want to learn something, read a little further. You'll find a few completely voluntary extra details or some cross-references to check out. There's no pressure, though. You won't be forced to learn anything that you don't want to or that you simply don't have time for.

If you have to type something into a little box on the computer screen, you see easy-to-follow text like this:

TYPE THESE LETTERS

In the preceding example, you type **TYPE THESE LETTERS** into the little box on-screen and then press the keyboard's Enter key. Typing words into a computer can be confusing, so a description of what you're supposed to type usually follows. That way, you can type the words exactly as they're supposed to be typed.

You won't, for example, accidentally type **"TYPE THESE LETTERS"** — complete with quotation marks. Computers are awfully picky about quotation marks and can do odd things when they see them.

Whenever we describe a message or information that you see on the screen, We present it like this:

```
This is a message on-screen.
```

Or if a relevant picture or message pops up onto the screen, you see the picture or message in the book.

This book doesn't wimp out by saying, "For further information, consult your manual." No need to pull on your wading boots. This book covers everything you need to know to use Windows 2000 Professional. The only thing you don't find is technical information about using Windows 2000 Server.

See, Windows 2000 comes in two flavors: Professional and Server. The administrator who runs the complicated network stuff uses the Server version of Windows 2000. That software comes with bunches of extra parts that make the administrators chew on pencil erasers and look worried. Instead, you use the Professional variety of Windows 2000. The Professional version is designed for people who use computers to get their work done — not for technical people who have turned computers into their line of work.

And What about You?

Well, chances are that you have a computer. You have Windows 2000 — you use it at your office or perhaps in your home. You know what you want the computer to do. The problem is making the computer do what you want it to do. You've gotten by one way or another, hopefully with the help of a computer guru — either a friend at the office or somebody down the street. Unfortunately, though, that computer guru isn't always around. This book can be a substitute for the computer guru during your times of need. Keep a fresh bag of Doritos in your desk drawer, however, just in case you need a quick bribe.

How This Book Is Organized

The information in this book has been well sifted. The book contains six parts, and each part is divided into chapters related to the part's theme. Each chapter is divided into short sections to help you navigate the stormy seas of Windows 2000. Sometimes, you may find what you're looking for in a small, boxed tip. Other times, you may need to cruise through an entire section or chapter. It's up to you and the particular task at hand.

Here are the categories (the envelope, please).

Part I: Intro to Windows 2000 (Bare-Bones Stuff)

This book starts out with the basics. You find out how to turn on your computer and log onto the network. You examine all your computer's parts and what Windows 2000 does to them. This part explains all the Windows 2000 stuff that everybody thinks you already know; plus, it explains all that networking stuff the company's Network Administrator assumes you already know.

You discover whether your computer has enough oomph to run Windows 2000, or whether its lack of horsepower would make decent water-cooler conversation. And you end this part (with great relief) by turning off your computer.

Part II: Making Windows 2000 Do Something

The biggest problem with using Windows 2000 isn't opening programs or moving windows around on-screen. It's making Windows 2000 do something useful. Here, you find ways to overcome the frustratingly playful tendencies that Windows 2000 displays so you can force it to shovel the walkway or blow leaves off the driveway.

Or if your computer is connected to everybody else's computer, you find out how to send and receive files from Jerry and Kathy's computer across the hall, all the while using e-mail to decide where to eat lunch that day.

Part III: Using Windows 2000 Applications

Windows 2000 comes with a whole bunch of free programs. In this part, you find practical information about your new word processor, automatic phone dialer, Paint program, calculator, and bunches of other goodies. (If your computer has a CD-ROM drive, you even find out how to smuggle in some earphones and listen to your favorite jazz CDs while working.)

Part IV: Been There, Done That: Quick References for Moving to Windows 2000

Millions of people are using other versions of Windows, like Windows NT 4, Windows 95, and Windows 98. That means millions of people are muttering, "How do I make Windows 2000 work like my other version of Windows?" This part of the book offers quick tips, work-arounds, and quick-reference charts to help you get up and running with Windows 2000 Professional.

Part V: Getting Help

Are your windows stuck? Broken? Do you need new screens? Although glass doesn't shatter when Windows 2000 crashes, those crashes can still hurt. In this part, you find some soothing salves for the most painful and irritating maladies.

Part VI: The Part of Tens

Everybody loves lists (unless they're published by the IRS and your name is on them). This part contains lists of Windows 2000-related trivia: ten new features in Windows 2000, ten Windows 2000 flaws (and how to work around them), and ten (or so) Windows 2000 icons and what they mean — things like that.

Icons Used in This Book

Already seen Windows 2000, or any other version of Windows? Then you've probably noticed its icons, which are little pictures for starting various programs. The icons in this book fit right in. They're even a little easier to figure out:

Watch out! This signpost warns you that pointless technical information is coming around the bend. Swerve away from this icon, and you're safe from the nerdy technical drivel.

This icon alerts you to information that makes computing easier. For example, swinging your mouse overhead like a lasso is a great way to distract your coworkers when you don't want them to know you've forgotten your password for the third time that week.

Don't forget to remember these important points. (Or at least dog-ear the pages so you can look them up again a few days later.)

The computer itself won't explode while you're performing the delicate operations associated with this icon. Still, wearing gloves and proceeding with caution is a good idea when this icon is near.

Face it: Some computer stuff definitely falls squarely into the realm of the pocket-protector crowd. Don't even bother attempting any of the maneuvers marked by this stuff. Just lean back in your chair, raise your hand, and slowly wave it back and forth until the office's Network Administrator comes over to fix the problem.

Where to Go from Here

Now you're ready for action. Give the pages a quick flip and maybe scan through a few sections that you know you'll need later. And remember: This is your book — your weapon against the computer criminals who've inflicted this whole complicated computer concept on you. So personalize your sword: Circle the paragraphs you find useful, highlight key concepts, cover up the technical drivel with sticky notes, and draw smiley faces in the margins. The more you mark up the book, the easier it will be for you to find the important stuff when you need it a few weeks later.

Part I

Intro to Windows 2000 (Bare-Bones Stuff)

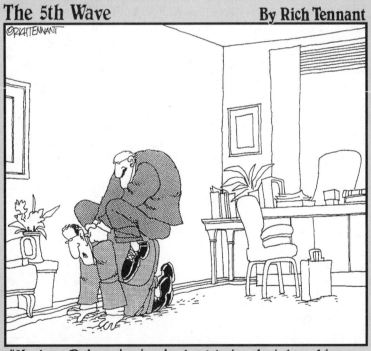

"You know, Phil, most network administrators don't demand horsey-rides in exchange for helping users remember their password."

In this part . . .

Windows 2000 is an exciting, modern way to use the computer. That means it's as confusing as a VCR's remote control. Even the most wizened old computer buffs can stumble in this land of logons, logoffs, and bizarre oddities like *peer-to-peer networking*.

Have you been thrust in front of a computer at work, where the Person in Charge told you that Windows 2000 is "easy-to-use"? Well, Windows 2000 can be intuitive, but that doesn't mean it's as easy to figure out as a hammer.

In fact, most people are dragged into Windows 2000 without a choice. Maybe the gurus installed Windows 2000 at the office, where everyone had to learn it except for John, who cashed out his stock options and escaped to Fiji the night before it was installed.

You can adjust to Windows 2000, however, just like you eventually learned to live with the awful-tasting tap water when you visited your friends in San Diego.

Whatever your situation, this part keeps things safe and sane, with the water flowing smoothly. If you're new to computers, the first chapter answers the question you've been afraid to ask around the lunch room: "Just what is this Windows thing, anyway?"

Chapter 1

What Is Windows 2000?

Many years ago, a tiny company called Microsoft created a strange piece of computer software called Windows. It didn't catch on real fast because it looked weird and barely worked.

Microsoft kept trying, however, and now Windows software comes already installed on millions of new computers around the world. In fact, Windows is more than just software — it has become a way of life. When a new version is due, it's like *Star Wars* for computer junkies — hordes of them stay up all night just to be first in line when the computer stores open.

Many people will tell you that Microsoft Windows has grown into a computer paradise, filled with beautiful graphics and relaxing menus. But be prepared: Windows is no panacea, no matter how you want to pronounce that word. When software becomes more friendly, computers seem to become more complicated.

Besides, the simplest-looking things are often the most treacherous. Remember the first time you ate with chopsticks?

This chapter looks at a version of Windows called Windows 2000. The chapter explains what Windows 2000 is and what it's supposed to do. It explains how Windows 2000 differs from other versions of Windows you may have heard about.

Plus, you find out how Windows 2000 is really *two* programs — the relatively simple Windows 2000 Professional and the hugely complicated Windows 2000 Server. (Thank goodness you only have to mess with Windows 2000 Professional in this book. . . .)

What Is This Windows Stuff, Anyway?

Windows is just another computer program, like zillions of other pieces of software lining the store shelves. But it's not a program in the normal sense — a letter-writing program, for example, or a cheery game like *Death Rocket Flame Killers.* Rather, Windows completely changes the way you work with your computer.

In the early days, computer programs clung to a "typewriter" look. People typed letters and numbers on a keyboard . The computer listened and responded by placing letters and numbers on a screen. This time-tested system worked well. But it took a long time to learn, and it was as boring as an oral hygiene pamphlet.

Of course, these text-based systems were boring — they were designed by computer geeks for other computer geeks. They thought that computers would be forever isolated in windowless rooms where tedious fellows in white lab coats jotted down notes while the big reels whirled. Nobody expected normal people to use computers — especially not in their offices, their dens, or, heaven help us, their kitchens.

 ✔ Windows software dumps the old typewriter analogy and updates the *look* of computers. Windows replaces the words and numbers with pictures and buttons. It's splashy and modern, like an expensive new coffeemaker.

 ✔ Because Windows software looks and acts so differently from the old software, learning it can take a few days. After all, you probably couldn't make perfect coffee the first day you tried, either.

 ✔ Windows 2000 is the latest version of Windows NT software. Windows 2000 is the version that updates Windows NT 4, which updated Windows NT 3.51, which updated Windows NT 3.50 — you get the idea.

What Does Windows 2000 Do?

Like the mother with the whistle in the lunch court, Windows controls all the parts of your computer. You turn on your computer, Windows 2000 starts and you start running Windows programs. Each program runs in its own little *window* on-screen. Yet Windows keeps things safe, even if the programs start throwing food at each other.

Windows 2000 is usually on a *network,* meaning it can let your computer talk to other computers, squirting information through little cables.

While it's keeping order, Windows makes computing quite a bit easier. Back in the bad old days, computers were instructed by means of the *command line.* If you wanted to copy a file, you had to tell the computer exactly what you wanted to do and exactly where to find the file. So, for example, to copy a file from your computer's hard drive to a floppy disk, you could easily find yourself having to type:

```
COPY C:\WORDS\REPORTS\CORP\BOON\JULY15.DOC A:\CORP
```

One little letter out of place and you'd get a rude error message, like `File Not Found`. These were tense times for computer users. You had to memorize all the programs' names and remember where the programs lived on the computer. When it came to giving directions or offering tips, the computer was as useless as a Pittsburgh phone book in Paris.

Windows replaces most of the text with little pictures, or *icons,* as shown in Figure 1-1. To copy a file onto a floppy disk in Windows, for example, you look for the picture representing your file. It may look something like Figure 1-1.

Figure 1-1:
Windows replaces the text-based commands with little push-button pictures.

Then you look for the picture of the floppy drive, as shown in Figure 1-2.

Figure 1-2:
By manipulating the pictures, you can manipulate your files; here, a file is being copied to a floppy disk, for example.

By pointing at the picture of the file with the mouse, holding down the mouse button, dragging the file to the floppy drive, and letting go of the mouse button, you can quickly and easily copy the file to the floppy disk. (Chapter 18 shows how to copy files — and do just about anything else — in four steps or less.)

- ✔ Windows fills the screen with lots of fun little boxes, pictures, and push-buttons; older-style computers were for no-nonsense minimalists who never put bumper stickers on their cars.

- ✔ A computer environment like Windows that uses little pictures and symbols is called a *graphical user interface,* or GUI (pronounced *gooey,* believe it or not). Pictures require more computing horsepower than letters and numbers, so Windows 2000 requires a relatively powerful computer. (You can find a list of its requirements in Chapter 2.)

- ✔ Windows gets its name from all the cute little windows on-screen. Each window shows some information: a picture, perhaps, or a program you're running. You can put several windows on-screen at the same time and jump from window to window, visiting different programs. (Actually, the windows look like little squares, but who would buy a program called Squares?)

- ✔ When the word *Windows* starts with a capital letter, it refers to the Windows program. When the word *windows* starts with a lowercase letter, it refers to windows you see on-screen. When the word Windows ends with 2000, it refers to Windows 2000 specifically.

Because Windows uses graphics, it's much easier to use than to describe. To tell someone how to move through a document in a text-based program, you simply say, "Press the PgDn key." In Windows, you say, "Click in the vertical scroll bar beneath the scroll box." Those directions sound awfully weird, but after you've done it, you'll say, "Oh, is that all? Golly!" (Plus, you can still press the PgDn key in Windows if you don't want to use the mouse.)

With Windows 2000, your Desktop doesn't have to look like a typewritten page *or* a desktop — instead you can dress it up like an Internet Web page as shown in Figure 1-3. (More about Web pages in Chapter 16.) Using the "Active Desktop," you can have connections to Internet sites that update on schedule.

In fact, you can have your screen look like the "classic" Windows desktop or customize it any of a zillion ways. (More on fiddling around with the Desktop in Chapter 12.)

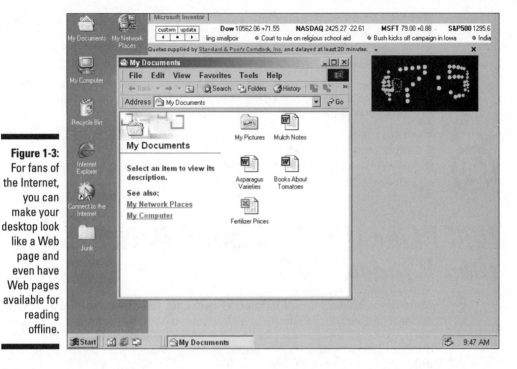

Figure 1-3:
For fans of
the Internet,
you can
make your
desktop look
like a Web
page and
even have
Web pages
available for
reading
offline.

Why Should I Bother Using Windows 2000?

Most Windows 2000 users don't have a choice. They have to use Windows 2000, or they don't get a paycheck. See, Windows 2000 is designed for large *networks* — huge groups of linked computers that live in large buildings decorated along the top with gargoyles and artichokes. Windows 2000 isn't particularly designed for home users or small offices with small networks — though it's certainly used in such places.

If you or your company isn't running a large network, then plain old Windows 95 or Windows 98 probably meets your needs better than Windows 2000.

✔ Any version of Windows can be networked. In fact, Windows 95 and Windows 98 are used on networks even more than Windows 2000 Professional. However, Windows 2000 can be made more secure (snoopproof), so corporations like it.

✔ While Windows 95 and Windows 98 can be networked, they're primarily used on freestanding desktop machines. Windows 2000 Professional can also be used as a freestanding machine, but its main function in life is to be on a big network.

- Both Windows 95 and Windows 98 are a little easier to set up and configure than Windows 2000. Now that Windows 2000 comes with a feature called "Plug and Play," modems, sound cards, and printers are just about as easy to install as on Windows 95 and Windows 98 machines.

- Windows 2000 takes a lot more disk space than Windows 95 or Windows 98. Even with a *big* hard drive, who wants to give up more than 500 MB just for Windows 2000?

- Don't know what version of Windows 2000 you're running? Click on the My Computer icon with your right mouse button, then choose Properties from the menu that appears. You should spot the version number hidden in the screen that appears.

Will I Like Windows 2000 Better than Windows NT?

Down in the coffee room, Windows NT users are exchanging nervous glances and whispering the Big Question: Will Windows 2000 be a total pain, crash the network, clog the e-mail, and make it impossible for Kathy and Jeff to organize the party at the pizza pub? Not likely. Windows 2000 actually offers many improvements over Windows NT.

- Windows 2000 is easier to install and works with more different kinds of hardware. Got a scanner? A digital camera? Both will work with less hassle than ever before. And everyday hardware such as printers and soundcards are a piece of cake because Windows 2000 has the Plug and Play technology pioneered in Windows 95 and improved for Windows 98.

- You'll see lots more little buttons with pictures on them — *icons* — used in Windows 2000 programs. Don't know what the icon with the little policeman picture is supposed to do? Unlike earlier versions of Windows NT, Windows 2000 lets you rest your mouse pointer over the icon and, after a few seconds, a window pops up on-screen, explaining the icon's reason for living.

- Got a regular Internet connection? Not only can you make your Desktop look like a Web page, you can have bits of Web pages imbedded on your Desktop — running in the background — and listen to the Internet radio all at the same time.

- Windows 2000 can automatically schedule maintenance tasks in the background, to keep itself tuned up and in good running condition. Using your Internet connection, Windows 2000 can automatically grab files needed to keep it up-to-date.

What's the Difference between Windows 2000 Professional and Windows 2000 Server?

Windows 2000 software, like Windows NT, comes in two versions. One is called *Windows 2000 Server,* and the other is called *Windows 2000 Professional.* They look quite similar but perform very different functions.

Think of them like this: Windows 2000 Professional works sort of like a telephone. You use it to connect to other telephones and talk to other people. If you have a Touch-Tone phone, you can do fancy things, like call the water company and tell them to skip a delivery. Of course, Windows 2000 Professional isn't a telephone; but, like a telephone that places calls, Windows 2000 Professional links computers to a more centralized area in order to move information around.

That "centralized area" is where Windows 2000 Server lives, and it works more like a telephone switchboard. It's the device that controls all the incoming and outgoing calls and decides which callers get busy signals when two people call at the same time. No, it's not a real switchboard. But Windows 2000 Server runs on the computer that all the workstations connect to when sending and receiving information from each other.

Windows 2000 Server is much more complicated than Windows 2000 Professional. It's not just more expensive (though it is), it's also designed to carry the weight of network transactions, which Windows 2000 Professional is not. In fact, even at 500+ MB, Windows 2000 Professional is a lean, mean, fighting machine compared to Windows 2000 Server.

✔ If you *are* asked to use Windows 2000 Server, it's only because your boss plans to turn you into that most feared of creatures, the dreaded Network Administrator. Ask for a big raise. Then ask for a bigger one. Then think about emigrating.

✔ On the other hand, it may be that you're going to be a sort of assistant administrator — handling some very specific task that the real Network Administrator wants to get rid of. This can be even worse news because you'll have the responsibility and probably not get any of the credit.

✔ You may have occasion to log onto a computer running Windows 2000 Server, but unless your account on the network has administrator's rights, you won't be able to get at any of the truly dangerous stuff. In fact, whatever machine you use for logging onto the network, your Desktop will look just like it did the last time you logged off (anywhere on the network).

✔ Windows 2000 Server requires a more powerful computer than Windows 2000 Professional. This is partially because of the software and partially because administrators lust after powerful computers the way teenage boys lust after muscle cars.

Bracing Yourself for Windows 2000

When running Windows 2000, you'll notice that an awful lot happens at the same time. Its many different parts run around like hamsters with an open cage door. Programs cover each other up on the screen. They overlap corners, hiding each other's important parts. Occasionally, they simply disappear.

Be prepared for a bit of frustration when things don't behave properly. Of course, you'll occasionally be tempted to stand up, yell, and toss a nearby stapler across the room. After that, calmly pick up this book, find the trouble spot listed in the Index, and turn to the page with the answer.

✔ Windows software may be accommodating, but that can cause problems, too. For example, Windows 2000 often offers more than three ways for you to perform the same computing task. Don't bother memorizing each command. Just choose one method that works for you and stick with it.

✔ You can decorate the Desktop many different ways, but none of them will go away, so don't feel like you have to be in a big hurry to find every variation. You may end up liking something that didn't appeal to you at first.

✔ Windows 2000 runs best on a powerful computer with the key word *Pentium* (or maybe *testosterone*) somewhere in the description. It also runs on special types of computers called PowerPCs, Digital Alpha RISC, or MIPS RISC. You can find the impressive computer requirements for Windows 2000 in Chapter 2.

Chapter 2

Boring Hardware Talk

. . . .

In This Chapter

▶ Figuring out the names for the gizmos and gadgets on the computer

▶ Understanding what all those things do

▶ Finding out what stuff you need in order to use Windows 2000 Professional

. . . .

This chapter describes computer gizmos and gadgets. Go ahead and ignore it. Who cares what all your computer gadgetry is called? Unless your computer is beeping like a deranged microwave, don't bother messing with it. Just dog-ear the top of this page, say, "So that's where all that stuff is explained," and keep going.

In Windows 2000 Professional, you just press the buttons. Windows 2000 Professional scoots over to the right part of your computer and kick-starts the action. In case Windows 2000 Professional stubs a toe, this chapter holds the Band-Aids. And as always, the foul-smelling technical chunks are clearly marked; just hold your nose while gingerly stepping over them.

The Computer

Most likely, your computer is that beige box with all the cables. That box is probably connected to a bunch of other beige boxes, and they all most likely answer to names like IBM (or IBM-compatible), DEC Alpha, PowerPC, Silicon Graphics Workstation, or something with the word MIPS on the case. Whereas earlier versions of Windows — like Windows 95 and Windows 98 — could run only on IBM or IBM-compatible computers (the computers currently found in most homes and small offices), Windows 2000 Professional can run on much larger computers.

(Yawn. Hey, you were warned that this chapter would be boring.)

- Windows 2000 Professional is an operating system. An *operating system* functions as the computer's consciousness, so to speak, making sure that your computer's internal organs stay alive and ready to perform your computing tasks.

- Like earlier versions of Windows, Windows 2000 Professional can run on an IBM or IBM-compatible. But it can also run on larger, more powerful computers known as *workstations.* Costing megabucks, most workstations have macho names, like "FirePower X-Ultra ES4100" or "MIPS ArcSystem Magnum PC-5000."

- Thinking of grabbing a copy of Windows 2000 Professional from the DEC Alpha software shelf at work and running it on your Pentium at home? It won't work. See, Windows 2000 Professional works on a DEC Alpha and an Intel-based Pentium, and it looks the same on both systems. But you need a Pentium version of Windows 2000 Professional for the Pentium, and a DEC Alpha version of Windows 2000 Professional for the DEC Alpha workstation. The same version of Windows 2000 Professional won't run on both a Pentium and a DEC Alpha computer.

- PCs are called PCs because the original prototype of today's machines was the IBM PC. After a while, most of the computers being made were not from IBM — but the original PC was still around — so to make it clear what was being described, anything that wasn't an Apple was "IBM-compatible." Now that the original PC has gone to the great Nerd Museum in the Sky, all the heirs are again called PCs. (Hard to believe, but *some* people find this fascinating.)

- You can run Windows 2000 Professional on particularly muscular laptops and notebook computers, with Pentium microprocessors. At this point though, palmtops are relative weaklings and are limited to Windows CE — an itty-bitty version of Windows.

  Laptop users, rejoice: Windows 2000 Professional supports PC Cards (formerly known as PCMCIA cards) and advanced power management so it won't drain your batteries in a hurry.

The Microprocessor

The computer's brain is a small chip of silicon buried deep inside the computer's case. Resembling a Moon Pie with square corners (though not nearly as tasty), this little box is the *microprocessor,* but nerds tend to call it a *central processing unit,* or CPU. (You've probably seen flashy TV commercials with the punch line "Intel Inside," because Intel makes about 80 percent of the CPUs for IBM-style computers.)

The entire computer is sometimes described in terms of the processor. For example, it'll be called a Pentium II 450 or a Celeron 400. The first part is the name of the processor itself and the number refers to the CPU speed in millions of cycles per second. Within a given family of processors, the higher the speed number, the faster the processor — and the more expensive. But the slowest of the next-highest family of chip is usually faster than the fastest of the previous family.

Confused? To make matters worse, it's no longer easy to tell where a family of processors fits in the pecking order.

Windows 2000 Professional can run on a variety of microprocessors. Table 2-1 shows a list of some processor families — from the oldest to the newest.

Table 2-1		Microprocessor Families	
Chip Name	*Speeds*	*Vintage*	*Comments*
Pentium	60-200	1992	The minimum processor for Windows 2000. At speeds of 133 and below, you need lots of memory for acceptable performance.
Pentium Pro	150-200	1996	First microprocessor optimized to run 32-bit programs.
Pentium II	233-450	1997	Pentium Pros with special "MMX" (MultiMedia eXtensions) features to make graphics and videos run better.
Pentium II Xeon	400+	1998	A souped-up version of the Pentium II for great big server computers.
Celeron	300-466	1998	A slightly dumbed-down version of the Pentium II but much less expensive and just as good under most conditions.
Pentium III	450-550	1999	The highest of the high-end processors.
Pentium III Xeon	500-550	1999	The Pentium III optimized for servers.

Then there are RISC (Reduced Instruction Set Computer) processors, including the DEC Alpha microprocessors designed for heavy-duty workstations. Windows 2000 Professional likes these. The various forms of the PowerPC — RISC-based processors designed for workstations — are another set of processors which Windows 2000 Professional also likes.

The thing to remember is Windows 2000 Professional needs at least a Pentium with a big number. Preferably something over 200 MHz. On slower Pentiums, it probably *will* run — about as fast as an unambitious snail. You can't even install it on computers using microprocessors older and slower than the Pentium.

Disks and Disk Drives

Computer boxes often have various slots or openings called *drives* that work like the drawer at the bank's drive-up teller window. These openings are ways for you to send and retrieve information from the computer (other than the keyboard or mouse).

You can push anything that'll fit into a drive, but the computer recognizes only floppy disks, compact discs, and little thingies usually called "zip disks" even though not all of them are Zip disks (which is a particular brand name). Hang on — all are discussed in the next sections.

Floppy disk flipping

A floppy disk's disk drive spits little magnetic impulses onto a floppy disk to store information safely. The disk drive can slurp the information back off the floppy disk by reading the magnetic impulses. You simply push the disk into the disk drive and tell Windows whether to slurp or spit. That's known as *copy from* or *copy to* in computer parlance.

By copying information to or from floppies, you can transport snippets of information to and from computers.

Windows 2000 Professional is made primarily to run on networks — and it's much easier to copy information from one computer to another on a network (that is, via network cables instead of disks), a process described in Chapters 9 and 13. These days, floppies primarily come in handy for storing a backup copy of a few important files, installing new software, or moving files between a laptop and desktop computer.

✔ For security reasons, some networked computers don't come with floppy drives. That keeps people from making copies of information and taking it home. (It also keeps them from putting naughty stuff onto the network.) All the valuable data stays lodged in the computers and moves back and forth through the networking cables.

Many viruses infect a company network while riding on a floppy disk. That's another reason many workstations are floppyless.

✔ The disk drive automatically grabs the disk when you push it in far enough. You hear it clunk, and the disk sinks down into the drive. If it doesn't, you're putting it in the wrong way. (The disk's silver edge goes in first, with the little round silver thing in the middle facing down.) To retrieve the disk, push the button protruding from around the drive's slot and then grab the disk when the drive kicks it out.

✔ A disk you can carry around in your pocket is a floppy disk. A hidden disk that lurks deep in the bowels of the computer is a *hard disk* or *hard drive.*

Hard disks are thick little Frisbees inside the computer that can hold thousands of times more information than floppy disks. They're also much quicker at reading and writing information. (They're a great deal quieter, too, thank goodness.) Windows 2000 Professional insists on using a hard disk because it's such a huge program. The programs that run under Windows 2000 Professional can be pretty huge, too.

✔ Computer stores sell blank floppy disks so that you can copy your work onto them and put them in a safe place.

These days, floppy disks come in three flavors though they're all the same size on the outside. The disk's box describes what sort of disks are inside, but the bare disks rarely offer a clue as to their capacity. Table 2-2 provides a handy identification chart for that disk you found behind the bookcase.

Table 2-2		True-to-Life Floppy Disk Facts		
Size	*Name*	*Storage Capacity*	*Label Jargon*	*Looks Like This*
3½-inch	Low-density	720K	DS/DD DD 135 tpi	Square and rigid; has a little arrow in one corner. The arrow points away from a single, small square hole in another corner. (Rare now.)
3½-inch	High-density	1.44MB	DS/HD HD	Most common. Square and rigid; has a little arrow in one corner and two small square holes in corners opposite the arrow. The letters HD are often stamped on the disk. (Practically every floppy you're likely to see.)
3½-inch	Extended density	2.8MB	DS/ED ED	Square and rigid; very rare and you are not likely to ever see one. (If you think you may have one, though, look for little ED letters stamped on the disk.)

Disk do's and doughnuts

✔ Do label your disks so you know what's on them.

✔ Do at least make a valiant effort to peel off a disk's old label before sticking on a new one. (After a while, those stacks of old labels make the disk too fat to fit into the drive.)

✔ Do copy important files from your hard disk to floppy disks on a regular basis. (This routine is called *backing up* in computer lingo. You can buy special backup packages to make this chore a little easier. Not much easier, but a little. Or make the leap and buy a system that automates much of the backup process.)

✔ Do not listen to silver-tongued devils who say you can *notch* a low-density disk to turn it into a high-density disk. This method just doesn't work consistently and reliably.

✔ Do not leave disks lying in the sun.

✔ Do not place disks next to magnets. Don't place them next to magnets disguised as paper clip holders, either, or leftover trade show magnets, for that matter.

What disk drives does Windows 2000 Professional like?

Face it: Windows 2000 Professional is no cute little pot-bellied piglet — it's a hairy hog with big ears. First, it needs about 500MB of hard disk space and can easily take up 100MB more. To be comfortable, your computer had better have a 2GB or larger hard disk to accommodate Windows 2000 Professional and all your programs.

If you've never installed Windows 2000 Professional, you need a 3½-inch disk drive to run a few "setup boot disk" floppies and a CD-ROM drive. If you have a system that allows you to boot from the CD-ROM drive, you don't even need the floppies.

If you're buying a new computer or just a new CD-ROM drive, you definitely want one that allows you to start the computer from a CD-ROM. This is called a bootable CD-ROM drive and you want one that meets the *El Torito* standard. As usual, the name of the standard is more interesting than the standard itself. It came about because the technobrains who developed the standard did so over many burrito-based lunches at a local restaurant.

What does "write-protected" mean?

Write-protection is supposed to be a helpful safety feature, but most people discover it when Windows stops them with an abrupt warning. Figure 2-1 shows what happens when I try to copy a file to a write-protected disk.

Figure 2-1:
Windows
2000
Professional
won't write
to a disk
that's been
write-
protected.

A write-protected disk has simply been tweaked so that nobody can copy to it or delete the files it contains. Write-protection is a simple procedure, and surprisingly enough, requires no government permit. You can write-protect and un-write-protect disks in the privacy of your own office cubicle.

- ✔ To write-protect a 3½-inch disk, look for a tiny, black sliding tab in a square hole in the disk's corner. Slide the tab with a pencil or your thumbnail so that the hole is uncovered. The disk is now write-protected.

- ✔ To remove the write-protection on a 3½-inch disk, slide the little black plastic thingy so that the hole is covered up.

- ✔ If you encounter the write-protect error, wait until the drive stops making noise and the little light on the front of the drive goes out. Then click on OK to remove the Error message window. Remove the disk, un-write-protect the disk, and put the disk back in the drive. Finally, repeat what you were doing before you were so rudely interrupted.

Driving with compact discs

Compact discs look like the things you've been sliding into your stereo's CD player for the past decade. And in fact, if you slide an Allman Brothers CD into your computer's CD-ROM drive, you can whistle along to Dickey Betts' slide guitar while you work. (Hopefully your computer has a sound card and speakers.)

Instead of storing information in the form of magnetic impulses, CDs store information as little blips for a little focused beam of light to read. Because light-beam blips can be more precise than a floppy disk's magnetic impulses, CDs can hold a lot more information — about 680MB of information, in fact.

- ✔ Because CD-ROM drives can hold so much information, they're the premier way of installing Windows 2000 Professional and just about every other software package for sale these days.

✔ You can't write to a CD-ROM drive; you can only read information from it. That means a CD is always write-protected.

✔ I lied. You can write information to CDs with special CD-ROM drives called *CD Recordable drives.* You don't find those attached to Windows 2000 Professional workstations very often. Some Recordable CD-ROM drives (also called *CD-R drives*) can not only write stuff to a disc, they let you erase your old stuff and write new stuff. (They're called Read/Write, or *CD-RW drives.*)

✔ Compact disc is spelled with a *c* to confuse people accustomed to seeing disk spelled with a *k.*

Zippity-do-drives

Floppy disks don't hold a lot of information — and CD Recordable drives are still tricky to set up, so some years back a company called Iomega came up with *Zip drives.* These drives use special disks that each hold 100MB or more of information.

✔ Zip drives can be built into the computer box or can be portable gadgets about the size of a Sony Walkman. Zip disks hold 100MB or 250MB of information.

✔ *Jaz drives* are more like removable hard drives and have a capacity of 1GB or 2GB. They too can be portable or built-in.

✔ Iomega isn't the only one to make these kinds of removable storage devices — Syquest also makes a system that can store 230MB to 1.5GB at a time.

Plug and Play

In the past, adding or removing hardware from a computer has been about as much fun as your Cousin Edna's voice recitals. You had to have the right *driver* (a file containing info needed by a program to install and operate peripherals, such as printers and monitors) and feed it to the computer in just the right way, attach the hardware (or detach it) at just the right time, know the secret handshake, and perform other bizarre rituals. Starting with Windows 95, however, Microsoft incorporated a technology called Plug and Play. It was improved with Windows 98 and works pretty darn well now in Windows 2000 Professional.

Plug and Play (once unkindly dubbed "Plug and Pray") means that you plug in the new modem, soundcard, monitor, or other hardware device and the operating system reacts by throwing up a box on your screen that says, basically,

"Hey! There's new hardware!" It then installs the hardware without any help from you. (Well, you may have to supply your Windows 2000 Professional CD-ROM.)

Always let Plug and Play look for new hardware instead of trying to sidestep it and configure a new device by your lonesome. If Windows 2000 Professional is stumped and can't find, say, your new soundcard, you'll be given a chance to supply the information yourself.

The Mouse and Other Pointing Devices

The *mouse* is that rounded plastic thing that looks like a bar of electronic soap. Marketing people thought that the word mouse sounded like fun, so the name stuck. Actually, think of your mouse as your electronic finger because you use it in Windows 2000 Professional to point at stuff on-screen.

A mouse has a little roller, or mouse ball, embedded in its belly. (Ouch. Where were the animal rights people?) When you move the mouse across your desk, the ball rubs against electronic sensor gizmos. The gizmos record the mouse's movements and send the information down the mouse's tail, which connects to the back of the computer.

As you move the mouse, you see an arrow, or pointer, move simultaneously across the computer screen. Here's where your electronic finger comes in: When the arrow points at a picture of a button on-screen, you press, or click, the left button on the mouse. The button is selected, just as if you'd pressed it with your finger. It's a cool bit of 3-D computer graphics that makes you want to click buttons again and again.

- ✔ You control just about everything in Windows 2000 Professional by pointing at it with the mouse and pressing and releasing the mouse button, or clicking. (The mouse pitches in with a helpful clicking noise when you press its button.)

- ✔ The plural of mouse is mice, just like the ones cats chew on. It's not mouses.

- ✔ Fold-down airline trays don't have enough room for a laptop, a mouse, and a beverage, so laptops often substitute a touchpad in place of the mouse. You slide your finger around the pad and the pointer on the screen copies your motion. (You have to practice — the pointer races around like a drunken gerbil until you get the hang of it.) Some laptops have a little doohickey embedded in the keyboard that looks like a pencil eraser. You push it around with the tip of a finger and the pointer runs around the screen accordingly. You use your other hand to inadvertently spill your beverage.

✔ Most mice run in two modes: Microsoft-compatible mode or some funky third-party way. Microsoft created Windows, so you have fewer problems if you run the mouse in the Microsoft-compatible mode. Also, mice come in three breeds: bus, PS/2, and serial. Windows 2000 Professional works with all three breeds, so it doesn't care which you have, and neither should you.

✔ A mouse won't work by itself; it needs software called a *driver*. Fortunately, Windows 2000 Professional comes with whatever driver you need and installs the driver without any help from you. Visit Chapter 11 for more on mouse manipulation.

The mouse arrow changes shape, depending on what it's pointing at in Windows. When it changes shape, you know that it's ready to perform a new task. Table 2-3 is a handy reference for the different uniforms the mouse pointer wears for different jobs. (Beware, however, that you can customize your mouse pointers; your pointers may not look exactly like the ones in the table. Head to Chapter 11 for mouse-pointer customization tips.)

Table 2-3	The Various Shapes of the Mouse Pointer	
Shape	*What It Points At*	*What to Do When You See It*
↖	Just about anything on-screen	Use this pointer for moving from place to place on-screen.
✛	A single window	Uh-oh. You've somehow selected the annoying size or move option from the Control menu. Moving the mouse or pressing the cursor-control keys now makes the current window bigger or smaller. Press Enter when you're done or press Esc if you want to get away from this uncomfortable bit of weirdness.
↕	The top or bottom edge of a window	Hold down the mouse button and move the mouse back and forth to make the window grow taller or shorter. Let go when you like the window's new size.
↔	The left or right edge of a window	Hold down the mouse button and move the mouse back and forth to make the window fatter or skinnier. Let go when you like the window's new size.
↖	The corner of a window	Hold down the mouse button and move the mouse anywhere to make the window fat, skinny, tall, or short. Let go when you're through playing.

Shape	What It Points At	What to Do When You See It
I	A program or box that accepts text	Put the pointer where you want words to appear; then click on the button and start typing the letters or numbers. (This pointer is called an *I-beam,* in techno terms.)
☝	A *link* to some other related information. In Windows 2000, it's usually a connection to a definition in the Help files. In Internet Explorer, it's a connection to another place on the Web.	Click the mouse, and Windows trots out some more helpful information about that particular subject. If you're in Internet Explorer, you jump to some related information. Use the Back button to return to the spot you jumped from.
⧗	Nothing (Windows is working and is busy ignoring you.)	Move the mouse in wild circles and watch the hourglass spin around until Windows 2000 Professional catches up with you. This usually happens when you are loading large files or copying stuff to a floppy disk.

The breeds of mice

A serial mouse, a bus mouse, and a port mouse all look the same: They're all little plastic things with tails stretching toward the computer's rear. When the tails reach the back of the computer, the mice's tails differ subtly. A serial mouse plugs into an oblong doodad called a *serial port.* Almost all computers come with a preinstalled serial port that nerds call *COM1.*

The tails from bus and port mice don't head for the serial port. Instead, each of those tails has a little round end that plugs into a little round hole in the computer's rear. If your mouse says "PS/2" or "PS/2 compatible" on its belly, you have a port mouse. If your mouse plugs into a hole mounted on a silver card, you have the rarer bus mouse design.

Windows 2000 Professional can tell which mouse you have, and it installs the mouse automatically. But if you accidentally yank your mouse cord from the back of your computer, now you know which hole to plug it back into.

Some cordless mice don't have tails at all. But they have a receiving unit — a little box that plugs into one of the three areas discussed above.

Finally, some people prefer an IntelliMouse — a PS/2 mouse with the edge of a wheel protruding from its back. By spinning the wheel, you automatically scroll down the page. No more clicking on the window's borders! Plus, pushing down on the wheel equals a double-click. Such modern conveniences.

Don't worry about memorizing all the various shapes that the pointer takes on. The pointer changes shape automatically at the appropriate times. I've described the shapes here just so you won't think that your pointer's goofing off when it changes shape.

Cards and Monitors

The monitor is the thing you stare at all day until you go home to watch TV. The front of the monitor, called its *screen* or *display,* is where all the Windows 2000 Professional action takes place. The screen is where you can watch the windows as they bump around, occasionally cover each other up, and generally behave like nine people eyeing a recently delivered eight-slice pizza.

Monitors have two cords so they won't be mistaken for a mouse. One cord plugs into the electrical outlet; the other cord heads for the video card, a special piece of electronics poking out from behind the computer. The computer tells the video card what it's doing; the card translates the events into graphics information and shoots it up the cable into the monitor, where it appears on-screen.

- ✔ Like herbivores and cellulose-digesting gut microorganisms, monitors and video cards come in symbiotic pairs. Neither can function without the other, and it's best to buy them in matched sets so that you know in advance that they get along. If you're buying a new flat panel monitor, it's even more important because the digital monitors are very picky about which video cards they're willing to work with.

- ✔ Unlike other parts of the computer, the video card and monitor don't require any special care and feeding. Just wipe the dust off the screen every once in a while.

Spray plain old glass cleaner on a rag and then wipe off the dust with the newly dampened rag. If you spray glass cleaner directly on the screen, the fluid drips down into the monitor case, annoying the trolls who sleep under the bridge.

- ✔ Some glass cleaners contain alcohol, which can cloud the antiglare screens found on some fancy new monitors. When in doubt, check your monitor's manual to see whether glass cleaner is allowed.

- ✔ When you first install Windows 2000 Professional, it interrogates the video card and monitor until they reveal their brand name and orientation. Windows 2000 Professional usually gets the right answer from them and sets itself up automatically so that everything works the first time. (A little tweaking later on may help, though, as described in Chapter 11.)

- ✔ For such simple gadgets, monitors and cards command a dazzling array of nerdy terms. Ignore them all. Windows picks the appropriate video settings automatically and moves on to the hard stuff, like mouse drivers.

Ignore these awful graphics terms

Some people describe their monitors as *boxy* or *covered with cat hair;* others use the following strange scientific terms:

✔ **Pixel:** A *pixel* is a fancy name for an individual dot on-screen. Everything on-screen is made up of bunches of graphic dots, or pixels. Each pixel is a different shade or color, which creates the image. (Squint up close to the screen, and you may be able to make out an individual pixel.) Monochrome monitors are often called *gray-scale monitors* because their pixels can show only shades of gray.

✔ **Resolution:** The *resolution* is the number of pixels on a screen — specifically, the number of pixels across (horizontal) and down (vertical). More pixels mean greater resolution: smaller letters and more information packed onto the same-sized screen. People with small monitors usually use 640x480 resolution. People with larger monitors often switch to 1024x768 resolution so that they can fit more windows on-screen and impress their coworkers.

✔ **Color:** The term *color* describes the number of colors that the card and monitor display on-screen. The number of colors can change, however, depending on the current resolution. When the card runs at a low resolution, for example, it can use its leftover memory to display more colors. At a 1024x768 resolution, you may see only 256 colors on-screen. With a lower resolution of 640x480, you may be able to see 16.7 million colors. Windows 2000 Professional usually runs fastest with 256 colors, and unless you're using a high-resolution color photo of your first-born child for your monitor's background, you won't need more colors than that.

✔ **Mode:** A predetermined combination of pixels, resolution, and colors is described as a *graphics mode.* Right out of the box, Windows 2000 Professional can handle the mode needs of most people. If the video card hails from a weird mode planet, you need a *driver* from the folks who made the card.

You don't need to know any of this stuff. If you're feeling particularly modular, however, you can change the Windows graphics modes after reading Chapter 11.

Keyboards

Computer keyboards look pretty much like typewriter keyboards with a few dark growths around the perimeter. In the center lie the familiar white typewriter keys. Other keys with obtuse code words live along the outside edges. They're described next.

Groups of keys

Obtuse code-word sorters divvy those outside-edge keys into key groups:

- **Function keys:** These F keys either sit along the top of the keyboard in one long row or clump together in two short rows along the keyboard's left side. Function keys boss around programs. For example, you can press F1 to demand help whenever you're stumped in Windows 2000 Professional.

- **Numeric keypad:** Zippy-fingered bankers like this thingy: a square, calculator-like pad of numbers along the right edge of most keyboards. (You have to press a key called Num Lock above those numbers, though, before they work. Otherwise, they're cursor-control keys, described next.)

- **Cursor-control keys:** If you haven't pressed the magical Num Lock key, the keys on that square, calculator-like pad of numbers are the cursor-control keys. These keys have little arrows that show which direction the cursor will be moved on-screen. (The arrowless *5* key doesn't do anything except try to overcome its low self-esteem.) Some keyboards have a second set of cursor-control keys next to the numeric keypad. Both sets do the same thing. Additional cursor-control keys are Home, End, PgUp, and PgDn (or Page Up and Page Down). To move down a page in a word-processing program, for example, you press the PgDn key.

- **Windows keys:** A new breed of keyboard, the 104-key Windows keyboard, has a few extra keys. (But they're real yawners.) The little Windows symbol key simply brings up the Start menu — just as if you'd clicked on the Start button. The key with the little menu symbol brings up the menu for the currently open window.

More key principles

Other keyboard keys you need to be familiar with follow:

- **Shift:** Just as on a typewriter, this key creates uppercase letters or the symbols %#@$, which make great G-rated swear words.

- **Alt:** Watch out for this one! When you press Alt (which stands for Alternate), Windows 2000 Professional moves the cursor to the little menus at the top of the current window. If you're trapped up there and can't get out, you probably pressed Alt by mistake. Press Alt again to free yourself.

- **Ctrl:** This key (which stands for Control) is used for weird computer combinations. For example, holding down the Ctrl key while pressing Esc (described next) brings up the Windows 2000 Professional Start button menu, in case your mouse has died or isn't handy.

✔ **Esc:** This key, which stands for Escape, was a pipe dream of the computer's creators. They added Esc as an escape hatch from malfunctioning computers. By pressing Esc, the user was supposed to be able to escape whatever inner turmoil the computer was currently going through. Esc doesn't always work that way, but give it a try. It sometimes enables you to escape when you're trapped in a menu or a dastardly dialog box. (Those traps are described in Chapter 6.)

✔ **Scroll Lock:** No one knows what this key does. Ignore it. (It's no relation to a scroll bar, we do know that at least.) If a little keyboard light glows next to your Scroll Lock key, press the Scroll Lock key to turn it off. (The key is often labeled Scrl Lk or something equally obnoxious.)

✔ **Delete:** Press the Delete key (sometimes labeled Del), and the unlucky character sitting to the right of the cursor disappears. Any highlighted information disappears as well. Poof.

✔ **Backspace:** Press the Backspace key, and the unlucky character to the left of the cursor disappears. The Backspace key is on the top row, near the right side of the keyboard; it has a left-pointing arrow on it. Oh, and the Backspace key deletes any highlighted information, too.

✔ **Insert:** Pressing Insert (sometimes labeled Ins) puts you in Insert mode. As you type, any existing words are scooted to the right, letting you add stuff. The opposite of Insert mode is Overwrite mode, where everything you type replaces any text in its way. Press Insert to toggle between these two modes.

   Ugly disclaimer: Some Windows-based programs, such as Notepad, are always in Insert mode. You simply cannot move to Overwrite mode, no matter how hard you pound the Insert key.

✔ **Enter:** This key works pretty much like a typewriter's Return key but with a big exception: Don't press Enter at the end of each line. A word processor can sense when you're about to type off the edge of the screen. It herds your words down to the next line automatically. So just press Enter at the end of each paragraph.

   You also want to press Enter when Windows 2000 Professional asks you to type something — the name of a file, for example, or the number of pages you want to print — into a special box.

✔ **Caps Lock:** If you've mastered the Caps Lock key on a typewriter, you'll be pleased to find no surprises here. (Okay, there's one surprise. Caps Lock affects only your letters. It has no effect on punctuation symbols or the numbers along the top row.)

✔ **Tab:** You won't find any surprises here, either, except that Tab is equal to five spaces in some word processors and eight spaces in others. Still other word processors enable you to set Tab to whatever number you want. Plus, a startling Tab Tip follows.

✔ Press Tab to move from one box to the next when filling out a form in Windows 2000 Professional. (Sometimes, these forms are called dialog boxes.)

A mouse works best for most Windows 2000 Professional tasks, like starting programs or choosing among various options. Sometimes the keyboard comes in handy, however. Windows comes with shortcut keys to replace just about anything you can do with a mouse. Pressing a few keys can be quicker than wading through heaps of menus with a mouse. (The shortcut keys are described in Chapter 5, in the section on when to use the keyboard.)

If you don't own a mouse or a trackball, you can control Windows exclusively with a keyboard. But it's awkward — like Barney trying to floss his back molars.

Those little bumps on your *F* and *J* keys are there so you can put your fingers on the right keys when you're typing in the dark.

Print Screen: The one fun, weird code key

In the old days of computing, pressing the Print Screen key sent a snapshot of the screen directly to the printer. Imagine the convenience! But, if a screen showed graphics, or anything other than straight text, pressing the Print Screen key sent a wild jumble of garbled symbols to the printer. And if the printer wasn't connected, turned on, and waiting, the computer stopped cold.

You no longer need to worry about the Print Screen woes of yore. Pressing the Print Screen key now sends a picture of the screen to a special place in Windows that is known as the *Clipboard*. When the image is in the Clipboard, you can paste the image into your programs or save it to disk. You can see the image by calling up the Clipbook Viewer. You can even print the screen's picture if you paste the image from the Clipboard into Paint, the Windows 2000 Professional drawing program.

  ✔ With some older computers, you have to hold down Shift while you press Print Screen, or you get just an asterisk on-screen. Not nearly as much fun.

  ✔ The Clipbook Viewer and Clipboard are described in Chapter 10.

Sound Cards (Making Disgusting Bioactive Noises)

For years, PC owners looked enviously at Macintosh owners — especially when the Macs ejected a disk. The Macintosh could make a cute barfing sound when ejecting a disk. Macs come with sound built in; they can barf, giggle, and make really disgusting noises that won't be mentioned here. (Any Mac owner will be happy to play them back for you.)

But the tight collars at IBM decided there was no place for sound on a Serious Business Machine and the PC was quite quiet. Windows finally fixed that mistake, so now the accounting department's computers can giggle as loudly as the ones in the art department down the hall.

- ✔ Windows 2000 Professional can certainly barf (or giggle, or play excerpts from *Swan Lake*), but it needs a computer with two things: a sound card and a speaker. And unfortunately, some computers around the office lack these amenities. Fortunately, more and more *new* computers have these goodies built in.

- ✔ Windows 2000 Professional comes with some pleasant sounds already included, but it doesn't have any really offensive ones. However, if you have an Internet connection, you can easily find and fetch any number of disgusting sounds.

- ✔ Just like the Macintosh, Windows 2000 Professional enables you to assign cool sounds to various functions. For example, you can make your computer scream louder than you do when it tosses out an error message. For more information, refer to the section in Chapter 11 on making cool sounds with multimedia.

Scanners and Cameras

Scanners and cameras that work with computers are both in the business of taking visual information and translating it into digital information that your computer can read and display. Scanners take a picture of drawings, photos, or text and turn it into a file that you can see on screen, print, save on a hard disk, or attach to e-mail. Digital cameras work like other cameras except that their pictures are delivered in digital form to your computer.

Part of the bonus that comes with the Plug and Play technology that we talk about earlier in this chapter is that scanners and digital cameras are much easier to install and use. You still want the particular program or programs that came with your toy, but Windows 2000 Professional gives you a hook into all sorts of other programs as well.

For example, you can open the Imaging program that's part of Windows 2000 Professional and run your scanner from there. Other programs such as Microsoft Excel and PowerPoint also let you take pictures directly from your scanner or camera and plop them down into a spreadsheet or presentation.

Modems

Modems are little mechanical gadgets that translate a computer's information into squealing sounds that can be sent and received over plain, ordinary phone lines.

Because computers store sound, text, numbers, pretty pictures, and video, they can send and receive all that information over a modem as well. In fact, computers use this sophisticated technology when connected to the World Wide Web: Their owners use a modem to watch a live video of somebody's ant farm (www.atomicweb.com/antfarm.html), or connect to the Federal Bureau of Investigation's Ten Most Wanted Fugitives list (www.fbi.gov/mostwanted.htm) to see whether they recognize any relatives.

- ✔ The computers on both ends of the phone lines need modems in order to talk to each other. That's why people who want to talk on the World Wide Web need to pay money to an Internet service provider (ISP). The ISP provides a way for your modem to talk to other computers on the Internet, and the ISP charges money for that privilege. (This confusing stuff is made much more clear in Chapter 16, thank goodness.)

- ✔ On a network, your Internet connection is probably not made through the kind of modem you use at home. Most companies with Internet connections lease a "dedicated" phone line. This phone line is "on" all the time. It is also a much bigger pipeline for information than a regular phone line. Some are to your average modem connection as a fire hose is to a soda straw.

- ✔ Windows 2000 Professional comes with a communications program called Internet Explorer for probing the World Wide Web. This software, known as a Web browser, lets people "surf the Net." (Chapter 16 covers Internet Explorer.)

- ✔ Another program that comes with Windows 2000 Professional is called Outlook Express which can transport mail not only through modems but through the network. (Exchange gets its due in Chapter 16.)

- ✔ People also use modems to call America Online, CompuServe, and other online services. Online services are huge computers stuffed with information like stock prices, weather updates, news, and message areas, where people can swap talk about flatware, UFOs, and how much the online service is costing them. (Most online services cost about $20 a month for unlimited use, all charged to the user's credit card.)

Printers

Realizing that the paperless office still lies several years down the road, Microsoft made sure that Windows 2000 Professional can shake hands and make enthusiastic gestures with more than 200 types of printers.

If you're lucky, you have a printer in your office that you can use. If you're not lucky, you have a printer connected to the network, meaning you have to walk down the hall to grab your printed items.

✔ Even the fanciest printers must be turned on before Windows 2000 Professional can print to them. (You'd be surprised how easily you can forget this little fact in the heat of the moment.)

✔ Windows 2000 Professional prints in a WYSIWYG (what you see is what you get) format, which means that what you see on-screen is reasonably close to what you see on the printed page.

✔ When you click on the Print button in a Windows 2000 Professional program or use the menu to send something to the printer, a little picture of a printer appears in the bar that runs along the edge of your screen. Double-click on the picture of the printer, and you can see a list (known as a queue) of all the files waiting to be printed. (The longer the list, the longer you have to wait for your own file.)

Networks

Networks connect PCs so that people can share information. Coworkers can send stuff to a single printer, for example, or send messages to each other asking whether Esther has been by with the paychecks yet.

You're probably on a network if you can answer "yes" to any of these questions:

✔ Can your coworkers and you share a printer, data, or messages without standing up and yelling across the room?

✔ When your computer stops working, do you hear simultaneous batches of moans and groans from coworkers down the hall?

✔ Are you using Windows 2000 Professional?

✔ Do you have a *Network Administrator?*

- Most networks require a paid human attendant known as a Network Administrator. This person controls everything that happens on the network and can pass out additional privileges, like letting your files have priority in reaching the office printer.

- It pays to be nice to your Network Administrator.

- For what it's worth: You don't have to be running Windows 2000 Professional as your operating system to participate on an NT network. Windows 2000 Server and Windows NT Server can link Apple computers, UNIX computers, and PCs running Windows 98, Windows 95, Windows 3.1*x*, OS/2, or DOS.

- For more information about networks, start with Chapter 4.

Parts Required by Windows 2000 Professional

Table 2-4 compares what Windows 2000 Professional asks for on the side of the box with what you really need before it works well.

Table 2-4	What Windows Requires
Listed, Ethereal Requirements	*Normal, Human Requirements*
166 MHz Pentium or higher	200 MHz Pentium or higher
32MB RAM	64MB RAM (96-128MB is better)
VGA card and monitor	Fast SuperVGA card and 17-inch monitor
2GB Hard disk with 650MB free	2GB Hard disk with 650MB free
Quad-speed (4X) or faster CD-ROM drive	12X or faster CD-ROM drive
High-density 3½ inch disk drive, unless your CD-ROM drive is bootable	High-density 3½ inch disk drive, unless your CD-ROM drive is bootable
Options: Mouse	*Required:* Mouse, preferably Microsoft-compatible
Options: Network card and cables	*Required:* Network card and cables

Chapter 3

Windows 2000 Stuff Everybody Thinks You Already Know

*W*hen the first version of Windows hit the market in 1985, it was not exactly a success. The weakling computers of the day could barely add numbers, yet Windows forced them to paint the screen with heavy-duty graphics. Windows was slow and ugly, and most people didn't think it would last a year.

Today's powerhouse computers can not only calculate the trendiest financial forecast algorithms but create feature-length motion pictures as well. And Windows, with its fashionable color schemes — like Lilac, Maple, and Slate — has turned into a trendy worldwide best seller.

Because Windows has been around for so long, a lot of computer geeks have had a head start in learning its special language. To help you catch up; this chapter is a tourist's alphabetized guidebook to those Windows words that the nerds have been batting around for years.

Backing Up Your Work

A computer can store bunches of files on its hard disk. And that multitude of files can be a problem. When the hard disk eventually dies, it takes all its stored files down with it. Pfffft.

Computer users who don't like anguished pffffft sounds back up their hard disks religiously by making a second copy of it for safekeeping. They do so in four main ways:

- **Floppies:** Some people copy all their files from the hard disk to a bunch of floppy disks. Although custom-written backup programs make this task easier, it's still a time-consuming chore. Who wants to spend an extra hour backing up computer files after finishing a day's work?

  Using an older backup program that didn't come with Windows 2000? If your backup program doesn't claim to be "Windows 2000 compatible," don't use it. These old backup programs probably won't know how to back up files using Windows 2000's special ways of storing files. If you try to use an old backup program with Windows 2000, the backup won't be reliable.

- **Tape backup unit:** This special computerized tape recorder either lives inside the computer like a disk drive or plugs into the computer's rear. Either way, the gizmo tape-records all the information on your hard disk. Then when your hard disk dies, you still have all your files on tape. The faithful tape backup unit plays back all your information onto the new hard disk. No scrounging for floppy disks.

  The tape backup unit can cost from $150 to $1,000, depending on the size of your computer's hard disk. Some people back up their work every day, using a new tape for each day of the week. If they discover on Thursday that last Monday's report had important information, they can pop Monday's tape into the backup unit and grab the report.

- **Removable disks:** These guys work like floppy disks, but are usually a little larger in size. And although they're just a little larger, they can hold more than a hundred times as much information. (Look for the Ditto, Zip, and Jaz units.)

- **Automatic network backup:** The luckiest people don't need to worry about backing up their hard disks at all. They work on a network that handles all the backup chores automatically. Because Windows 2000 is primarily used on networks, you probably don't need to worry about backing up your hard disk.

  But a lot depends on how much you trust your Network Administrator to do a complete daily backup. Take this little test:

  1) Do you spot your Network Administrator playing "House of Cards" with floppy disks and tapes?

  2) Does your Network Administrator keep a packed suitcase in his or her office at all times?

  If your answer to either of these questions is "yes," you should at least consider copying your most valuable files to floppies.

Hey, when do I use the left mouse button, and when do I use the right mouse button?

When somebody tells you to "click" something in Windows 2000, it almost always means that you should "click with your left mouse button." That's because most Windows 2000 users are right-handed, and their index fingers hover over the mouse's left button, making that button an easy target.

Windows 2000, however, also lets you click your *right* mouse button, and it regards the two actions as completely different.

Pointing at something and clicking the right button often brings up a secret hidden menu with some extra options. Right-click on a blank portion of your Desktop, for example, and a menu pops up, enabling you to organize your Desktop's icons or change the way your display looks. Right-clicking on an icon often brings up a hidden menu as well.

The right mouse button is designed for users who like to feel that they're doing something sneaky. That's why clicking the right mouse button often brings up a hidden menu of extra options.

You'll rarely, if ever, have to use the right mouse button. Just about every option it offers can be accomplished in other ways. But once you experience the joys of being sneaky, you may find yourself using the right mouse button as often as the left.

Windows 2000 comes with Backup, a program that automatically copies files from your hard disk to whatever storage device you choose, such as floppy disks, network drives, or removable disks, to name a few.

Clicking

Computers make plenty of clicking sounds, but only one click counts: the one that occurs when you press a button on a mouse. You'll find yourself clicking the mouse hundreds of times in Windows 2000. For example, to push an on-screen button marked Push Me, you move the mouse until the mouse pointer rests over the Push Me button, and then you click the mouse button.

✔ When you hear people say, "Press the button on the mouse," they leave out an important detail: *Release* the button after you press it. Press the button with your index finger and release it, just as you press a button on a touch-tone phone. (See the "Dragging and Dropping" section for an important exception.)

✔ Most mice have two buttons; some have three, and some esoteric models for traffic engineers have more than 32. Windows 2000 listens mostly to clicks coming from the button on the left side of your mouse. It's the one under your index finger. Refer to Chapter 11 for more mouse button tricks (including how to turn your mouse into a left-handed mouse).

✔ Most Windows 2000 applications listen to clicks coming from the right button as well as from the left button.

✔ Don't confuse a click with a double-click. For more rodent details, see "Double-Clicking," "The Mouse," and "Pointers/Arrows," later in this chapter. The insatiably curious can find even more mouse stuff in Chapter 2.

The Control Panel

You can find the central control room for Windows 2000 Professional in the Control Panel — a handy repository for just about every tool you'll ever use to change how Windows 2000 Professional looks and operates.

To get a look at the Control Panel, click the Start button and, while holding the mouse button down, slide up the menu to Settings, then slide right to Control Panel. Let go of the button and you'll see a window like the one in Figure 3-1. Every one of those little pictures represents something you might want to do some day — or might have to do.

Cruise on over to Chapter 11 for the scoop on each of the Control Panel's icons.

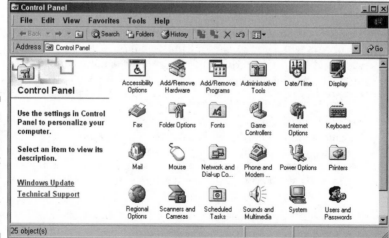

Figure 3-1: The Control Panel is full of icons that connect you to ways to set up your computer.

The Cursor

A typewriter has a little mechanical arm that strikes the page, creating the desired letter. Computers don't have little mechanical arms (except in science fiction movies), so they have *cursors:* little blinking lines that show where that next letter will appear in the text.

Cursors appear only when Windows 2000 is ready for you to type text, numbers, or symbols — usually when you write letters or reports.

- ✔ The cursor and the mouse pointer are different things that perform different tasks. When you start typing, text appears at the cursor's location, not at the pointer's location.

  You can distinguish between the cursor and the mouse pointer with one look: Cursors always blink steadily; mouse pointers never do. For more information, check out "Pointers/Arrows" in this chapter or Table 2-3 in Chapter 2.

- ✔ You can move the cursor to a new place in the document by using the keyboard's cursor-control keys (the keys with little arrows). Or you can point to a spot with the mouse pointer and click the button. The cursor leaps to that new spot.

Defaults (And the "Any Key")

Finally, a computer term that can be safely ignored. Clap your hands and square-dance with a neighbor! Here's the lowdown on the, er, hoedown: Some programs present a terse list of inexplicable choices and casually suggest that you choose the only option that's not listed: the default option.

Don't chew your tongue in despair. Just press Enter.

Those wily programmers have predetermined what option works best for 99 percent of the people using the program. So if people just press Enter, the program automatically makes the right choice and moves on to the next complicated question.

- ✔ The default option is similar to the oft-mentioned *any key* because neither of them appears on your keyboard (or on anyone else's, either — no matter how much money the person paid).

- ✔ When a program says to press any key, simply press the spacebar. (The Shift keys don't do the trick, by the way.)

- ✔ Default can also be taken to mean standard option or what to select when you're completely stumped. For example, "People riding in elevators often stare at their shoes by default."

Desktop (And Wallpapering It)

To keep from reverting to revolting computer terms, Windows 2000 uses familiar office lingo. For example, all the action in Windows 2000 takes place on the Windows 2000 Desktop. The *Desktop* is the background area of the screen, where all the programs pile up.

Windows 2000 comes with a drab green Desktop. To jazz things up, you can cover the Desktop with pictures, or *wallpaper.* Windows 2000 comes with several pictures you can use for wallpaper (and Chapter 11 can help you hang one of them up).

You can customize the wallpaper to fit your own personality: pictures of dogs playing poker, for example, or giant cantaloupe slugs. You can even draw your own wallpaper with the built-in Windows 2000 Paint program.

Double-Clicking

Windows 2000 places a great significance on something pretty simple: pressing a button on the mouse and releasing it. Pressing and releasing the button once is known as a *click.* Pressing and releasing the button twice in rapid succession is a *double-click.*

Earlier versions of Windows watched very carefully to see whether you clicked or double-clicked on its more sensitive parts because the two actions produced completely different results. Clicking usually selects something and double-clicking not only selects something, it also kick-starts it into action, like launching a program.

Windows 2000 Professional also cares how you click, but for the first time, you can decide if you want to double-click at all! (Don't let the excitement make you hyperventilate or anything.) There are two ways to mouse about:

  ✔ Click once to select something and double-click to make it do something (the default setting).

  ✔ Or move the pointer over something to select it, then click once to force it into action (also known as *point and click*).

Scurry over to the section on mouse behavior in Chapter 11 to change from the default to point and click. Some other mouse points to ponder:

✔ A double-click can take some practice to master, even if you have fingers. If you click too slowly, Windows 2000 thinks you're clicking twice — not double-clicking. Try clicking a little faster next time, and Windows 2000 will probably catch on.

✔ Is your mouse pointer moving around too slowly? Or dashing headlong around the screen way too impetuously? Then tiptoe to the section on tinkering with the mouse in Chapter 11; you can find mouse adjustment instructions there.

Dragging and Dropping

Although the term *drag and drop* sounds as if it's straight out of a hitman's handbook, it's really a nonviolent mouse trick in Windows 2000. Dragging and dropping is a way of moving something — say, a picture of an emu egg — from one part of your screen to another.

To drag, put the mouse pointer over the egg and hold down the mouse button. As you move the mouse across your desk, the pointer drags the egg across the screen. Put the pointer/egg where you want it, and then release the mouse button. The egg drops, uncracked. If you hold down the right mouse button while dragging, Windows 2000 tosses a little menu in your face, asking whether you're *sure* that you want to move that egg across the screen. (The menu also gives you the option of copying or creating a shortcut to the dragged item.)

For more mouse fun, see "Clicking," "Double-Clicking," "The Mouse," and "Pointers/Arrows," in this chapter and, if you're not yet weak at the knees, the information on the parts of your computer in Chapter 2.

Drivers

Although Windows 2000 does plenty of work, it hires help when necessary. When Windows 2000 needs to talk to unfamiliar parts of your computer, it lets special drivers do the translation. A *driver* is a piece of software that enables Windows 2000 to communicate with parts of your computer.

Hundreds of computer companies sell computer attachables, from printers to sound cards to milking machines. In the past, these companies had to write drivers for their products so that Windows could chat with them and persuade them to work correctly. These days, most companies have agreed to let Windows talk to their hardware using Plug and Play technology so you hardly ever have to bother with drivers. Still, it's possible that the old modem you inherited from Fred in Accounting may need a driver of its very own.

> ✔ Sometimes computer nerds say that your mouse driver is all messed up. They're not talking about your hand, even though your hand is what steers the mouse. They're talking about the piece of software that helps Windows 2000 talk and listen to the mouse.

> ✔ Changing to Windows 2000 may require a new driver for your old hardware. If you send a begging letter to the company that made your mouse, the company may mail you a new, updated driver on a floppy disk. It's much easier to find the company's site on the World Wide Web and fetch the driver from there. But don't start changing drivers without the knowledge and consent of your network's administrator — you could suffer unexpected consequences. (This is the computer term that translates as "You're in hot water now, boyo.")

Files and Folders

A *file* is a collection of information in a form that the computer can play with. A *program file* contains instructions telling the computer to do something useful; like add up the money you spent on take-out food last month. A *data file* contains information you've created, like a picture of a golf ball you drew in the Windows 2000 Paint program.

> ✔ Files can't be touched or handled; they're invisible, unearthly things. Somebody figured out how to store files as little impulses on a round piece of specially coated plastic, or disk.

> ✔ A file is referred to by its filename. Early versions of Windows made people call files by a single word containing no more than eight characters. For example, FILENAME could be the name of a file, as could REPORT, SPONGE, or X. Yes, thinking up descriptive filenames back in those days was difficult.

> Windows 95 finally broke the barrier and Windows 98, Windows NT 4, and Windows 2000 came spilling in too. Now you can call files by bunches of words, as long as the words (and spaces) don't total more than 255 characters.

✔ Filenames have optional extensions of up to three letters that usually refer to the program that created them. For example, the Windows 2000 Notepad program automatically saves files with the extension TXT. Microsoft realized that most people don't care about file extensions, so Windows 2000 no longer lists a file's extension when it's displaying filenames.

You'll still see a file extension when Windows 2000 is confused about what program created a particular file — then Windows 2000 displays that confusing file's file extension on the screen, and asks you to choose which program created it. Once you tell Windows 2000 which programs create which files, it usually remembers which extensions come from which programs.

✔ Filenames still have nearly as many rules and regulations as the Department of Motor Vehicles, so for more information than you'll ever want to know about filenames, flip to Chapter 13.

Folders and Directories

In your everyday paper world, files are stored in folders in a cabinet. In the computer world, files are stored in a *directory* on a disk. Dusty old file cabinets are boring, but directories are even more dreadfully boring: They'll never hold any long-lost baseball cards.

So Windows 2000 swapped metaphors. Instead of holding files in directories, Windows 2000 holds files in folders. You can see the little pictures of the folders on your monitor.

The folders in Windows 2000 are really just directories, if you've already grown used to that term.

Maintaining files and working with folders can be painful experiences, so they're explained in Chapter 13. In the meantime, just think of folders and directories as separate work areas to keep files organized. Different directories and folders hold different projects; you move from directory to directory as you work on different things with your computer.

Older versions of Windows stored files in directories. Ever since Windows 95, Windows has been storing files in folders. The two terms mean the same thing.

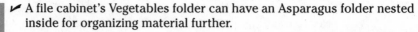

✔ A file cabinet's Vegetables folder can have an Asparagus folder nested inside for organizing material further.

✔ Technically, a folder in a folder is a nested *subfolder* that keeps related files from getting lost. For example, you can have subfolders for Butter and Lemon in the Asparagus subfolder, which lives in the Vegetables folder.

Hardware and Software

Alert! Alert! Fasten your seat belt so you don't slump forward when reading about these two particularly boring terms: *hardware* and *software*.

Your CD player is hardware; so are the stereo amplifier, speakers, and batteries in the boombox. By itself, the CD player doesn't do anything but hum. It needs music to disturb the neighbors. The music is the software, or the information processed by the CD player.

✔ Now you can unfasten your seat belt and relax for a bit. Computer hardware refers to anything you can touch, including hard things like a printer, a monitor, disks, and disk drives.

✔ Software is the ethereal stuff that makes the hardware do something fun. A piece of software is called a *program*. Programs come on disks or CDs.

✔ Software has very little to do with lingerie.

✔ When somber technical nerds (STNs) say, "It must be a hardware problem," they mean that something must be wrong with your computer itself: its disk drive, keyboard, or central processing unit (CPU). When they say, "It must be a software problem," they mean that something is wrong with the program you're trying to run from the disk. When they say, "It's a configuration problem," it means that they don't have the foggiest notion what's going on.

Icons

An icon is a little picture. Windows 2000 fills the screen with icons. You choose among them to make Windows 2000 do different things. For example, you choose the Printer icon, the little picture of the printer, to make your computer print something. Icons are just fancy names for cute buttons.

You'll find icons in just about every Windows 2000-based program.

✔ Windows 2000 relies on icons for nearly everything, from opening files to releasing the winged monkeys.

✔ Some icons have explanatory titles, like Open File or Terrorize Dorothy. Others make you guess (for example, the big blue "e" which opens the Internet Explorer browser).

✔ Can't figure out an icon's function in life? Rest your mouse pointer over it for a few moments; in many Windows 2000-based programs, a box pops up to give you helpful material explaining what the icon is supposed to do.

Kilobytes, Megabytes, and So On

Figuring out the size of a real file folder is easy: Just look at the thickness of the papers stuffed in and around it. But computer files are invisible, so their size is measured in *bytes* (which is pronounced like what Dracula does).

A byte is pretty much like a character or letter in a word. For example, the word *sodium-free* contains 11 bytes. (The hyphen counts as a byte.) Computer nerds picked up the metric system a lot more quickly than the rest of us, so bytes are measured in kilos (1,000), megas (1,000,000), gigas (a thousand megas), and teras (too big to think about).

A page of double-spaced text is about 1,000 bytes, known as 1 kilobyte, which is often abbreviated as 1K. One thousand of those kilobytes is a megabyte, or 1MB. Your computer's hard disk is full of bytes; most hard disks today contain between 200MB and 1GB (a gigabyte).

Big Warning Department: Today's software sticks a bunch of special coding and graphics into documents these days: A single page of text can easily consume 40K of space.

If you're working on a large network, your own computer may not have a large hard disk. Instead, the hard disk (or hard disks — some computers have a whole bunch of them) may be attached to a big computer — the computer running Windows 2000 Server. Everybody in the office then accesses the information on the server through the network cables, like four people sharing one milkshake with a handful of straws.

✔ Unlike hard disks, which come in a wide variety of sizes to meet different needs, almost all floppy disks hold 1.4MB of information. (A few older varieties hold less.)

✔ All files are measured in bytes, regardless of whether they contain text. For example, that Windows 2000 logo some people use as background art for their Desktop is 129,831 bytes. (For information on using that Windows 2000 logo, see Chapter 11. Chapter 11 also shows how to use your own files for wallpaper.)

✔ The Windows Explorer or My Computer window can tell you how many bytes each of your files consumes. (Or click on the file's name with your right mouse button and choose Properties from the menu that pops up.) To find out more, check out Chapter 13.

One kilobyte doesn't really equal 1,000 bytes. That would be too easy. Instead, this byte stuff is based on the number two. One kilobyte is really 1,024 bytes, which is 2 raised to the 10th power, or 2^{10}. (Computers love mathematical details, especially when a 2 is involved.) For more byte-size information, see Table 3-1.

Table 3-1	Ultra-Precise Details from the Slide-Rule Crowd		
Term	**Abbreviation**	**Rough Size**	**Ultra-Precise Size**
Byte	1 byte	1 byte	
Kilobyte	K or KB	1,000 bytes	1,024 bytes
Megabyte	M or MB	1,000,000 bytes	1,048,576 bytes
Gigabyte	G or GB	1,000,000,000 bytes	1,073,741,824 bytes
Terabyte	T or TB	1,000,000,000,000 bytes	1,099,511,627,776 bytes

Loading, Running, Executing, and Launching

Paper files are yanked from a file cabinet and placed onto a desk for easy reference. On a computer, files are loaded from a disk and placed into the computer's memory so you can do important stuff with them. You can't work with a file or program until it has been loaded into the computer's memory.

When you run, execute, or launch a program, you're merely starting it up so you can use it. Load means pretty much the same thing, but some people fine-tune its meaning to describe when a program file brings in a data file.

The Windows 2000 Start button enables picture lovers to start programs by using icons. The Windows Explorer enables text-and-word lovers to start programs by clicking on names in a list (although Explorer lets you click on icons, too, if you prefer).

Memory

Whoa! How did this ugly memory stuff creep in here? Luckily, it all boils down to one key sentence:

The more memory a computer has, the more pleasantly Windows 2000 behaves.

- Memory is measured in bytes, just like a file. All computers sold today have at least 640 kilobytes, or 640K, of memory; most come with much, much more memory — usually 32MB or more.

- Windows 2000 requires 32MB of memory, or it won't even bother to come out of the box. And it won't play nicely with others unless you provide 64MB or more of memory.

Memory and hard disk space are both measured in bytes, but they're two different things: Memory is what the computer uses for quick, on-the-fly calculations when programs are up and running on-screen. Hard disk space is what the computer uses to store unused files and programs.

Everybody's computer contains more hard disk space than memory because hard disks — also known as hard drives — are a lot cheaper. Also, a hard disk remembers things even when the computer is turned off. A computer's memory, on the other hand, is washed completely clean whenever someone turns the computer off or pokes its reset button.

The Mouse

A mouse is a smooth little plastic thing that looks like Soap on a Rope. It rests on a little roller, or ball, and its tail plugs into the back of the PC. When you push the mouse across your desk, the mouse sends its current location through its tail to the PC. By moving the mouse around on the desk, you move a corresponding arrow across the screen.

You can wiggle the mouse in circles and watch the arrow make spirals. Or to be practical, you can maneuver the on-screen arrow over an on-screen button and click the mouse button to boss Windows 2000 around. (Refer to "Clicking," "Double-Clicking," and "Pointers/Arrows" in this chapter and, if you haven't run out of steam, turn to Chapter 2 for information on the parts of your computer.)

Multitasking and Task Switching

Windows 2000 can run two or more programs at the same time, but computer nerds take overly tedious steps to describe the process. So skip this section because you'll never need to know it.

Even though the words task switching and multitasking often have an exclamation point in computer ads, there's nothing really exciting about them.

When you run two programs and switch back and forth between them, you're task switching. For example, if Terry calls while you're reading a book, you put down the book and talk to Terry. You are task switching: stopping one task and starting another. The process is similar to running your word processor and then stopping to look up a phone number in the Exchange program.

But when you run two programs simultaneously, you're multitasking. For example, if you continue reading your book while listening to Terry talk about the fabulous special on string beans at the grocery store, you're multitasking: performing two tasks at the same time. In Windows 2000, multitasking can be as simple as playing a Solitaire game while printing something in the background.

These two concepts differ only subtly, and yet computer nerds make a big deal out of the difference. Everybody else shrugs and says, "So what?"

Networks

Networks connect PCs with cables so that users can share equipment and information. Users can all send stuff to one printer, for example, or they can send messages back and forth talking about Jane's weird new hairstyle.

Windows 2000, which was built for networks, does something a little strange: It makes networks almost invisible to their users. When you open a file on your computer, the network automatically fetches that file from another computer way down the hall — yet the file pops onto your screen quickly and easily, just as if it were stored inside your own computer.

Of course, this explanation assumes that the network is working correctly and that somebody else in the office hasn't already grabbed that file onto his or her own computer. It also assumes that you've been granted access to that file, that you haven't forgotten your logon password, and that your computer's network cable hasn't fallen out.

Just be glad that you, as a Windows 2000 beginner, are safely absolved from knowing anything about networks. Leave network stuff to that poor person in charge known as the Network Administrator.

Plug and Play

Historically, installing new hardware devices has required substantial technical expertise to configure and load hardware and software. Basically, that means only geeks could figure out how to fix their computers and add new gadgets to them.

So a bunch of computer vendors hunched together around a table and came up with Plug and Play — a way for Windows to set up new gadgets for your computer automatically, with little or no human intervention. You plug in your latest gadget, and Windows "interviews" it, checking to see what special settings it needs. Then Windows automatically flips the right switches.

Because Windows keeps track of which switches are flipped, none of the parts have to argue over who got the best settings. Better yet, users don't have to do anything but plug the darn thing into their computers and flip the On switch.

Gadgets that say "Plug and Play" on their boxes should be a lot easier to install under Windows 2000 than gadgets that don't feature those words. But not every manufacturer has gotten it all together, so sometimes you may have to do some switch-flipping yourself.

Pointers/Arrows

This one sounds easy at first: When you roll the mouse around on your desk, you see a little arrow move around on-screen. That arrow is also known as your pointer. (Almost everything in Windows 2000 has two names.)

The pointer serves as your electronic index finger. Instead of pushing an on-screen button with your finger, you move the pointer over that button and click the left button on the mouse.

So what's the hard part? Well, that pointer doesn't always stay an arrow. Depending on where the pointer is located on the Windows 2000 screen, it can turn into a straight line, a two-headed arrow, a four-headed arrow, a little pillar, or a zillion other things. Each of the symbols makes the mouse do something slightly different. Luckily, you can find these and other arrow-heads covered in Chapter 2.

Programs, Accessories, and Applications

Most people call a computer program a program. In Windows 2000, programs are called *applications* or *accessories*.

 ✔ We dunno why.

 ✔ Those free programs that came with Windows 2000 (Calculator, WordPad, Phone Dialer, and so on) are called accessories. The programs sold for Windows 2000 are called applications.

 ✔ This book uses the terms program and application interchangeably, because they're pretty much the same thing. But we hardly ever use the word accessory, because it sounds like something you might pick up at Neiman Marcus.

Quitting or Exiting Programs

Done working with a program? Then feel free to "turn it off" by quitting or exiting the program.

Exiting Windows programs is fairly easy because all the programs are supposed to use the same special exit command. You simply click on the little X in the upper-right corner of the program's window. Or if you prefer using the keyboard, you hold down the Alt key (either one of them, if you have two) and press the key labeled F4. (The F4 key is a function key; function keys are either in one row along the top of your keyboard or in two rows along its leftmost edge. Check out Chapter 2 for more function key fun.)

If you're done with a program but think you may need to use it again really soon, just minimize the program: Find the three little squares in the program's topmost right corner and click in the square with the little bar. The window shrinks itself down into a little icon along your computer's taskbar — that bar running along an edge of your screen. (Click on that minimized program's icon when you're ready to use the program again.)

Don't quit a program by just flicking off your computer's power switch. Doing so can foul up your computer's innards. Instead, you must leave the program responsibly so that it has time to perform its housekeeping chores before it shuts down.

 ✔ When you press Alt+F4 or click on the little X in the upper-right corner, the program asks whether you want to save any changes you've made to the file. Normally, you click on the button that says something like "Yes, by all means, save the work I've spent the last three hours trying to create." (If you've muffed things up horribly, click on the No button.

Windows 2000 disregards any work you've done and lets you start over from scratch.)

✔ If by some broad stretch of your fingers you press Alt+F4 by accident, click on the button that says Cancel, and the program pretends that you never tried to leave it. You can continue as if nothing happened.

✔ Early Windows programs have a square button, located in the upper-most left corner, that looks like an aerial view of a single-slot toaster. Double-clicking on that toaster exits the program. Windows 2000 still lets you close most Windows programs by either double-clicking in the uppermost left corner (although the programs don't have that toaster anymore). However, single-clicking on the X in the program's uppermost right corner is usually easier. But either action tells the program that you want to close it down.

✔ Save your work before exiting a program or turning off your computer. Many programs aren't smart enough to save your work automatically (although they're usually polite enough to ask if you'd like them to save it for you).

Quitting or Exiting Windows 2000 Professional

When you're ready to throw in the computing towel and head for greener pastures, you need to stop, or quit, any programs you've been using. The terms quit and exit mean pretty much the same thing: make the current program on-screen stop running so you can go away and do something a little more rewarding.

To quit Windows 2000, click on the Start button and choose the Shut Down command. A box pops up, as shown in Figure 3-2.

Figure 3-2: Choosing the Shut Down command brings up a variety of options.

Each option does something slightly different:

- **Log off *yourname*:** Click on the downward-pointing arrow and choose this option if you're unsure of what else to choose. It "logs you off" the computer, essentially locking up your own account. Other people can use the computer — in fact, the computer tells passersby that they can press Ctrl+Alt+Delete to log on if they'd like to use the computer. But they have to log on with their own passwords and use their own accounts.

- **Shut down:** This option "logs you off" the computer and prepares the animal for being turned off. The computer shuts down all your currently running Windows-based programs (politely asking whether you'd like to save any unsaved work) and then leaves a message on the screen saying that turning off the computer is safe. (If you arrive at the Shut Down Windows box by mistake, simply click on the Cancel button to return to what you were doing.)

  Although you should always turn off your monitor when you're through computing for the day, ask your Network Administrator whether or not you should turn off your computer. Network Administrators treat matters like that very seriously.

- **Restart:** Click on the downward-pointing arrow and choose this option if the computer seems to be acting weird. Windows 2000 basically saves all your work, shuts down your programs, and restarts the computer from scratch. Something akin to taking off your shoe and shaking it, this option can often knock out the pebble that was causing so much grief.

Save Command

Save means to send the work you just created on your computer to a disk for safekeeping. Unless you specifically save your work, your computer thinks you've just been fiddling around for the past four hours. You need to specifically tell the computer to save your work before it will safely store the work on a disk.

Thanks to Microsoft's snapping leather whips, all Windows-based programs use the same Save command, no matter what company wrote them. Press and release the Alt, F, and S keys in any Windows program, in that order, and the computer saves your work.

If you're saving something for the first time, Windows 2000 asks you to think up a filename for the work and pick a folder to stuff the new file into. Luckily, we cover this stuff in Chapter 5.

✔ You can save files to a hard disk, floppy disk, or any special gadgets attached to your computer, such as writable CDs, Zip disks, or other removable media.

✔ If you prefer using the mouse to save files, click on the word File from the row of words along the top of the program. When a menu drops down, choose Save.

✔ Choose descriptive filenames for your work. Windows 2000 gives you 255 characters to work with, so a file named "June Report on Squeegee Sales" is generally more helpful than one named "Stuff."

✔ Some programs, such as Microsoft Word for Windows, have an autosave feature that automatically saves your work every five minutes or so.

Save As Command

Huh? Save as what? A chemical compound? Naw, the Save As command just gives you a chance to save your work with a different name and in a different location.

Suppose that you open the July 1999 Financial Report file in your Stuff folder and change a few numbers so that it's now the August 1999 Financial Report. You want to save the changes, but you don't want to lose the original report for July. So you choose Save As and type in the new name, August 1999 Financial Report.

✔ The Save As command is identical to the Save command when you're first trying to save something new: You can choose a fresh name and location for your work.

✔ Windows 2000 uses the same Open and Save box for all programs, so you only have to figure it out *once*.

✔ 'Tis better to have loved and lost than to have choked on a meatball and coughed.

Shortcuts

The shortcut concept has appealed to most people since childhood: Why bother walking around the block to get to school when a shortcut through Mr. McGurdy's backyard can get you there twice as fast?

The same goes for Windows 2000. Instead of wading through a bunch of menus to get somewhere, you can create a shortcut and assign it to an icon. Then when you double-click on the shortcut icon, Windows 2000 immediately takes you there and loads the file.

You can create a shortcut to your word processor, for example, and leave the shortcut icon sitting on your Desktop within easy reach. A shortcut is simply a push button that loads a file or program. You can even make shortcuts for accessing your printer, disk drive, or a popular folder. In fact, shortcuts are so much fun, we cover them again in Chapter 12.

✔ The ever-helpful Start button automatically makes a shortcut to the last 15 documents you've opened. Click on the Start button, choose Documents, and you see shortcuts waiting for you to discover them.

✔ Unfortunately, the Start button keeps track of only the last 15 documents you've opened. If you're looking for the sixteenth one, you won't find a shortcut waiting. Also, not all programs tell the Start button about recently opened documents; the shortcuts then don't appear on the list. (It's not your fault, if that makes you feel any better.)

✔ Shortcuts are no more than a push button that starts a program. If you delete a shortcut, you haven't deleted a program; you've just removed a button that started that program. And since they're just a push button, you can make a dozen shortcuts to, let's say your favorite spreadsheet, and put them anywhere you want without causing any trouble. You can find much more information about shortcuts in Chapter 12.

Taskbars

Windows 2000 converts your screen to a Desktop but, of course, your screen is a lot smaller than any *real* desktop. That means that after you open a few windows, your screen can end up looking like a particularly untidy In Box.

To keep track of what's happening, Windows 2000 Professional uses the *taskbar.* It's usually stuck to the bottom of your screen and shows what windows are open. If you've found the Start button, you've found the taskbar because the Start button lives at the taskbar's far left end.

✔ Open a window or a program and Windows 2000 Professional tosses a miniature version of the window onto the taskbar. Open a lot of windows and the taskbar will shrink the buttons so that they all fit on the taskbar.

✔ If the window you want to see is hiding somewhere on your Desktop, just click its corresponding button on the taskbar and your missing window pops to the top.

✔ Don't like having the taskbar at the bottom of the screen? Just click on one of its naked parts (a bare spot) and, while holding the mouse button down, drag it to the side or top of the screen, then let go.

✔ You can set up the taskbar with other things that you use all the time — like your favorite programs. Chapter 7 has all you need to make the taskbar as crowded as the subway at rush hour.

The Windows

Windows 2000 lets you run several programs at the same time by placing them in windows. A window is just a little box.

You can move the boxes around. You can make them bigger or smaller. You can make them fill your entire screen. You can make them turn into little icons at the bottom of your screen. You can spend hours playing with windows. In fact, most frustrated new Windows 2000 users do.

✔ You can put as many windows on-screen as you want, peeping at all of them at the same time or just looking into each one individually. This activity appeals to the voyeur in all of us. (Window peeking, moving, and resizing information appears in Chapter 7.)

✔ For instructions on how to retrieve a lost window from the pile, head immediately to Chapter 8.

Chapter 4

Network Things Administrators Think You Already Know

. . . .

In This Chapter

▶ Understanding the network terms used in connection with Windows 2000

▶ Cross-referencing chapters where topics introduced are talked about in detail

. . . .

*P*eople who run networks are distracted, sometimes distraught, and generally bursting at the seams with jolly jargon and acronyms. They love this alien language so much, they've even got an acronym for acronyms — TLA — which stands for Three-Letter Acronym!

However, you don't have to adopt a foreign tongue. Just practice a look of alert intelligence and always be prepared to demonstrate the look. After you have that look down, whip it out when you hear a term that is totally meaningless to you. Nod — alertly and intelligently — and scoot back to your cubicle and this chapter.

Account or User Account

In most corporate settings, security is a big issue. Like everybody else, businesses have secrets, including financial records, personnel files, and even real-live trade secrets — all things that some people should see and others shouldn't.

All these things have to be on the network somewhere. Not only do the corporate bigwigs need to keep spies from finding out the secret recipe for the company's Super Salsa, but they also need to keep you from finding out that Roger (the weasel!) is making more money than anyone else in the department.

The primary way to control who can access different things on the network is the *account* (also called user account), which is what the Network Administrator sets up for you on your first day of work. You're given a user-name (like RathboneA or SharonC) and a password.

- ✔ Your first password is given to you by the Network Administrator, but you're required to provide your own, secret password as soon as you log on for the first time.

- ✔ Without an account, you can't use any machine on the network. The computers all ignore you. The administrator defines your user account and pretty much says what you can and can't do on the network.

- ✔ The Network Administrator, being all-powerful, can change just about any of the settings in your account, so appeal to that person when you want to check out the new color printer or play with the CD-ROM tower, because you won't be able to play with these toys without permission.

Active Directory

Active Directory is a new way of organizing information in Windows 2000, and it's a hot topic of discussion among network administrators and that ilk. It is not something that a normal person needs to know anything about. Whether your network does or does not use Active Directory — it won't make any difference to you.

Client/Server

Client/server is the term for the kind of network Windows 2000 Server sets up. Here's how it works: The *server* is the big machine or machines that store great big files, applications, or other types of information. Your own computer is the *client*. The network is the medium by which you get at these big files. After you've done what you need to do, the files are saved back on the server.

Think of it as going into a restaurant to eat. That makes you the client. Your server (who in California is probably named Brad or Ronni) hands over your soup. There's a fly in it, so you send it back. The server takes it into the kitchen, fishes out the fly, and brings the same soup back. This is the basic client/server relationship — in the end, the server has the last word, whether you know it or not.

Servers are the machines on a network that provide services to other computers so that these other computers can spend their time doing their regular business. Here are two examples:

One, two, many controllers

On a network with *domains* (described later in this chapter), each domain has at least one domain controller. The *domain controller* is the computer that stores all the information about the domain — details about users, computers, security settings, and so forth.

The controller is where all the clients check in at logon, logoff, and many times in between. (Don't worry — this "logon, logoff" stuff gets its own explanation later in this chapter.) That's why in big domains there are many controllers. That way if a controller is busy (or overworked, or just plain too tired to function at the moment), another controller can jump in and keep everything operational.

The point? If a computer freaks out, all the company's important information won't freak out with it. At least, that's what Microsoft means when it says Windows 2000 is a very "stable environment."

✔ *File servers* mean that workstations don't have to have humongous hard disks. You can fetch files from servers and return the files when you're done.

✔ *Print servers* handle directing printing traffic to the right printers and determining what prints first and what can wait. This means not only that printers can be shared, but also that your computer doesn't have to wait for a printer to be free before getting rid of the print job and moving on to other tasks.

On a Windows 2000 network, the server always runs Windows 2000 Server. Because you're reading this book, you're probably running Windows 2000 Professional — the client portion of Windows 2000.

Computer Name

Just like people, pets, and some beloved automobiles, every networked computer has its own name. With all the information flowing back and forth on the network, the names let Windows 2000 Server keep track of where everything is coming from and where it's going to. Also, names are much nicer than numbers. For example, RECEPTIONIST is easier to recognize than AC432SUB5695. Computer names are usually pretty short but can be as long as 15 characters.

To see the names of computers on your network, click on the icon labeled My Network Places, which we describe later in this chapter.

Domain

A *domain* is a collection of computers on a network. It's usually set up to group together all the people in one department or all the people doing the same kind of work. Many networks have only one domain; a really big network can have many domains.

- ✔ Knowing what domain you're in is important only if you want to play Hearts with your friend in another domain. In that case, the administrator has to give you permission to talk to the other domain (try to come up with a reason that doesn't include recreational topics).

- ✔ To qualify as a domain, the group of computers must designate at least one of its number to be a controller — the computer that bosses around everyone else in the domain.

Computers in a domain need to have only a couple of things in common: They all use the same servers, and they all have the same rules about security.

Like most businesses, a domain can have many controllers (bosses). Unlike most bosses, however, all domain controllers in Windows 2000 are equal.

Home Directory

A *home directory* is where you store all your computer files; everyone on the network has one. The home directory can be on your own machine, but more often, it's on one of the servers. Under most conditions, where it is doesn't make any difference to you.

If you can log on from more than one computer, your home directory is on a server somewhere. Very handy. Not so handy when the server in question is out of action, because then you can be out of action, too.

Logoff

When your computer is on, you are known to be on the network because you used your account to sign on. So if you go away and leave your computer on, some nefarious person (or the three-year-old child of a nice person) can come along and mess things up. And if your user account is the one that's active, guess who gets blamed?

That's why it's important to log off when leaving your computer in any area where other people can get to it. Logging off is simply telling the operating system that you're leaving and that it should break the network connections in an orderly fashion. (Very important to networks — order.)

Just going to the lunchroom for a caffeine fix? See the logging-off section in Chapter 5 for a way to protect your computer without having to log off completely.

 Quick answer department: For a quick way to log off your computer, click the Start button in the bottom-left corner of your screen and choose Shut Down from the menu. Then choose the option that says Log off *yourname* and click OK. That quickly logs you off the network and lets you head for the deli.

Logon

As with a top-secret military base, you can't just wander onto a network. A network has a sentry here, too, only it's called the *domain controller*. You identify yourself (your username) and supply your password. If everything's okay, you're allowed to pass. If it's not, you're shot dead. No, wait, that's not done on networks anymore. Instead, you just get a rude sort of message that says something's wrong, and you're denied entry.

Maybe you typed in your password incorrectly (remember, the password is *case sensitive,* meaning it considers Bullfrog and bullfrog to be two different passwords). Or perhaps you misspelled your username. Try again.

 If repeated tries don't get you on, it's time to wave your hand for help. (The administrator probably did something dumb but unintentional, so don't be hard on the poor schlub.)

 If your computer is not connected to a network, the logon procedure isn't even installed. No username, no password. You just turn the machine on and go.

Mapped Drive

A *mapped drive* is a hard drive (hard disk) on another computer that shows up in Explorer (or My Computer) as if it were on your own machine. For instance, Nancy's C drive could show up on your computer as your own F drive. When you copy things to your F drive, it automatically is mapped to Nancy's C drive. The drive has to be shared for you to map it. (See "Sharing" later in this section.)

If you have a powerful urge to map a hard disk that's on another computer so that it looks just like one of your hard drives, saunter over to Chapter 9 for the step-by-step on how to do it.

With Windows 2000, mapped drives are a lot less necessary than they used to be, because of the addition of My Network Places. You can access any of the shared drives, files, and folders by just clicking your way through the computers, drives, and folders listed in My Network Places. If you find yourself constantly using a particular drive or folder on another person's computer, however, you may want to map that drive so it appears as a letter on your own computer. Mapped drives are sort of a cumbersome, network version of shortcuts.

Member Server

A member server is a computer running Windows 2000 Server that's not a controller. A machine like that probably holds big databases or other files that a lot of people have to be able to get at — and get at quickly. A member server is good for that because it doesn't have to do any of the controller work and can dedicate itself to serving up files (or whatever its main role in life is).

✔ For the most part, whether a computer is a plain member server or a controller server makes no difference to you. Breathe a sigh of relief.

✔ "Member server" is really a Microsoft term. Most people just say, "server" or "file server," either of which works just as well.

My Network Places

Right on your Desktop is an icon labeled My Network Places.

Double-click on the icon, and you see all the computers on your domain (at least the ones you're allowed to see), including your own. By clicking your way through the folders, you can get at any document, file, folder, or program that's being shared.

My Network Places has an icon for your computer, and you can use it to get at things on your own machine. Yes, it is a very roundabout way to open a file. Using My Network Places to get what you want is covered in Chapter 9.

Changing the name of My Network Places to something less (or even more) silly is covered in Chapter 13.

Network

A *network* is no more than a bunch of computers connected together to share information of some sort. The connection can be permanent, in the form of cables, or it can be temporary, using phone lines or even wireless links. Networks can include all sorts of bells and whistles — huge masses of technology so Barbara can send you e-mail asking whether you wanna have lunch on Tuesday.

You can find more info on Networks in Chapters 9 and 16.

Network Administrator

Every network needs an administrator to keep the network going. This is the haggard-looking person you see scuttling down the corridor to fix a non-working printer or the accounting department's e-mail.

Sometimes the administrator is laid-back Larry in the next cubicle, who spends an hour a day maintaining the network. More likely, it's stressed-out Stella, who's there when you arrive for work and is the last one to leave at night.

The administrator (though a network may have more than one) is the person you go to when you can't log on or log off, when you can't find other computers on the network, or when your system has collapsed in some undignified way.

Network Administrators, being very much like real people, respond differently to different stimuli. Until you know whether your administrator is a charming fellow or a real pickle-puss, it's important to tread carefully. And regardless of the administrator's personality, always provide the occasional small offering, such as Doritos or Jolt cola (which is mother's milk to them).

Outlook Express

Outlook Express is the part of Windows 2000 that handles messaging — in other words, all your internal and external electronic mail goes through Outlook Express.

Have a look at Chapter 16 for advice on using Outlook Express.

Password

A password, along with your username, is what you need whenever you want to fire up your computer and log onto the network. Your first password is probably given to you, but then you're required to make up one of your very own almost immediately.

Everything you'd ever care to know about passwords is at the very beginning of Chapter 5.

Find out early what your network's policy is about passwords. In some cases, you may be required to change yours every 60 days or so. You don't want to be caught unaware one morning when you're in a desperate hurry and the logon procedure cheerily announces that you have to provide a new password before proceeding. Yikes.

Peer-to-Peer

Peer-to-peer is a type of network that doesn't have controllers. Every machine in the network is equal. It seems very democratic, but someone still has to administer the network, even if it's not a very big job. Otherwise, people give different names to printers and hard disks, and soon your office starts looking like the floor of the New York Stock Exchange, with people standing around yelling at each other.

 ✔ Peer-to-peer is a perfectly good way to set up any computer network with ten or fewer computers, even if they're not running Windows 2000. Each computer acts as both a client and a server.

 ✔ Peer-to-peer networks are sometimes called workgroups.

Permissions

Permissions are bestowed by the Network Administrator (and a few other honchos) and basically say who gets to use what things in what way. For example, you need permission to use either a printer on the network or the cool Games folder on Nick's computer. Nick can't do it himself.

Permissions are also graciously granted for you to open particular folders or get an Internet connection. Permissions are so specific that they can be assigned down to individual files (but only on a hard disk that's using complicated NTFS stuff — which I'm sure you'd rather not know about).

- ✔ The usual kind of permission is called *full control*, which means that you can do whatever you like with the object: Read it, change it, save it, and even delete it.

- ✔ Other levels of permission, commonly found with files and folders, let you read the files but not change them, or both read and change but not delete. Yep, those Network Administrators are attending to some pretty bothersome details. (And those details get a good shakedown in Chapter 9.)

- ✔ Permissions are talked about interchangeably with rights, but they're not the same thing. Permissions apply to particular things; rights apply to the system as a whole. This only matters in the administrator's alternate universe. In the real world, you can use whichever word pops into your head first.

Remote Access

If you've ever called up CompuServe or America Online, you've already done remote access. It just means that you can use a computer to connect to another computer (or network of computers) even if you're not directly connected by a network cable.

Windows 2000 has remote access built in. If your company uses remote access, you (or somebody) can phone in from Beijing or Biloxi, connect to the network, and do whatever business you need to do, just as if you were in the next cubicle.

Remote access business is sometimes handled by a Remote Access server, which is a computer that receives the phone calls, handles the verification process (keeping strangers out), and directs traffic. Any old computer can be a Remote Access server because even the pokiest computer can handle data a zillion times faster than a phone line.

Resource

Resource is just a generic name to cover anything that's shared over the network — a file, a folder, a printer. If you can see it on your screen, it's a resource. Just because it's a resource doesn't necessarily mean you have permission to use it. See the section, "Permissions," in this chapter.

Server

Server is an annoying term because it's used to mean different things. Most of the time, it means a controller on the network. But you can also have computers called file servers, print servers, fax servers — on and on.

Even so, you're safe in assuming that every server on a Windows 2000 network does the following things:

- ✔ Uses Windows 2000 Server or Windows NT Server as its operating system
- ✔ Provides something to the workstation (that's you) that the workstation doesn't have

The second item sums up the strength of a network with servers: Expensive hardware can be shared, and processor work can be farmed out to computers that have little else to do. The "Client/Server" entry earlier in this chapter has more on the relationship between you and the server.

Sharing

Unless you're a member of the Network Administrator's inner circle, you have nothing to say about what's shared. The administrator and a few other cronies with some of the administrator's powers are the only ones who can determine that.

But once something's shared, you can make use of shared folders (directories) on other computers. And you can use any of the shared printers or other resources on the network — providing you also have permission to use them.

TCP/IP

TCP/IP is a term that the technically tiresome throw around with great abandon. Simply put, TCP/IP is the protocol that the Internet works on — and probably your network, too. A protocol is a set of rules about how data is transmitted back and forth. Computers using different protocols can't talk to each other.

Okay, here it comes. TCP/IP stands for Transmission Control Protocol/Internet Protocol.

Username

You need two pieces of information to log onto the network: your password and your username. Your username is not exactly the same as your real name, because most networks have a standard way of assigning usernames.

For example, every username on one network may be a person's last name plus a first initial, or each one may be a first name plus some number of letters from the last name. The standard was determined when the network was set up to provide some consistency. So Kathy O'Dea may end up being KathyO, or Wayne Wong's username could be WongWay, depending on the network.

> ✔ You may be able to change a truly unfortunate username if you appeal at once to the administrator's good graces. But don't wait — the longer you have it, the harder it is to change.
>
> ✔ You're assigned a username at the same time you get your starting password.
>
> ✔ Passwords will (and should) change, but your username goes on forever.

Workgroup

A workgroup is a collection of Windows computers that are grouped together because they're all doing the same kind of work or they're all in the same department. Within the workgroup, all the computers are peers, and the users themselves decide what is shared with other members of the group. Workgroups can be part of an actual client/server network.

If you're assigned to a workgroup, you log on to the workgroup or you log onto the domain you're part of. You can't be in two places at once, as Lt. Columbo loved to point out.

Workstation

In general, when people talk about a workstation, they mean some big, powerful hotshot computer that can calculate rocket trajectories in real time. True, some workstations can do all that and more. But in the world of Windows 2000, a workstation is any computer that's running Windows 2000 Professional as its operating system.

That the two types of computers may coincide is irrelevant.

Part II
Making Windows 2000 Do Something

The 5th Wave — By Rich Tennant

"WE SORT OF HAVE OUR OWN WAY OF PREDICTING NETWORK PROBLEMS."

In this part . . .

After you get used to its rough edges, Windows 2000 can be more fun than a plastic snap-together stegosaurus from the bottom of a Cracker Jack box. It's especially fun to show neighboring co-workers the built-in screen savers, like the one that straps you into a starship and cruises toward the Fifth Quadrant's snack shop at warp speed. You can even adjust the ship's speed through the Windows 2000 Control Panel.

Unfortunately, some spoil-sport will eventually mutter the words that bring everything back to Earth: "Let's see Windows 2000 do something useful, like send e-mail, or teach Bill to remove his old sandwiches from the lunch room refrigerator *before* they turn green."

Toss this eminently practical part at them to quiet 'em down.

Chapter 5

Getting to Work with Windows 2000 Professional

• •

• •

*W*elcome to the world of Windows 2000, where your computer lives in social contact with bunches of other computers. Here, networking no longer refers to people at cocktail parties looking to find better jobs. No, in the Windows 2000 world, networking refers to how the computers interact, hopefully coexisting in peace and harmony.

Consider this chapter a guide toward Social Etiquette in Windows 2000. Here, you discover how to make Windows 2000 not only recognize you but also treat you politely when you sit in front of your computer. You find out where the programs live and how to address them properly. You see where some of the other computers live and how to find the right ones.

The chapter explains how to coax Windows 2000 into running two or more programs simultaneously without complaining. It also shows how to send your work to the printer so you can convince doubting coworkers that you are, indeed, capable of making Windows 2000 do something useful.

Finally, you find out how to log off Windows 2000 — a required method of bidding your computer adieu until you meet again.

Logging Onto Windows 2000

When a Windows 2000 computer starts its day, the system goes through its usual ritual of checking to see that all of its parts are still present and working. After going through a certain amount of clicking and clacking, the whole shebang stops dead at a screen that says "press Ctrl+Alt+Delete to begin."

Go ahead and hold down all three keys simultaneously. (Most people use both hands for this.) This key combination opens the Log On to Windows box, where you're asked to type in your username and password. Enter them into the appropriate boxes and click on OK.

- ✔ Pressing Ctrl+Alt+Delete while running some earlier versions of Windows or DOS causes the computer to die violently, taking all your unsaved work down with it. Windows 2000 uses the magical Ctrl+Alt+Delete sequence in a much more benign way, so don't be scared if the computer tells you to press those keys — it's okay now.

- ✔ The User Name box already contains the name of the last person to use the computer. If that isn't you, double-click on the name in the User Name box to highlight it, and type your username instead.

- ✔ Remember that passwords are case-sensitive. If your password is WormHead and you type in Wormhead, the network, already disgusted, refuses to let you in.

- ✔ If you can't log on the first time, try again. After several tries, if you still can't get access, it's time to raise your hand and play Ask the Network Administrator.

- ✔ If you ever see a box labeled Domain, don't change what's there — unless you've been specifically told to. Even if other domains are on the network, you probably can't log onto them directly anyway.

Changing your password

Even if it's not required, changing your password every few months is a good idea. To do so, log in using your old password, and then press Ctrl+Alt+Delete to open the Windows 2000 Security box. Click on Change Password and type in your old password, then your new one (twice). Click OK and the next time you log on, you start using the new password.

Oh, NO! I can't remember my password

If you suddenly can't remember your password, don't panic. Just stop for a minute and don't think. Get a drink of water. Call your mom like you promised. Write down your choices for the football pool.

Still can't remember? *Now* you can try thinking. Did you write it down somewhere safe? So safe, you don't know where? What kinds of passwords do you usually choose? What were you doing when you changed it the last time?

If in the end, you can't come up with your password, you will have to go to the Network Administrator. The administrator can change your password to a new one, tell you what the new one is so you can log on, and require you to change the new password into a private one that only you know. (Again!)

- ✔ The administrator can't find out what your password is and tell you.
- ✔ The administrator can only delete private passwords and assign new ones.
- ✔ It's true that this is a pretty easy administrative task, but if you require it too often, your reputation as a Responsible Person is bound to suffer.

Do I even need a password?

If your Windows 2000 Professional is on a computer that's all by its lonesome — no network to snuggle up to — then you won't be asked for a username and password at all. But if the computer has expectations of being part of a network — even if it's only every now and then, you'll need a username and password.

Starting Your Favorite Program

When Windows 2000 first takes over your computer, it turns your screen into a Desktop. However, "Desktop" is merely a fancy name for a plate of buttons with labels underneath them. Click on a button, and a program hops to the screen in its own little window.

Click on the Start button in the bottom-left corner of the screen, move the mouse pointer over the menus, and you'll see even more buttons to choose from (see Figure 5-1).

Because the buttons have little pictures on them, they're called icons. An icon offers clues to the program it represents. For example, the icon on the Desktop with the computers and cables stands for My Network Places, a program that lets people talk to other computers on their network.

See the dark bar shading Windows Explorer in Figure 5-1? The bar means that the Windows Explorer program is *highlighted:* It's queued up and ready to go. As long as you leave the mouse pointer on the highlighted name, it'll stay ready. If you click your left mouse button anywhere on the highlighted portion, Explorer hops to the forefront. (Don't do it now though, because Explorer is too boring to play with right now. Just slide the pointer off the menu and it collapses. Click on a blank spot on the Desktop and the whole menu goes away.)

Now, it's time to try some of this stuff yourself. Roll your mouse around until its arrow hovers over the Start button.

Click your mouse button, and the Start menu pops up on the screen. Next, roll your mouse pointer up to Programs, and another menu full of buttons shoots out. Slide over to Accessories to see yet another menu (your screen now looks a lot like Figure 5-1). Keep sliding to Games to see the last menu on the chain. And if you're not too exhausted, click on Freecell (as shown in Figure 5-2) and play a few hands of the Windows 2000 card game.

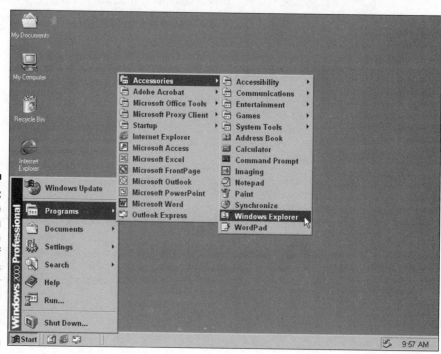

Figure 5-1:
Click on the
Start button
to see
menus of
programs
and other
options in
Windows
2000.

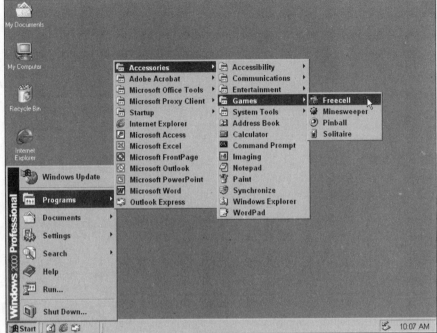

Figure 5-2:
Click on
your
program's
name or
icon to
load it.

✔ The Start button is just a big panel of buttons. When you press one of the buttons by pointing at it and clicking with the mouse, the program assigned to that button heads for the top of the screen and appears in a little window.

✔ Probably when you were sliding your mouse around, if you paused long enough, a little label popped up with a description of what you were pointing to. You can keep these pop-up description labels around for as long as you like, but when you get tired of them, Chapter 6 tells you how to turn 'em off.

✔ Icons can stand for files as well as for programs. Clicking on Documents in the Start menu usually brings up shortcut buttons that take you to 15 of your most recently used documents.

✔ Microsoft has already set up the Start button to include icons for the most popular programs and files that Windows 2000 found when it installed itself on your computer — stuff like Excel and WordPerfect. If you want to add some other programs and files, however, check out the section in Chapter 12 on customizing your Start button.

✔ If you're kind of sketchy about all this double-click stuff, head to the mouse section in Chapter 2.

Bond . . . James Bond — to the white courtesy telephone, please!

Passwords are the cloak-and-dagger part of the network business because keeping out unauthorized folk is a security focus for most institutions. Passwords are also the bane of both network users and administrators, and here's why.

The administrator wants you, the user, to change your password frequently in case other people discover it and use it, to refrain from writing it down, and to choose something that's hard for other people to guess. On the other hand, you, the user, want an easy-to-remember password that never has to be changed. Those two different goals can create a slight conflict, but not one that's impossible to deal with.

Passwords can be as long as 14 characters, but unless you're a speed typist, you'll be happier in the 6 to 8 character range.

A good password is

- At least six characters long

- A mix of lowercase and uppercase characters, with at least one non-alphabetic character

Bad passwords are

- Your name or initials

- Names or initials of family members

- Your dog's name or initials

- Your birth date or the birth date of a family member

- A variation on your username

- Your phone number or phone numbers of friends or family

- Popular obscenities — even when spelled backwards.

One good method is to turn a catch phrase or family joke into an acronym. For example, I've used the password *Wk?Wc?*, which is just a shortened version of "Who knows? Who cares?" Or do the same with a song or a book title. (Don't use the title of the book that's on your desk next to the computer.)

Passwords, unlike usernames and filenames, are *always* case-sensitive. If your password is *Wk?Wc?* and you type in WK?WC?, the password won't be recognized.

Overall password policy is set by the administrator. So passwords may be required to have a minimum length, and you may have to change your password at regular intervals.

- Despise mice? You don't need a mouse for the Start button. Hold down the Ctrl key and press the Esc key to make the Start menu appear. Then press the arrow keys to navigate the various menus. Highlighted the program you want? Press Enter, and the program begins to run.

- If the icon you're after in the Start menu has a dark background, it's highlighted. If you just press the Enter key, the highlighted program loads itself into a window. Or you can still click on it to load it. Windows 2000 lets you do things in a bunch of different ways.

- This chapter gives you just a quick tour of Windows 2000. You can find glowing descriptions of the Start button in Chapter 12.

Using pull-down menus

Windows 2000, bless its heart, makes an honest effort toward making computing easier. For example, the Start button puts a bunch of options on the screen in front of you. You just choose the one you want, and Windows 2000 takes it from there.

But if Windows 2000 put all its options on the screen at the same time, it would be more crowded than the 14-page menu at the House of Hui restaurant. To avoid resorting to fine print, Windows 2000 hides some menus in special locations on the screen. When you click the mouse in the right place, more options leap toward you, like whether you'd prefer your Dim Sum chicken feet to be spicy or incendiary.

For example, load the Windows 2000 word-processing program, WordPad, by clicking on the Start button, choosing Programs, sliding onto the Accessories area, and choosing WordPad.

See the row of words beginning with File that rests along the top edge of WordPad? You'll find a row of words — called a *menu bar* — across the top of every Windows program. Move your mouse pointer over the word File and click once.

A menu opens from beneath File. This menu is called a *pull-down menu,* if you're interested, and it looks like what you see in Figure 5-3.

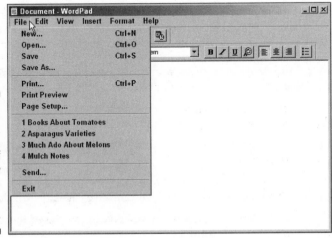

Figure 5-3: Click on a word along the top of any window to reveal a secret pull-down menu.

- Pull-down menus open from any of those key words along the top of a window. Just click the mouse on the word and the menu tumbles down like shoeboxes falling off a closet shelf.

- To close the menu, click the mouse someplace away from the menu. (Or press the Esc key on the keyboard.)

- Different Windows 2000-based programs have different words across the menu bar, but almost all the bars start with File on the left. The File pull-down menu contains file-related options, such as Open, Save, Print, and Push Back Cuticles.

- You'll find pull-down menus sprinkled liberally throughout Windows 2000.

- Oh yeah — to close that WordPad program, click on the box with the little X in the program's upper-right corner.

Loading a file

First, here's the bad news: Loading a file into a Windows 2000-based program can sometimes be a mite complicated. Second, loading a file means the same thing as opening a file.

Now that those trifles have been dispensed with, here's the good news: All Windows 2000-based programs load files in the exact same way. So once you know the proper etiquette for one program, you're prepared for all the others!

Here's the scoop: The problem with loading a file is that you have to find the file first. So to open a file in any Windows 2000-based program, do the following:

1. **Look for the program's menu bar, that row of important-looking words along its top. Because you're after a file, click on File.**

   A most-welcome pull-down menu descends from the word File. The menu has a list of important-looking words.

2. **Because you want to open a file, move the mouse to the word Open and click once again.**

   Yet another box hops onto the screen, as shown in Figure 5-4 — you'll see this box named Open appear over and over again in Windows 2000.

3. **See the list of filenames inside the box? Point at one of them with the mouse and click the button.**

   By default, the first place a Windows program looks for files is the My Documents folder.

4. Click on the Open button.

The program opens the file and displays it on-screen.

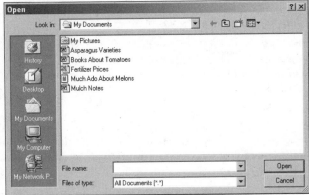

Figure 5-4:
Almost
every
Windows
2000-based
program
tosses this
box at you
when you
open or
save a file.

You've done it! You've loaded a file into a program! Those are the same stone steps you'll walk across in any Windows 2000-based program, whether it was written by Microsoft or by the teenager down the street. All the programs work in the same way.

✔ You can speed things up by simply double-clicking on a file's name; that does the same thing as single-clicking on the filename and then clicking on the Open button. Or you can click on the name once to highlight it (it acquires a dark background), and then press the Enter key. Windows 2000 is full of multiple options like that. (Different strokes for different folks and all.)

Can't see a thing in the Open box? Look at the bottom of the Open box next to a little window labeled Files Of Type. Click the little downward arrowhead on the right side and then click All Documents (some programs show a slightly different option, such as All Files) from the list. Every file in the current folder pops out of hiding — even if they're not the right file type for your program.

✔ If you've changed an open file, even by an accidental press of the spacebar, most programs take it for granted that you've changed the file for the better. When you try to close the file, the program cautiously asks whether you want to save the changes you've made. Click on the No button unless you do, indeed, want to save that version you've haphazardly changed.

✔ The Open box has a bunch of options in it. You can open files that are stored in different folders or on other disk drives. You can also call up files that were created by certain programs, filtering out the ones you won't be needing. All this more complicated Open box stuff is explained in Chapter 6.

✔ If you're still a little murky on the concepts of files, folders, directories, and drives, flip to Chapter 13 for the best ways to explore.

✔ Trying to load a file that you've recently opened? If you opened it in the same program, it shows up on the program's File menu. (Take a look at Figure 5-3 again. The four most recent files loaded in WordPad are listed on the File menu.) Click on any one of these files to spring it back to life.

✔ Or, once you've opened the Open box (shown back in Figure 5-4), click the History button. This handy button shows you every place you've been in and around Windows 2000. To return, just double-click the file or folder you want to see.

✔ You can also click on Documents from the Start button menu. There, Windows 2000 lists the last 15 documents you opened. Click on your document's name, and Windows 2000 loads that document into the program that created it and brings both the program and document to the screen. Modern convenience at its best.

✔ Or go at it from the other direction: Click on the Start button, choose Search and then choose For Files Or Folders. Type in the file's name or what little part of the name you know. Click on Search Now. A whole bunch of files will probably show up in the process of the search. Just double-click on the one you want to open. We cover all the uses for the Search program in Chapter 8.

Putting two programs on-screen simultaneously

After seeing the lavish amount of money spent for Windows 2000 and the computer systems powerful enough to cart it around, you're not going to be content with only one program on your screen. You want to fill the screen with programs, all running in their own little windows.

How do you put a second program on the screen? Well, if you've opened WordPad by clicking on its icon in the Start button's menu, then you're probably already itching to load Freecell, the card game that is a devilishly absorbing variant on solitaire. Simply click on the Start button and start moving through the menus, as described in the "Starting Your Favorite Program" section earlier in this chapter. When you spot Freecell in the Games area, click on it, and it hops to the screen.

✔ This section is intentionally short. When working in Windows 2000, you almost always have two or more programs on the screen at the same time. It's nothing really special, so belaboring the point here is unnecessary.

✔ The special part comes when you move information between the two programs, which we explain in Chapter 10.

✔ If you want to move multiple windows around on the screen, move yourself to Chapter 7.

✔ If you've started up Freecell, you may be wondering where the WordPad window disappeared to. The Freecell window is now covering up the WordPad window. To get WordPad back, check out the information on retrieving lost windows in Chapter 8. (Or if you see a button called WordPad along the bottom of your screen, click on it — WordPad is immediately resurrected from the bottom of the Desktop.)

✔ To switch between windows, just click on the one you want. When you click on a window, it immediately becomes the active window — the window where all the activity takes place. For more information on switching between windows, switch to Chapter 7.

Using the Keyboard

It's a good thing Microsoft doesn't design automobiles. Each car would have a steering wheel, a joystick, a remote control, and handles on the back for people who prefer to push. Windows 2000 offers almost a dozen ways for you to perform the simplest tasks.

For example, if you're a speedy typist and don't like to remove your fingers from the keys, you can take advantage of keyboard shortcuts to all the menus in Windows 2000 Professional. The secret weapon is hiding behind the Alt key.

Press (and release) the Alt key and keep an eye on the row of words in the menu bar. All the words suddenly have a letter underlined and the first word, File, looks like a button that's been depressed. No, it's not unhappy; you've selected it, just as if you'd clicked on it with the mouse.

Now, look a few steps to the right on the menu bar — see how the letter V in View is underlined? Press V on the keyboard, and the pull-down menu hidden below View falls down, like a mushroom off a pizza.

That's the secret underlined-letter trick! And pressing Alt and V is often faster than plowing through a truckload of mouse menus — especially if you think that the whole mouse concept is rather frivolous anyway.

✔ You can access almost every command in Windows 2000 by using the Alt key rather than a mouse. Press the Alt key and then press the key for the underlined letter. That option, or command, then begins to work.

✔ If you've accidentally pressed the Alt key and find yourself trapped in Menu Land, press the Alt key again to return to normal. If that doesn't work, try pressing the Esc key.

✔ As pull-down menus continue to appear, you can keep plowing through them by selecting underlined letters until you accomplish your ultimate goal. For example, pressing Alt and then V brings down the View pull-down menu. Pressing R subsequently activates the Ruler option from the View menu and immediately turns off the Ruler from the top of the word processor's screen. (If you liked the Ruler, press Alt, V, and R again to toggle the Ruler back on.)

To see the underlined letters, press and release your Alt key. Then press that underlined letter to choose that menu item.

Printing Your Work

Eventually, you'll want to transfer a copy of your finely honed work to the printed page so you can pass it around. Printing something from any Windows 2000-based program (or application, or applet, whatever you want to call it) takes only three keystrokes. Press and release the Alt key and then press the letters F and P. Click the Enter button, and what you see on your screen is whisked to a printer.

Pressing the Alt key activates the underlined letters in the words along the top, known as the menu bar. The letter F wakes up the File menu, and the letter P tells the program to send its stuff to the printer — pronto. (See the preceding section for more menu-oriented details.)

✔ Alternatively, you can use the mouse to click on the word File and then click on the word Print from the pull-down menu. Depending on the RPM of your mouse ball and the elasticity of your wrist, the mouse and keyboard methods can be equally quick.

✔ If nothing comes out of the printer after a few minutes, try putting in paper and making sure the printer's turned on.

✔ Some programs, like WordPad, have a little picture of a printer along their top. Clicking on that printer icon is a quick way of telling the program to shuffle your work to the printer. Because your work shoots directly to the printer, however, it bypasses all the menus that let you add fancy printing features: printing more than one copy, for example, or only printing page 3.

Saving Your Work

Any time you create something in a Windows 2000-based program, be it a picture of a spoon or a letter to *The New York Times* begging for a decent comics page, you want to save it to disk.

But I don't have a printer attached to my computer!

Printing is a breeze in Windows 2000 whether you have a printer attached to your computer or you use a printer that's all the way down the hall. Depending on your position in the food chain, you may be able to print to one or to many printers.

To find out what printers are available to you, double-click on your Desktop's My Computer icon and then double-click on the Printers folder. If you see a bunch of printers, look for the icon that has a white check mark in a black circle. That's the printer your computer uses if you're printing something from Notepad or another program that doesn't let you pick a particular printer.

It's also the automatic choice of your programs. When you choose Print from the File menu, though, you can choose any other printer that's been made available to you. That means you can print to the nearest ordinary printer for most things, specify the fancy color printer for your charts, and choose the special high-speed printer for those 1,000-page printing jobs.

To use printers other than the default one, choose Print from your program's File menu. In the window that opens, the default printer is shown in the box labeled Name. But just click on the little downward arrow next to the text box, and a list of the available printers opens. Pick the one you want and then click on the OK button.

Now here's the hard part: Usually, the name that the Network Administrator chooses for the printer is good enough to tell you the type of printer involved. But nothing in any of these boxes is likely to tell you where the printer is actually *located.* A smart and caring administrator may name a printer Tektronix Color Printer in Editorial Department, but much more commonly, the printer is called Unity 1200XL v.47.0. Most helpful, yes?

In these cases, you have no choice but to ask. Start, as usual, with the person in the next cubicle and work your way up. Sure, it takes a little more effort, but then again, you're trying to do something a little fancier than print to the *normal* printer.

For more on network printing, see Chapter 9.

Saving your work means placing a copy of it onto a disk, be it the mysterious hard disk inside your computer or a floppy disk, one of those things you're always tempted to use as beverage coasters. (They make lousy coasters, so don't try it.)

Luckily, Windows 2000 makes it easy for you to save your work. You need only press three keys, just as if you were printing your work or opening a file. To save your work, press and release the Alt key, press F, and then press S.

If you prefer to push the mouse around, click on File in the menu bar. When the secret pull-down menu appears, click on Save. Your mouse pointer turns into an hourglass, asking you to hold your horses while Windows 2000 shuffles your work from the program to your hard disk or a floppy disk for safekeeping.

That's it!

✔ If you're saving your work for the first time, you see a familiar-looking box: It's basically the same box you see when opening a file. See how the letters in the File name box are highlighted? Windows 2000 helpfully suggests that you might want to name your file "Document." The computer is always paying attention to the highlighted areas, so anything you type appears in that box. Type in a name for the file and press Enter.

✔ If Windows 2000 throws a box in your face saying something like `This filename is not valid,` you haven't adhered to the filename guidelines discussed in Chapter 13.

✔ Just as you can load files from different directories and disk drives, you can save to them as well. You can choose among different directories and drives by clicking on various parts of the Save As box. All this stuff is explained in Chapter 13.

Logging Off Windows 2000

Ah! The most pleasant thing you'll do with Windows 2000 all day could very well be to stop using it. And you do that the same way you started: by using the Start button, the friendly little helper that popped up the first time you started Windows 2000.

Other Windows 2000-based programs come and go, but the Start button is always on your screen somewhere. (And if it's currently playing hide-and-go-seek, press Ctrl+Esc to make it reveal itself.)

To log off Windows 2000, click on the Start button and click on the Shut Down command from the Start button's menu. Windows 2000, not able to believe that you're leaving, asks just what you are planning, as shown in Figure 5-5.

Click on the little arrowhead to see your choices — we outline a few of these options in the following sections.

Figure 5-5:
Windows
2000
Professional
gives you
some
choices
when you
decide to
close down.

For the day

If you're planning to turn off the computer completely, choose Shut down, which means that you want Windows 2000 Professional to pick up its toys and close down completely because you're turning the computer off. If you mean business, click on the OK button or press Enter. Windows 2000 starts to put all its parts away, preparing to leave the screen of your computer. If, by some odd mistake, you've clicked on the Shut Down button in error, click on the Cancel button, and Windows 2000 ignores your faux pas. (Keyboard users must press Tab to highlight the Cancel button, and then press Enter.)

For a minute

You don't always have to log off completely. If you're just going down the hall to find out whether Linda has any jujubes and you don't want anyone messing with your machine, press Ctrl+Alt+Delete to open the Windows 2000 Security box, and then click the Lock Workstation button. When you come back with your teeth all stuck together, you need to press Ctrl+Alt+Delete again and type in your password. When you do, your computer screen reappears looking the same as it did when you left.

For a while longer

If your machine might be used by someone else while you're away, just choose Log Off <yourname> and click the OK button. When you come back, you log on as you did before, pressing Ctrl+Alt+Del and typing in your password.

For lazy users

For a fast way to log off, put the Log Off option right on your Start button menu.

1. **Right-click on a bare spot on the taskbar and click Properties on the menu that pops up.**

2. **Click the Start Menu Options tab.**

3. **At the bottom of the page, look for "Display Logoff" and click the box next to it.**

   A check mark appears in the box.

4. **Click the OK button.**

   Next time you click the Start menu, the Log Off option waits for you.

For a quick fix

Restart is the third option in the Shut Down Windows box. Restart shuts down the computer and starts it up again. The restart makes it check all its parts which gives it a clean start. Restart is the computer equivalent of burping a colicky baby. It's not a guaranteed fix, but it does cure a lot of problems.

For your information

When you shut down Windows 2000, you need to follow all the shutdown rules to keep your files and programs happy. Newer programs are good at recovering from unexpected shutdowns, but some just lose their little minds — and that can mean they lose some of your work. Not good.

✔ Be sure to shut down Windows 2000 through its official Shut Down program before turning off your computer. Otherwise, Windows 2000 can't properly prepare your computer for the event, which leads to future troubles.

✔ Holding down Alt and pressing F4 tells Windows 2000 that you want to stop working in your current program and close it down. If you press Alt+F4 while no programs are running, Windows 2000 figures you've had enough for one day, and it acts as if you chose its Shut Down command.

✔ When you tell Windows 2000 you want to quit, it searches through all your open windows to see whether you've saved all your work. If it finds any work you've forgotten to save, it tosses a box your way, letting you click on the OK button to save the work. Whew!

✔ If you happen to have any of those old DOS-based programs running, Windows 2000 stops and tells you to quit your DOS programs first. See, Windows 2000 knows how to shut down Windows 2000-based programs because they all use the same command. But all DOS programs are different. You have to shut the program down manually, using whatever exit sequence you normally use in that program.

✔ If your computer has a sound card, you hear a pleasant wind-chimes sound telling you that it's time to go home and relax. (Or time to buy a sound card if you haven't yet succumbed to the urge.)

Chapter 6

Examining Buttons, Bars, and Boxes

As children, just about all of us played with elevator buttons until our parents told us to knock it off. An elevator gave such an awesome feeling of power: Push a little button, watch the mammoth doors slide shut, and feel the responsive push as the spaceship floor begins to surge upward. What fun!

Windows 2000 takes the elevator-button concept to an extreme, and it loses something in the process. First, some Windows 2000 buttons don't even look like buttons. They're ambiguous little symbols without labels. And the worst of it comes with their terminology: The phrase "push the button" becomes "click the scroll bar above or below the scroll box on the vertical scroll bars." Yuck!

When braving your way through Windows 2000, don't bother learning all these dorky terms. Instead, treat this chapter as a field guide, something you can grab when you stumble across a confusing new button or box. Just page through until you find its picture. Read the description to find out whether that particular object is deadly or just mildly poisonous. Then read to find out where you're supposed to poke it with the mouse pointer.

You get used to the critter after you click on it a few times. Just don't bother remembering the scientific name *vertical scroll bar,* and you'll be fine.

A Typical Window

Nobody wants a field guide without pictures, so Figure 6-1 shows a typical window with its parts labeled.

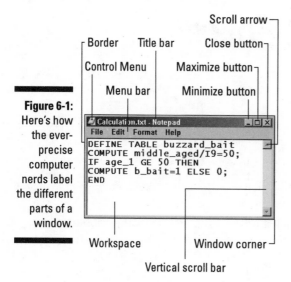

Figure 6-1: Here's how the ever-precise computer nerds label the different parts of a window.

Just as boxers grunt differently depending on where they've been punched, windows behave differently depending on where they've been clicked. The following sections describe the correct places to click and, if that doesn't work, the best places to punch.

- ✔ Windows 2000 is full of little weird-shaped buttons, borders, and boxes. You don't have to remember their Latin or Greek etymologies. The important part is just knowing what part you're supposed to click on.

- ✔ After you click around a bit, you'll see how easy it all is. The hard part is at the beginning, just like when trying to pronounce Ermenegildo Zegna.

Bars

Windows 2000 is filled with bars; perhaps that's why some of its programs seem a bit groggy and hung over. *Bars* simply are thick stripes along the edges of a window. Windows 2000 comes with several varieties of bars.

The title bar

The *title bar* is that topmost strip in any window (see Figure 6-2). It lists the name of the program as well as the name of any open file. For example, the title bar in Figure 6-2 comes from Windows 2000 Notepad.

Figure 6-2:
A title bar.

`Untitled - Notepad                                              _ |□| x|`

If you open Notepad and just start creating a file, Windows 2000 assigns the imaginative "Untitled" as the file name until you save the file and can think of something a little more descriptive. (For example, an untitled file may be full of notes you've jotted down from an energetic phone conversation with Ed McMahon.) Then when you type in the new name for the file, your newly created filename replaces the admittedly vague Untitled in the title bar.

✔ The title bar shows the name of the current program and file. If you've just started to create a file, the title bar displays a generic default filename, such as Untitled, Document1, or some other equally dull name.

✔ The title bar can serve as a handle for moving a window around on-screen. Point at the title bar, hold down the mouse button, and move the mouse around. The window moves as you move the mouse. Let go of the mouse button and the window stays where you put it.

✔ When you're working on a window, its title bar is *highlighted,* meaning that it's a different color from the title bar of any other open window. By glancing at all the title bars on-screen, you can quickly tell which window you're currently using. The window with the highlighted title bar is also called the *active* window.

The menu bar

Windows 2000 has menus everywhere. But if menus appeared all at once, everybody would think about deep-fried appetizers rather than computer commands. So Windows 2000 hides its menus in something called a *menu bar* (see Figure 6-3).

Figure 6-3:
A menu bar.

`File   Edit   Format   Help`

Lying below the title bar, the menu bar keeps those little menus hidden behind little words. To reveal secret options associated with those words, click on one of the words.

If you think mice are for milksops, then use the brawny Alt key instead. A quick tap of the Alt key activates the menu words across the top of the window. Press the arrow keys to the right or left until you've selected the word you're after; then press the down-arrow key to expose the hidden menu.

For example, to see the entrees under the word Edit, click your mouse button on Edit (or press Alt and then E). A secret menu tumbles down from a trap door, as shown in Figure 6-4, presenting all sorts of edit-related options.

Figure 6-4:
Select any
word in the
menu bar to
reveal its
secret
hidden
menu.

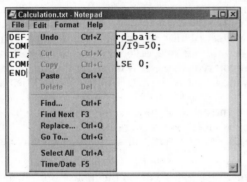

✔ When you select a key word in a menu bar, a menu comes tumbling down. The menu contains options related to that particular key word.

✔ Just as restaurants sometimes run out of specials, a window sometimes isn't capable of offering all its menu items. Any unavailable options are grayed out, as the Cut, Copy, and Delete options are in Figure 6-4.

✔ If you've accidentally selected the wrong word, causing the wrong menu to jump down, just sigh resignedly. (S-i-i-i-i-igh.) Then select the word you really want. The first menu disappears, and the new one appears below the new word.

✔ If you want out of Menu Land completely, click the mouse pointer back down on your work in the window's workspace — usually the area where you've been typing stuff. (Or press the Alt key, whichever method comes to mind sooner.)

✔ Some menu items have shortcut keys listed next to them, such as the Ctrl+Z key combination next to the Undo option in Figure 6-4. Just hold down the Ctrl key and press the letter Z to undo your last effort. The Undo option takes place immediately, and you don't have to wait for the menu to tumble down.

The toolbars

Though they sound like something that you'd see on *This Old House*, toolbars are just another window bar you find in most programs — but with an assortment of handy-dandy tools you can choose from. Typically, toolbars consist of a number of related icons plunked side by side, usually near the top of your screen. The handy icons enable you to perform frequently used tasks with speedy, single-click shortcuts — as fast as a carpenter can say #@%$! after pounding a thumb with a ball-peen hammer.

For example, some programs have a formatting toolbar containing an assortment of icons that you can use to tinker with the format of documents, spreadsheets, and the like. WordPad, for example, makes it easy to change the typeface, apply italics, or add a bullet list — among other things — all from the formatting toolbar shown in Figure 6-5. Simply highlight the text you want to format, then click a button.

Figure 6-5:
A formatting toolbar puts the decorative elements right at hand.

The scroll bar

The *scroll bar,* which looks like an elevator shaft, is along the edge of a window (see Figure 6-6). Inside the shaft, a little freight elevator (the scroll box) travels up and down as you page through your work. In fact, by glancing at the little elevator, you can tell whether you're near the top of a document, the middle, or the bottom.

For example, if you're looking at stuff near the top of a document, the elevator box is near the top of its little shaft. If you're working on the bottom portion of your work, the elevator box dangles near the bottom. You can watch the little box travel up or down as you press the PgUp or PgDn key. (Yes, distractions are easy to come by in Windows 2000.)

Figure 6-6:
Scroll bars
enable you
to page
through
everything
that's in a
window.

Here's where the little box in the scroll bar comes into play: By clicking in various places on that scroll bar, you can quickly move around in a document without pressing the PgUp or PgDn key.

✔ Instead of pressing the PgUp key, click in the elevator shaft above the little elevator (the scroll box). The box jumps up the shaft a little bit, and the document moves up one page, too. Click below the scroll box, and your view moves down, just as with the PgDn key.

✔ To move your view up line by line, click on the boxed-in arrow (scroll arrow) at the top of the scroll bar. If you hold down the mouse button while the mouse pointer is over that arrow, more and more of your document appears, line by line.

✔ Scroll bars that run along the bottom of a window move your view from side to side rather than up and down. They're handy for viewing spreadsheets that extend off the right-hand side of your screen.

✔ Some scroll bars don't have a little scroll box inside them, and then you have to use the little arrows to move around. There's no little elevator to play with. Sniff. Sniff.

✔ Want to move around in a hurry? Then put the mouse pointer on the little elevator box, hold down the mouse button, and drag the little elevator box up or down inside the shaft. For example, if you drag the box up toward the top of its shaft and release it, you can view the top of the document. Dragging it and releasing it down low takes you near the end.

✔ Windows 2000 adds another dimension to some scroll bars: the little elevator's size. If the elevator is swollen up so big that it's practically filling the scroll bar, then the window is currently displaying practically all the information the file has to offer. But if the elevator is a tiny box in a huge scroll bar, then you're viewing only a tiny amount of the information contained in the file.

✔ If you don't have a mouse, you can't play with the elevator. To view the top of your document, hold down Ctrl and press Home. To see the bottom, hold down Ctrl and press End. Or press the PgUp or PgDn key to move one page at a time.

Undoing what you've just done

Windows 2000 offers a zillion different ways for you to do the same thing. Here are three ways to access the Undo option, which unspills the milk you've just spilled:

✔ Click on the word Edit and then click on the word Undo from the menu that falls down. (This approach is known as wading through the menus.) The last command you gave is undone, saving you from any damage.

✔ Press and release the Alt key, then press the letter E (for Edit), and then press the letter U (for Undo). (This Alt key method is handy when you don't have a mouse.) Your last bungle is unbungled, reversing any grievous penalties.

✔ Hold down the Ctrl key and press the Z key. (This little quickie is known as the shortcut-key method.) The last mistake you made is reversed, sparing you from further shame.

Don't feel like you have to learn all three methods. For example, if you can remember the Ctrl+Z key combination, you can forget about the menu method and the Alt key method.

Or if you don't want to remember anything, stick with the menu method. Just pluck the Undo command as it appears on the menu.

The taskbar

Windows 2000 converts your computer monitor's screen into a desktop. But because your newly computerized desktop is probably only 14 inches wide, all your programs and windows cover each other up like memos tossed onto a spike.

To keep track of the action, Windows 2000 supplies the *taskbar*, which lies along the bottom of your screen and shows miniature versions of the windows that are currently open. If you've found the Start button, you've found the taskbar — the Start button lives on the taskbar's left end.

✔ To switch from one window to another, just click on the desired window's name from its button on the taskbar. Wham! That window shoots to the top of the pile.

✔ You can find more information about the taskbar in Chapter 12.

The Quick Launch bar

Also living on the taskbar is the Quick Launch bar — look for it nestled up next to the Start button. When Windows 2000 Professional is first installed, the Quick Launch bar looks like Figure 6-7. The icons represent programs you can start by clicking on them.

Figure 6-7:
The Quick
Launch bar.

The first icon — the one that looks like a desk blotter (a desk blotter!) is the quickest way to unclutter your Desktop. Click this icon and every open window gets swept up and put (in miniature form) on the taskbar. Click the desk blotter icon again and everything's back on the Desktop.

The second icon — the big blue "e" — opens Internet Explorer. The third icon is for Outlook Express, the Windows 2000 mail program. More on both of those in Chapter 16.

- ✔ The Desktop icon minimizes every open window — even windows and dialog boxes that can't otherwise be shrunk down.

- ✔ After you shrink everything to the Desktop, you can selectively pick windows to reopen on the Desktop by clicking their icons on the taskbar.

- ✔ To add an icon to the Quick Launch bar, click on a program or other icon with the right mouse button and, holding down the button, drag the icon to the Quick Launch bar. Release the mouse button, choose Create Shortcut from the popup menu, and presto — it's attached.

- ✔ Removing a shortcut from the Quick Launch bar is as easy as clicking on it once with the right mouse button and dragging it off to the Desktop. When the menu pops up, click Move Here.

Borders

A *border* is that thin edge enclosing a window. Compared with a bar, it's really tiny.

- ✔ You use borders to change a window's size. You can find out how to do that in Chapter 7.

- ✔ You can't use a mouse to change a window's size if the window doesn't have a border.

- ✔ If you like to mess about with details, you can make a border thicker or thinner through the Windows 2000 Control Panel, which is discussed in Chapter 11. In fact, some large-fingered laptop owners thicken their windows' borders to make them a little easier to grab with those awkward touchpads.

Other than that, you won't be using borders much.

The Button Family

Three basic species of buttons flourish throughout the Windows 2000 environment: command buttons, option buttons, and minimize/maximize buttons. The three species are closely related, and yet they look and act quite differently.

Command buttons

Command buttons may be the simplest buttons to figure out — Microsoft labeled them! Command buttons are most commonly found in _dialog boxes,_ which are little pop-up forms that Windows 2000 makes you fill out before it will work for you.

For example, when you ask Windows 2000 to open a file, it often sends out a form in a dialog box. You have to fill out the form, telling Windows 2000 what file you're after and where it's located.

Table 6-1 identifies some of the more common command buttons that you encounter in Windows 2000.

Table 6-1	Common Windows 2000 Command Buttons	
Command Button	_Habitat_	_Description_
OK	Found in nearly every pop-up dialog box	A click on this button says, "I'm done filling out the form, and I'm ready to move on." Windows 2000 then reads what you've typed into the form and processes your request. (Pressing the Enter key does the same thing as clicking on the OK button.)
Cancel	Found in nearly every pop-up dialog box	If you've somehow loused things up when filling out a form, click on this Cancel button. The pop-up box disappears, and everything returns to normal. Whew! (The Esc key does the same thing.)

(continued)

Table 6-1 *(continued)*

Command Button	Habitat	Description
	Found in nearly every pop-up dialog box	Stumped? Click on this button. Yet another box pops up, this time offering help on your current situation. (The F1 function key does the same thing.) **Extremely Cool Tip:** If you see a question mark in the top-right corner of the window, click on it and then click on the part of the window that says something confusing. If you're lucky, Windows 2000 tosses out an extra bit of helpful information.
Setup... Settings... Pizza...	Found less often in pop-up dialog boxes	If you encounter a button with arrowheads or ellipsis dots (...) after the word, brace yourself: Selecting that button brings yet another box to the screen. The arrowheads mean there's more to see. The dots mean that you get even more choices of settings, options, or toppings.

✔ When you click on a command button, you're telling Windows 2000 to carry out the command that's written on the button. (Luckily, no command buttons are labeled Explode.)

✔ Instead of scooting your mouse to the Cancel button when you've goofed in a dialog box, just press your Esc key. It does the same thing.

If you've clicked on the wrong command button but haven't yet lifted your finger from the mouse button, stop! There's still hope. Command buttons take effect only after you've lifted your finger from the mouse button. So keep your finger pressed on the button and scoot the mouse pointer away from the button. When the pointer no longer rests on the button, gently lift your finger. Whew! Just try that trick on an elevator.

Option buttons

Sometimes Windows 2000 gets ornery and forces you to choose just a single option. For example, you can finish the report that's due on Monday, or you can spend your time playing Freecell. You can't do both, so Windows 2000 won't let you select both of the options.

Windows 2000 handles this situation with an option button. When you choose one option, the little dot hops over to it. If you choose the other option, the little dot hops over to it instead. You find option buttons in many locations. Figure 6-8 shows an example.

✔ Although Windows 2000 tempts you with several choices in an option box, it lets you select only one of them. It moves the dot back and forth between the options as your decision wavers. Click on the OK button when you've reached a decision. The dotted option then takes effect.

✔ If you can choose more than one option, Windows 2000 won't present you with option buttons. Instead, it offers the more liberal *check boxes,* which we describe in a separate section later in this chapter.

✔ Option buttons are round. Command buttons, described in the previous section, are rectangular.

Figure 6-8:
When you choose an option, the black dot hops to it.

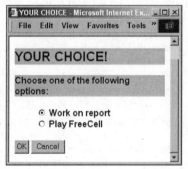

Some old-time computer engineers refer to option buttons as *radio buttons,* after those push buttons on car radios that switch from station to station, one station at a time.

Minimize/maximize buttons

All the little windows in Windows 2000 often cover each other up like teenagers in the front row at a Backstreet Boys concert. To restore order, you need to separate the windows by using their minimize/maximize buttons.

These buttons enable you to enlarge the window you want to play with or shrink all the others so they're out of the way.

The *minimize button* (shown in the margin) is one of three buttons in the upper-right corner of every window.

A single click on the minimize button makes its window disappear and then reappear as a tiny button on the taskbar along the bottom of your screen. (Click on that taskbar button to return the window to its normal size.) Keyboard users can press Alt, the spacebar, and then N to minimize their current window.

> ✔ Minimizing a window doesn't destroy its contents; it just transforms the window into a little button on the bar that runs along the bottom of the screen (the taskbar).
>
> ✔ To make the button on the taskbar turn back into an on-screen window, click on it. The button reverts to a window in the same size and location as before you shrank it. (Keyboard users can hold down Alt while pressing Tab — a little box will start showing the currently running programs. Let go of the Alt key when the box chooses your program.)
>
> ✔ *Closing a window* and *minimizing a window* are two different things. Closing a window purges it from the computer's memory. In order to reopen it, you need to load it from your hard drive again. Turning a window into an icon (minimizing it) keeps it handy, loaded into memory, and ready to be used at an instant's notice.

The *maximize button* (shown in the margin) is in the upper-right corner of every window, too.

A single click on the maximize button makes the window swell up something fierce, taking up as much space on-screen as possible. Keyboard users can press Alt, the spacebar, and then X to maximize their windows.

> ✔ If you're frustrated with all those windows that are overlapping each other, click on your current window's maximize button. The window muscles its way to the top, filling the screen like a real program.
>
> ✔ Immediately after you maximize a window, its little maximize button turns into a restore button (which we describe momentarily). The restore button lets you shrink the window back down when you're through giving it the whole playing field.

You don't have to click on the maximize button to maximize a window. Just double-click on its *title bar,* the thick strip bearing the window's name along the window's top. That double-click does the same thing as clicking on the maximize button, and the title bar is a lot easier to aim for.

In the upper-right corner of every maximized window is the *restore button* (shown in the margin). When a window is maximized, a click on this button returns the window to the size it was before you maximized it. (Keyboard users can press Alt, the spacebar, and then R.)

✔ Restore buttons appear only in windows that fill the entire screen (which is no great loss because you need a restore button only when the window is maximized).

✔ When a window is maximized, you can't drag it around by the title bar. You need to click the Restore button first.

The Disappearing Control-Menu Button

Just as all houses have circuit breakers or fuse boxes, all windows have Control-menu buttons. This button hides in the top-left corner of almost every window, where it looks like an inconspicuous hood ornament. (Sharp-eyed readers will notice that the button is actually a miniature icon representing the program.)

That little hood ornament hides a menu full of functions, but they're all pretty dopey, so ignore them all except for this one here: Double-click on the Control-menu button whenever you want to leave a window.

Dialog Box Stuff (Lots of Gibberish)

Sooner or later, you'll have to sit down and tell Windows 2000 something personal. You'll want to tell Windows 2000 the name of a file to open, for example, or the name of a file to print. To handle this personal chatter, Windows 2000 sends out a dialog box.

A dialog box is merely another little window. But instead of containing a program, it contains a little form or checklist for you to fill out. These forms can have bunches of different parts, which are discussed in the following sections. Don't bother trying to remember the names of the parts, however — *how* they work is more important.

Text boxes

A text box works just like a fill-in-the-blanks test in history class. You can type anything you want into a text box — even numbers. For example, Figure 6-9 shows a dialog box that pops up when you want to search for some words or characters in WordPad.

When one just isn't enough

Because Windows 2000 can display only one pattern on your Desktop at a time, you can select only one pattern from the Desktop's list box. Fortunately, other list boxes, like those in Explorer, let you choose a bunch of things simultaneously. Here's how:

✔ To select more than one item, hold down the Ctrl key and click on each item you want. Each item stays highlighted.

✔ To select a bunch of adjacent items from a list box, click on the first item you want. Then hold down Shift and click on the last item you want. Windows 2000 immediately highlights the first item, last item, and every item in between. Pretty sneaky, huh?

Figure 6-9: This dialog box from WordPad contains a text box.

Find	? X
Find what: the missing link	Find Next
☐ Match whole word only	Cancel
☐ Match case	

When you type words or characters into this box and press the Enter key, WordPad searches for them. If it finds them, it shows them to you on the page. If it doesn't find them, it sends out a robotic message saying it's finished searching.

✔ Two clues let you know whether a text box is *active* (that is, ready for you to start typing stuff into it): The box's current information is highlighted, or a cursor is blinking inside the box. In either case, just start typing the new stuff. (The older highlighted information disappears as the new stuff replaces it.)

✔ If the text box isn't highlighted, or no blinking cursor is inside it, then it's not ready for you to start typing. To announce your presence, click inside it. Or press Tab until the box becomes highlighted or has a cursor. Then start typing.

✔ If you click inside a text box that already contains words, you must delete the information with the Delete or Backspace key before you can start typing in new information. (Or you can double-click on the old information; that way, the incoming text automatically replaces the old text.)

Regular list boxes

Some boxes don't let you type stuff into them — they already contain information. Boxes containing lists of information are called appropriately enough, *list boxes.* For example, click Format and then Font in WordPad to see a list box of the available typefaces. (See Figure 6-10.)

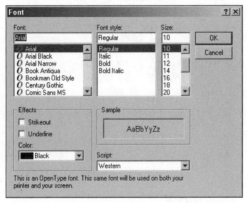

Figure 6-10:
The Font list box shows all the typefaces available in WordPad.

✔ See how the Arial font is highlighted? It's the currently selected font. Press Enter (or click on the OK command button), and WordPad uses that font in your current paragraph.

✔ See the scroll bars along the side of the list box? They work just as they do anywhere else: Click on the little scroll arrows (or press the up or down arrow on your keyboard) to move the list up or down, and you can see any names that don't fit in the box.

✔ Many list boxes have a text box above them. When you click on a name in the list box, that name hops into the text box. Sure, you can type the name into the text box yourself, but that's not nearly as much fun.

✔ When confronted with a bunch of names in a list box, type the first letter of the name you're after. Windows 2000 immediately scrolls down the list to the first name beginning with that letter.

Drop-down list boxes

List boxes are convenient, but they take up a lot of room. So, Windows 2000 sometimes hides list boxes, just as it hides pull-down menus. Then if you click in the right place, the list box appears, ready for your perusal.

So where's the right place? It's that downward-pointing arrow button, just like the one shown next to the box beside the Font option in the WordPad format bar (shown back in Figure 6-5). Figure 6-11 shows the drop-down list that appears when you click on the downward-pointing arrow button.

✔ To make a drop-down list box drop down without using a mouse, press the Tab key until you highlight the box next to the little arrow. Hold down the Alt key and press the down-arrow key, and the drop-down list starts to dangle.

✔ To scoot around quickly in a drop-down list box, press the first letter of the item you're after. The first item beginning with that letter is instantly highlighted. You can press the up- or down-arrow key to see the ones nearby.

✔ Another way to scoot around quickly in a drop-down list box is to click on the scroll bar to its right. (We discuss scroll bars earlier in this chapter, if you need a refresher.)

✔ You can choose only one item from the list of a drop-down list box.

Figure 6-11:
Click on the downward-pointing arrow next to the Font box to see a drop-down list box.

Check boxes

Sometimes you can choose from a whopping number of options in a dialog box. A check box is next to each option, and if you want that option, you click in the box. If you don't want it, you leave the box blank. (Keyboard users can press the up- or down-arrow key until a check box is highlighted and then press the spacebar.) For example, with the check boxes in the dialog box shown in Figure 6-12, you pick and choose how the Windows 2000 taskbar behaves.

✔ By clicking in a check box, you change its setting. A click in an empty square turns on that option. If the square already has a check mark in it, a click turns off that option, removing the check mark.

✔ You can click in as many check boxes as you want. With option buttons, those things that look the same but are round, you can select only one option.

Sliding controls

Rich Microsoft programmers, impressed by track lights and sliding light switches in luxurious model homes, included a few sliding controls in Windows 2000. These "virtual" light switches are easy to use and don't wear out nearly as quickly as the real ones do. To slide a control in Windows 2000 — to adjust the volume level, for example — just drag and drop the sliding lever, like the one shown in Figure 6-13.

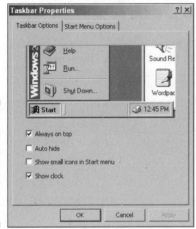

Figure 6-12:
A check mark appears in each check box you've chosen.

Figure 6-13:
To slide a lever, drag it until the lever moves to where you want it.

Point at the lever with the mouse and, while holding down the mouse button, move the mouse in the direction you want the sliding lever to move. As you move the mouse, the lever moves, too. When you move the lever to a comfortable spot, let go of the mouse button, and Windows 2000 leaves the lever at its new position. That's it.

✔ Some levers slide to the left and right; others move up and down. None of them moves diagonally.

✔ To change the volume in Windows 2000, click on the little speaker near the clock in the bottom-right corner. A sliding volume control appears, ready to be dragged up or down.

✔ No mouse? Then go buy one. In the meantime, whenever you encounter a sliding control, press Tab until a little box appears over the sliding lever; then press your arrow keys in the direction you'd like the lever to slide.

Just Tell Me How to Open a File!

Enough with the labels and terms. Forget the buttons and bars. How do you load a file into a program? This section gives you the scoop. You follow these same steps every time you load a file into a program.

Opening a file is a file-related activity, so start by finding the word File in the window's menu bar (see Figure 6-14).

Figure 6-14:
To open a file, you first select the word File in the window's menu bar.

Then do the following:

1. Click on the word File (or press Alt and then F) to knock down that word's hidden little menu.

Figure 6-15 shows the File pull-down menu.

Figure 6-15:
When you select File, the File pull-down menu appears.

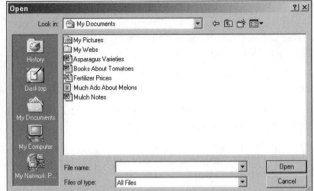

Figure 6-16:
This type of
Open dialog
box appears
whenever
you open a
file in any
recent
Windows-
based
program.

2. **Click on the word Open (or press O) to bring up the Open dialog box.**

    You can predict that the word Open will call up a dialog box because of the trailing ... things beside the word Open on-screen. (Those ... things are called an *ellipsis* or *three dots,* depending on the tightness of your English teacher's hair bun.)

Figure 6-16 shows the Open dialog box that leaps to the front of the screen. In fact, a similar dialog box appears almost any time you mess with the Open option on the File pull-down menu in any program.

✔ If you find your filename listed in the list box that appears the first time you click Open, you're in luck. Double-click on the file's name, and it automatically jumps into the program. Or hold down Alt and press N, type in the file's name, and press Enter. Or click on the file's name once and press Enter. Or curse Windows 2000 for giving you so many options for such a simple procedure.

✔ If you don't find the file's name, it's probably in a different *folder* (also known as a directory). Click on the little arrow next to the box along the top, and Windows 2000 displays a bunch of other folders and drives to examine. Each time you click on a different folder, that folder's contents appear in the first list box.

✔ At first, the Open box only lists the files that were made in the program you're running. To force Windows 2000 to disclose all the files in the folder, click the down arrow next to the Files Of Type box and select All Files.

✔ Don't know what those little icons along the top are supposed to do? Then rest your mouse pointer over the one that has you stumped. After a second or so, the increasingly polite Windows 2000 brings a box of explanatory information to the screen.

✔ The icons on the left of the box represent other folders that you use all the time:

- **History:** Everywhere you've been recently — it includes files, folders, and Internet sites.

- **Desktop:** Yes, the Desktop is actually a folder, so click this icon to get at all the files you may have deposited there.

- **My Documents:** Somewhat like the History folder, but it lists only the files in your My Documents folder.

- **My Computer, My Network Places:** Just like the icons on the Desktop, which give you access to the files on your hard drive and the network.

Hey! When Do I Click, and When Do I Double-Click?

When do you just click and when do you double-click is certainly a legitimate question, and Microsoft says that you should click when you're selecting something in Windows 2000 and you should double-click when you're carrying out an action. Huh?

Well, you're *selecting* something when you're highlighting it. For example, you may select a check box, an option button, an icon, or a file's name. You click on it to select it, and then you look at it to make sure that it looks OK. If you're satisfied with your selection, you click on the OK button to complete the job.

But I'd rather die than double-click!

Happy days are finally here for those of us who'd rather go bald than have to double-click. Windows 2000 gives us the option of a simple point and click. Point at an item and it's selected. No click necessary. Click just once on something and it's chosen.

To put the point-and-click into operation, take your mouse over to the My Computer and use your last-ever double-click to open the My Computer window. Then click the Tools menu and select Folder Options. On the General page, you see an area at the bottom labeled Click Items As Follows. Zip over and click the option button next to the text Single-Click To Open An Item (Point To Select).

Yikes! One more decision. Decide if you want the icons to be underlined all the time or only when you point at them. What a tough one. But you can test it out. Choose the first underline option and click Apply. In just a second or two, the underlines appear.

Don't like 'em? Then click the second underline option and click Apply. In an instant, the underlines are gone.

Click OK when you're done and your double-click days are *over*.

To select something is to set it up for later use.

When you *choose* something, however, the response is more immediate. For example, if you double-click on a filename, that file immediately loads itself into your program. The double-click says, "I'm choosing this file, and I want it now, buster." The double-click alleviates the need to confirm your selection by clicking on the OK button.

You choose something you want to have carried out immediately.

- ✔ If you accidentally double-click rather than single-click, it usually doesn't matter. But if something terrible happens, hold down the Ctrl key and press Z. You can usually undo any damage.

- ✔ If Windows 2000 keeps mistaking your purposeful double-click for two disjointed single-clicks, then head for the section in Chapter 11 on tinkering with the Control Panel. Adjusting Windows 2000 so that it recognizes a double-click when you make one is pretty easy.

- ✔ Don't know when you're supposed to use your left mouse button and when you're supposed to use your right mouse button? Everybody assumes you already know this important tidbit of information, so we cover it in Chapter 3.

Chapter 7

Moving the Windows Around

● ●

In This Chapter

▶ Moving a window to the top of the pile

▶ Moving a window from here to there

▶ Making windows bigger or smaller

▶ Shrinking windows onto the taskbar

▶ Turning taskbar icons back into windows

▶ Switching from window to window

▶ Fiddling with the taskbar

● ●

A h, the power of Windows 2000 Professional. Using separate windows, you can put a spreadsheet, a drawing program, and a word processor on-screen at the same time.

You can copy a hot-looking graphic from your drawing program and toss it into your memo. Stick a chunk of your spreadsheet into your memo, too. And why not? All three windows can be on-screen at the same time.

You have only one problem: With so many windows on-screen at the same time, you can't see anything but a confusing jumble of programs.

This chapter shows how to move those darn windows around on-screen so you can see at least one of them.

Moving a Window to the Top of the Pile

Take a good look at the mixture of windows on-screen. Sometimes you can recognize a tiny portion of the window you're after. If so, you're in luck. Move the mouse pointer until it hovers over that tiny portion of the window and then click the mouse button. Shazam! Windows 2000 Professional immediately brings the clicked-on window to the front of the screen.

That newly enlarged window probably covers up strategic parts of other windows. But at least you can get some work done, one window at a time.

Can't see any part of your misplaced window? Then look for its name along the buttons that usually live along the bottom of your screen. (That's called the taskbar, and it's discussed later in this chapter.) Click on the name, and the window magically appears.

Windows 2000 Professional can place a lot of windows on-screen simultaneously. But unless you have two heads, you'll probably use just one window at a time, leaving the remaining programs to wait patiently in the background. The window that's on top, ready to be used, is called the *active window*.

✔ Although many windows may be on-screen, you can enter information into only one of them: the active window. To make a window active, click on any part of it. The window rises to the top, ready to do your bidding.

✔ The active window is the one with the most lively title bar along its top — this title bar is a brighter color than all the others.

✔ The last window you've clicked on is the active window. All your subsequent keystrokes and mouse movements affect that window.

✔ Some programs can run in the background, even if they're not in the currently active window. Some communications programs can keep talking to other computers in the background, for example, and some spreadsheets can merrily crunch numbers, unconcerned with whether they're the currently active window. Imagine!

Another way to move to a window is by clicking on its name in the Windows 2000 Professional taskbar. See "The Window-Manipulating Taskbar and Its Cohorts" section later in this chapter.

Moving a Window from Here to There

Sometimes you want to move a window to a different place on-screen (the screen is known in Windows 2000 Professional parlance as the Desktop). Maybe part of the window hangs off the edge of the Desktop, and you want it centered. Or maybe you want to put two windows on-screen side by side, so you can compare their contents.

In either case, you can move a window by grabbing its title bar, that thick bar along its top. Put the mouse pointer over the window's title bar and hold down the mouse button. Now use the title bar as the window's handle. When you move the mouse around, you tug the window along with it.

When you've moved the window to where you want it to stay, release the mouse button to release the window. The window stays put and on top of the pile.

 ✔ The process of holding down the mouse button while moving the mouse is called *dragging*. When you let go of the mouse button, you're *dropping* what you've dragged.

 ✔ When placing two windows next to each other on-screen, you usually need to change their size as well as their location. The very next section tells how to change a window's size, but don't forget to read "The Window-Manipulating Taskbar and Its Cohorts" section later in this chapter. It's full of tips and tricks for resizing windows as well as moving them around.

Making a Window Bigger or Smaller

Moving the windows around isn't enough sometimes — they still cover each other up. Luckily, you don't need any special hardware to make them bigger or smaller. See that thin little border running around the edge of the window? Use the mouse to yank on a window's corner border, and you can change its size.

First, point at the corner with the mouse arrow. When the mouse arrow is positioned over the corner, the arrow becomes two-headed. Now hold down the mouse button and drag the corner in or out to make the window smaller or bigger. The window's border expands or contracts as you tug on it with the mouse, so you can see what you're doing.

When you're done yanking and the window's border looks about the right size, let go of the mouse button. The window immediately redraws itself, taking the new position.

Here's the procedure, step by step:

1. **Point the mouse pointer at the edge of the corner.**

   It turns into a two-headed arrow, as shown in Figure 7-1.

Moving windows a real drag?

If your computer borders on the slow side, dragging windows by the title bar can be very ugly. If a window drag quivers and shakes like Aunt Lola's Jello Surprise, you can have Windows 2000 Professional just move an outline of the window while you drag. After you place the outline in the new spot and let go of the mouse, the insides of the window catch up.

To make this change, find a blank spot on the Desktop and click the right mouse button. Then select Properties from the menu that pops up. In the Display Properties box that appears, click on the Effects tab. Clear the check box in front of Show Window Contents While Dragging. Click OK.

Figure 7-1:
When the
mouse
points at the
window's
bottom
corner, the
arrow
grows a
second
head.

**2. Hold down the mouse button and move the two-headed arrow in or
out to make the window bigger or smaller.**

Figure 7-2 shows how the new outline takes shape when you pull the
corner inward to make the window smaller.

Figure 7-2:
As you
move the
mouse, the
window's
border
changes to
reflect its
new shape.

3. Release the mouse button.

The window shapes itself to fit into the border you just created. That's it!
(See Figure 7-3.)

If a window is hanging off the edge of the screen and you can't seem to position it so that all of it fits on-screen, try shrinking it first. Grab a visible corner
and drag it toward the window's center. Release the mouse button, and the
window shrinks itself to fit in its now smaller border. Then grab the window's
title bar and hold down the mouse button. When you drag the title bar back
toward the center of the screen, you can see the whole window once again.

Figure 7-3:
Release the mouse button, and the window fills its newly adjusted border.

Making a Window Fill the Whole Screen

Sooner or later, you get tired of all this New Age, multi-window mumbo jumbo. Why can't you just put one huge window on-screen? Well, you can.

To make any window grow as big as it gets, double-click on its title bar, that topmost bar along the top of the window. The window leaps up to fill the screen, covering up all the other windows.

To bring the pumped-up window back to normal size, double-click on its title bar once again. The window shrinks to its former size, and you can see everything that it was covering up.

✔ When a window fills the entire screen, it loses its borders. That means you can no longer change its size by tugging on its title bar or dragging its borders. Those borders just aren't there anymore.

✔ If you're morally opposed to double-clicking on a window's title bar to expand it, you can expand it another way: Click on the window's maximize button, the middlemost of the three little boxes in its top-right corner. The window hastily fills the entire screen. At the same time, the maximize button turns into a restore button; click on the restore button when you want the window to return to its previous size.

See Chapter 6 for more information on the maximize, minimize, and restore buttons.

Shrinking Windows to the Taskbar

Windows spawn windows. You start with one window to write a letter to Mother. You open another window to check her address, for example, and then yet another to see whether you've forgotten any recent birthdays. Before you know it, four more windows are crowded across the Desktop.

To combat the clutter, Windows 2000 Professional provides a simple means of window control: You can stuff a screen-cluttering window into a tiny button at the bottom of the screen.

See the three buttons lurking in just about every window's top-right corner? Click on the minimize button — the button with the little line in it. Whoosh! The window disappears — but a little button listing that window's name still lives on the bar running along the bottom of your screen (the taskbar). Click on that window's button on the taskbar, and your window hops back onto the screen, ready for action.

 Or if you have a whole lot of windows making a mess of your screen, you can shrink them all to the taskbar. Just click the little Desktop icon on the taskbar. The difference can be dramatic. Figure 7-4 shows a Desktop with a bunch of open windows.

Figure 7-5 shows that same Desktop after all windows have been packed into their buttons along the taskbar.

The windows are still readily available, mind you. Just click on a window's button from the taskbar along the bottom of the screen, and that window instantly leaps back to its former place on-screen (see Figure 7-6).

Figure 7-4:
A Desktop can be distracting if too many windows are open simultaneously.

Figure 7-5:
Here's the same Desktop that's shown in Figure 7-4. Seeing what's going on is easier when the open windows are turned into buttons.

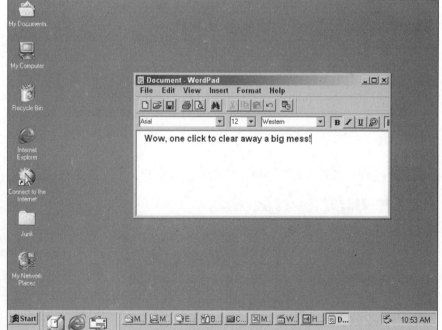

Figure 7-6:
Click on the icon for the program you want to see, and it pops open on your newly tidied Desktop.

- ✔ To shrink an open window so that it's out of the way, click on the left-most of the three buttons in the window's top-right corner. The window minimizes itself into a button and lines itself up on the taskbar.

- ✔ Each button on the taskbar has a label so that you can tell which program the button represents.

- ✔ When you minimize a window, you neither destroy its contents nor close it. You merely change its shape. It is still loaded into memory, waiting for you to play with it again.

- ✔ To put the window back where it was, click on its button on the taskbar. It hops back up to the same place it was before.

- ✔ Whenever you load a program by using the Start button or Explorer, that program's name automatically appears on the taskbar. If one of your open windows ever gets lost on your Desktop, click on its name on the taskbar. The window immediately jumps to the forefront.

- ✔ Want to shrink just one window? Click the window's icon on the taskbar and zoom! It's minimized.

Dispersing a Crowd of Windows

Sometimes the mess gets so dense on the desktop that you just want to sweep everything to the floor and start over. Windows 2000 Professional lets you do that without creating an even bigger mess.

Just click the Desktop icon at the end of the taskbar and all your windows shrink down to manageable miniatures on the taskbar. Then you can click on them one at a time and selectively open them.

Click the Desktop icon a second time and all the windows on the taskbar rush onto the Desktop and pile up much as they were before.

Turning Taskbar Buttons Back into Windows

To turn a minimized window at the bottom of the screen back into a useful program in the middle of the screen, just click on its name on the taskbar. Pretty simple, huh?

- ✔ If you prefer wading through menus, just click on the shrunken window's button with your right mouse button. A Control menu shoots out the top of the button's head. Choose the menu's Restore option, and the program leaps back to its former window position.

✔ In addition to using a click, you can use a few other methods to turn icons back into program windows. The very next section describes one way, and "The Window-Manipulating Taskbar and Its Cohorts" section later in this chapter describes another.

Switching from Window to Window

Sometimes switching from window to window is easy. If you can see any part of the window you want — a corner, a bar, or a piece of dust — just click on it. That's all it takes to bring that window to the front of the screen, ready for action.

You can also just click on that window's button on the taskbar along the bottom of your screen. The following sections give a few extra tricks for switching from window to window to window.

The Alt+Tab trick

This trick is so fun that Microsoft should have plastered it across the front of the Windows 2000 Professional box instead of hiding it in the middle of the manual.

Keeping your icons straight

Don't be confused by a program's icon on your Desktop and a program's button on the taskbar along the bottom of your screen. They're two different things. The button at the bottom of the screen stands for a program that has already been loaded into the computer's memory; it's ready for immediate action. The icon on your Desktop or in Windows Explorer stands for a program that is sitting on the computer's hard disk, waiting to be loaded.

If you mistakenly double-click on the icon in Windows Explorer or on the Desktop rather than click the button on the taskbar at the bottom of the screen, you load a *second* copy of that program. That means two versions of the program

are loaded: one running as a window and the other running as a taskbar button waiting to be turned back into a window.

You'll see two buttons on the taskbar with the same name. Running two versions can cause confusion — especially if you start entering stuff into both versions of the same program. You won't know which window has the *right* version!

If two buttons on the taskbar say the same thing, you probably opened two copies of the same program. Click on each button to compare the windows, and close the one that you don't need so you don't get confused as to which is which!

Hold down the Alt key and press the Tab key. A most welcome box pops up in the center of the screen, naming all the programs currently loaded into your computer's memory.

If the program you're after has a little box around it, like the Root Pie Recipe icon in Figure 7-7, rejoice! And remove your finger from the Alt key. The window named in that box leaps to the screen.

Figure 7-7:
Hold down
Alt and keep
pressing
Tab until a
box appears
around your
desired
program;
then release
Alt to make
that pro-
gram come
to the top of
the screen.

Root Pie Recipe - WordPad

If you're looking for a different program, keep your finger on the Alt key and press the Tab key again. At each press of Tab, Windows 2000 Professional moves its little box around the name of another open program. When the box reaches the program that you want, release the Alt key and then hoot and holler. The program leaps to the screen, ready for your working pleasure.

✔ The Alt+Tab trick works even if you're running a DOS-based program full-screen with Windows 2000 Professional lurking in the background. The DOS program disappears while the pop-up box has its moment in the sun. (And the DOS program returns when you're done playing around, too.)

✔ The Alt+Tab trick cycles through all the currently open programs, whether the programs are running in on-screen windows or living their lives as buttons on the taskbar. When you release the Alt key, the program currently listed in the pop-up window leaps to life.

✔ Only running a single program? Then the Alt+Tab trick won't work; it only fills the screen with your current program. No programs running at all? Then Alt+Tab won't do anything. Your computer's not broken. This is a feature, not a bug, as Microsoft says so nobly.

The Alt+Esc trick

The concept is getting kind of stale with this one, but here goes: If you hold down the Alt key and press the Esc key, Windows 2000 Professional cycles through all the open programs but in a slightly less efficient way.

Instead of bringing the program's name to a big box in the middle of the screen, Windows 2000 Professional simply highlights the program, whether it's in a window or sitting as a button on the taskbar. Sometimes this method can be handy, but usually it's a little slower.

If Windows 2000 Professional highlights a program resting on the taskbar, the Alt+Esc trick simply highlights that program's button at the bottom of the screen. That's not much of a visual indicator, and most of the time it won't even catch your eye.

When the window you want is highlighted, release the Alt key. If it's an open window, it becomes the active window. But if you release the Alt key while a button's name is highlighted, you need to take one more step: You need to click on the button to get the window on-screen.

The Window-Manipulating Taskbar and Its Cohorts

This section is all about one of the handiest tricks in Windows 2000 Professional, so pull your chair in a little closer. Windows 2000 Professional comes with a special program that keeps track of all the open programs. Called the taskbar, it always knows what programs are running and where they are. Shown in Figure 7-8, the taskbar normally lives along the bottom of your screen, although Chapter 11 shows how to move it to any edge you want.

From the taskbar, you can perform powerful magic on your open windows, as shown in the next few sections.

✔ See how the button for Calculator looks "pushed in" in Figure 7-8? That's because Calculator is the currently active window on the Desktop. One of your taskbar's buttons always looks "pushed in" unless you close or minimize all the windows on your Desktop.

✔ At the left end of the taskbar is the Quick launch bar, where you can park shortcuts to programs for instant launching. What the heck are shortcuts, you ask? Check them out in Chapter 12.

✔ Don't see the taskbar? Then hold down Ctrl and press Esc. Windows 2000 Professional instantly brings the taskbar to the surface, ready to do your bidding.

Figure 7-8:
Always
handy, the
taskbar lists
your
currently
running
programs
and lets you
bring them
to the
forefront by
clicking on
their names.

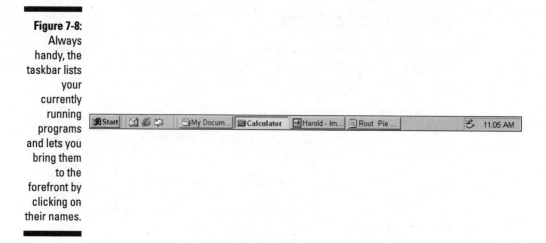

Figure 7-8:
Always
handy, the
taskbar lists
your
currently
running
programs
and lets you
bring them
to the
forefront by
clicking on
their names.

Switching to another window

See a window you'd like to play with listed on the taskbar? Just click on its name, and it rises to the surface. If the taskbar isn't showing for some reason, pressing Ctrl+Esc calls it to the forefront.

Closing a window from the taskbar

Mad at a program? Then kill it. Click on the program's name on the taskbar with your right mouse button and then click on the word Close from the menu that pops up (or press C). The highlighted program quits, just as if you'd chosen its Exit command from within its own window.

The departing program gives you a chance to save any work before it quits and disappears from the screen.

Want to close down *all* your programs at once? Hold down Ctrl and click each program listed on the taskbar; each program's taskbar button appears depressed after you click it. Right-click on one of the taskbar's programs, and choose Close from its pop-up menu. Whoosh! All the programs take a hint and shut themselves down.

Cascading and tiling windows

Sometimes those windows are piled up and you don't want to shrink them all — you just want to *see* them all. How to do it? Use the taskbar's Cascade and Tile commands. Right-click on a blank spot on the taskbar — the spot on or near the time display is usually good — and the Cascade and Tile commands appear.

The commands organize your open windows in drastically different ways. Figure 7-9 shows what your screen looks like when you choose the Cascade Windows command.

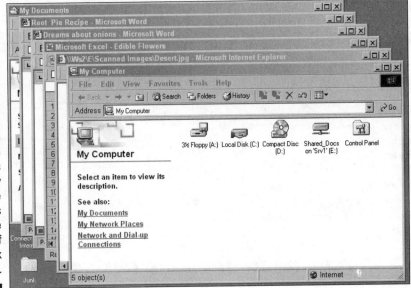

Figure 7-9: The taskbar's Cascade Windows command piles all the open windows neatly across the screen. It's a favorite command of blackjack players.

Talk about neat and orderly! The taskbar grabs all the windows and deals them out like cards across the Desktop. When you choose the taskbar's Cascade Windows command, all the open windows are lined up neatly on-screen with their title bars showing.

The Tile Windows Horizontally and Tile Windows Vertically commands rearrange the windows, too, but in a slightly different way (see Figure 7-10).

The Tile commands arrange all the currently open windows across the screen, giving each one the same amount of space. This arrangement helps you find a window that has been missing for a few hours.

Note: Both the Tile and Cascade commands arrange only windows already open on the Desktop. They don't open up any windows currently shrunken into buttons on the taskbar.

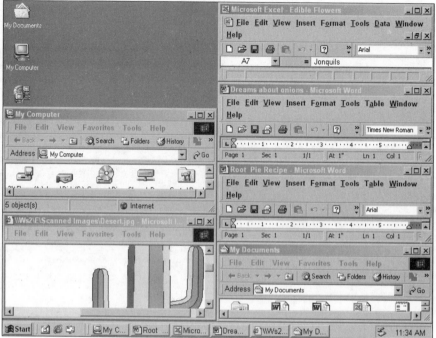

Figure 7-10:
The taskbar's Tile commands organize the open windows like tiles on the shower floor. You can see them all, but they're too small to be of much use.

Arranging icons on the Desktop

The taskbar can be considered a housekeeper of sorts, but it only does windows. It arranges the open windows neatly across the screen, but it doesn't touch any icons living on your Desktop.

If the open windows look fine but the Desktop's icons look a little shabby, click on a blank area of your Desktop with your right mouse button. When the menu pops up from nowhere, click the Arrange Icons command and choose the way you'd like Windows 2000 Professional to line up your icons: by Name, Type, Size, or Date.

Or simply choose the Auto Arrange option from the same menu. Then your Desktop's icons will always stay in neat, orderly rows.

Finding the taskbar

Taskbar not along the bottom of your screen? Then hold down Ctrl and press Esc, and the taskbar instantly appears. If you'd prefer that the taskbar not disappear sometimes, head for Chapter 12, where we explain how to customize your taskbar so it doesn't bail on you.

Not nearly enough windows?

Now that you've read all this stuff about managing windows, maybe you're feeling out of it because you really would like even *more* windows. Normally, as you poke into folders, Windows 2000 reuses the window. Open a folder inside a folder and the environmentally correct Windows 2000 recycles the window so that you have only one window showing.

Of course, if you're feeling profligate, you can open each folder in its own window.

Double-click the My Computer icon then click the Tools menu. Select Folder Options. Halfway down the page, you see a section labeled Browse Folders. Click on the option button next to Open Each Folder In Its Own Window. Click the OK button and you'll have all the windows your little heart could desire.

Chapter 8

I Can't Find It!

Sooner or later, Windows 2000 gives you that head-scratching feeling. "Golly," you say, as you frantically tug on your mouse cord, "that window was right there a second ago. Where did it go?"

When Windows 2000 starts playing hide-and-seek with your programs, files, windows, or other information, this chapter tells you where to search and how to make it stop playing foolish games. Then when you find your Freecell window, you can get back to work.

Plucking a Lost Window from the Taskbar

Forget about that huge, 1940s rolltop mahogany desk in the resale shop window. The Windows 2000 peewee Desktop can't be any bigger than the size of your monitor.

In a way, Windows 2000 works more like those spike memo holders than like an actual desktop. Every time you open a new window, you're tossing another piece of information onto the spike. The window on top is relatively easy to see, but what's lying directly underneath it?

If you can see a window's ragged edge protruding from any part of the pile, click on it. The window magically rushes to the top of the pile. But what if you can't see any part of the window at all? How do you know it's even on the Desktop?

You can solve this mystery by calling up your helpful Windows 2000 detective: the taskbar. The taskbar keeps a master list of everything that's happening on your screen (even the invisible stuff).

If the taskbar isn't squatting along one edge of your screen, hold down your Ctrl key and press the Esc key. The taskbar pops into action (see Figure 8-1).

Figure 8-1:
The mighty
taskbar
always
contains an
up-to-date
list of all
open
windows.

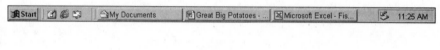

See the list of programs stamped onto buttons on the taskbar? Your missing window is somewhere on the list. When you spot it, click on its name, and the taskbar instantly tosses your newfound window to the top of the pile.

- ✔ Most of the time, the taskbar performs admirably in tracking down lost windows. If your window isn't on the list, then you probably closed it. Closing a window, also known as *exiting* a window, takes it off your Desktop and out of your computer's memory. To get that window back, you need to open it again, using the services of the Start button (see Chapter 12), the Explorer (see Chapter 13), or the My Computer program (also in Chapter 13).

- ✔ I lied. Sometimes a window can be running but not listed on the taskbar. Some utility programmers figure that people don't need to see their programs or their icons. Berkeley Systems' After Dark screen saver, for example, can be running on your screen and yet not show up on the taskbar. It simply runs in the background. (**Hint:** Sometimes pressing Alt+Tab brings up the program's icon, as explained in Chapter 7.)

- ✔ Sometimes you see your missing program listed on the taskbar, and you click on its name to dredge it from the depths. But although the taskbar brings the missing program to the top, you still can't find it on your Desktop. The program may be hanging off the edge of your Desktop, so check out the very next section.

Finding a Window That's off the Edge of the Screen

Even a window at the top of the pile can be nearly invisible. A window can be moved anywhere on the Windows 2000 Desktop, including off the screen. In fact, you can inadvertently move a big chunk of a window off the screen, leaving just a corner showing (see Figure 8-2). Clicking on the window's name in the taskbar won't be much help in this case, unfortunately. The window's already on top, but it's still too far off the screen to be of any use.

✔ If you can see any part of the rogue window's title bar, that thick strip along the window's top, hold the mouse button down and drag the renegade back to the center of the screen.

✔ Sometimes a window's title bar can be completely off the top of the screen. How can you drag it back into view? Start by clicking on any part of the window that shows. Then hold down your Alt key and press the spacebar. A menu appears from nowhere. Select the word Move, and a mysterious four-headed arrow appears. Press your arrow keys until the window's border moves to a more manageable location and then press Enter. Whew! Don't let it stray that far again!

Figure 8-2: Notepad is sticking off the top-right corner of the screen, making it difficult to work with.

> ✔ For an easier way to make Windows 2000 not only track down all your criminally hidden windows but also line them up on the screen in mug-shot fashion, check out the next two sections.

Cascading Windows (The Deal-All-the-Windows in-Front-of-Me Approach)

Are you ready to turn Windows 2000 into a personal card dealer who gathers up all your haphazardly tossed windows and deals them out neatly on the Desktop in front of you?

To turn the taskbar into a card dealer, click on a blank area of your taskbar — near the clock is good — with your right mouse button, and a menu pops up. Click on the Cascade Windows option, and the taskbar gathers all your open windows and deals them out in front of you, just like in a game of blackjack.

Each window's title bar is neatly exposed, ready to be grabbed and reprimanded with a quick click of the mouse.

> ✔ If the missing window doesn't appear in the stack of neatly dealt windows, perhaps it's been minimized. The Cascade Windows command gathers and deals only the open windows; it leaves the minimized windows resting as buttons along the taskbar. The solution? Click on the missing window's button on the taskbar before cascading the windows across the screen.
>
> ✔ For more about the Cascade Windows command, check out Chapter 7.

Tiling Windows (The Stick-Everything-on-the Screen-at-Once Approach)

Windows 2000 can stick all your open windows onto the screen at the same time. You can finally see all of them — no overlapping corners, edges, or menu flaps. Sound too good to be true? It is. Windows 2000 shrinks all the windows so they fit on the screen. And some of the weird-shaped windows still overlap. But, hey, at least you can see most of them.

Click on a blank area of the taskbar with your right mouse button and choose Tile Windows Vertically or Tile Windows Horizontally from the pop-up menu.

✔ The Tile commands pull all the open windows onto the screen at the same time. If you have two open windows, each of them takes up half the screen. With three windows, each window gets a third of the screen. If you have 12 windows, each window takes up one-twelfth of the available space. (They're very small.)

✔ The Tile Windows Vertically command arranges the windows vertically, like socks hanging from a clothesline. Tile Windows Horizontally arranges the windows horizontally, like a stack of folded sweatshirts. The difference is the most pronounced if you're tiling only a few windows, however.

✔ You can find more information about the Tile commands in Chapter 7. We cover the minimize button in Chapter 6.

Finding the Desktop

Sometimes you can have so many things open that just arranging them on the Desktop — either by tiling or cascading — is not enough. Or maybe it's the Desktop itself you need to get at.

 To shrink every open window down to the taskbar, click the Desktop icon on the taskbar. When you want to bring everything back to the Desktop, click the Desktop icon again.

Finding Lost Files or Folders (But Not Misplaced Laptops)

Windows 2000 has gotten much better at finding lost files and folders. And it should; after all, it's the one who's hiding the darn things. If one of your files, folders, or programs (or computers, if you're on a network) runs off into the electronic mists, make Windows 2000 do the work in getting the darn thing back by doing the following:

1. **Click on the Start button.**

2. **Choose the Search option.**

3. **Choose For Files or Folders from the pop-up menu, as shown in Figure 8-3.**

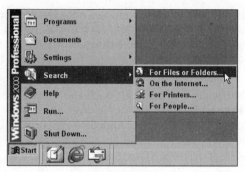

Figure 8-3:
Windows
2000 can
search your
computer
for lost files
and folders.

An incredibly detailed program pops up, letting you search for files meeting the minutest criteria. Best yet, it can simply search for missing files by their names. For example, suppose that your file called FISH EMULSION - FRIEND OR FOE disappeared over the weekend. To make matters worse, you're not even sure you spelled Emulsion correctly when saving the file.

The solution? Choose the Search program's Files or Folders command and type in any part of the filename you can remember. In this case, type **fish** into the box labeled Search For Files Or Folders Named, then click on the Search Now button. The Search program lists any file or folder with a name that contains *fish*, as shown in Figure 8-4. Quick and simple.

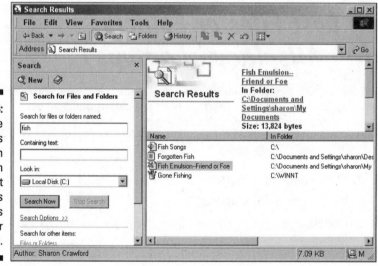

Figure 8-4:
Here, the
Windows
2000 Search
program
sniffed out
several files
with *fish* as
part of their
names.

✔ Highlight the filename and the top right window (labeled Search Results) tells you practically everything you'd ever want to know about the file. Double-click the filename to open it. Double-click the folder name to open the folder.

✔ Of course, you don't have to keep things quick and simple. For example, the Search program normally searches your computer's hard drives. If you prefer that it search every nook and cranny — all your hard disks and even any floppy disks or CD-ROM drives — click on the little downward-pointing arrow near the Look In box. After a menu drops down, click on the My Computer setting. That tells the Search program to look everywhere on your computer. Or click Browse and you can search anywhere on the network that you're allowed to go.

✔ Can't remember what you called a file but know approximately when you created it? Then click on Search Options, then Date. Then you can specify something you did to the file (modified, created, or last accessed) in some specific period of time — like the last day or month.

✔ Click on Computers under Search Options and you can locate any other computer on your network, providing you know the exact name of the computer, which may be something like ADMIN_B52_K2. Is that likely? A far, far easier way is to double-click on your Desktop's My Network Places icon and look for your missing computer listed in there. You still must know the name of the computer, but at least you don't have to spell it.

Finding Snippets of Stored Information

Help! You remember how much Mr. Jennings loved that wine during lunch, so you stealthily typed the wine's name into your computer. Now, at Christmas time, you don't remember the name of the file where you saved the wine's name. You don't remember the date you created the file, either, or even the folder where you stashed the file. In fact, the only thing you remember is how you described the wine's hard-hitting bouquet when typing it into your computer: "Smells much like compost heap."

Luckily, that's enough for Windows 2000 to find your file. All you have to do is the following:

1. **Click on the Start button.**

2. **Choose Search and then choose Files or Folders.**

3. **In the box labeled Containing Text, type the word you want to find.**

   In this example, type **compost**, as shown in Figure 8-5.

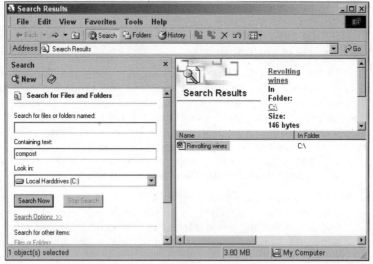

Once the file you're looking for pops up, click the Stop Search button and you won't have to wait around for the Search program to examine every recess of your computer.

When searching for files containing certain words, type in the words least likely to turn up in other files. For example, the word compost is far more unique than *much* or *like;* therefore, it's more likely to bring up the file you need — without spitting out dozens of unwanted files.

Other Fancy Searches

When you click on Start and then select Search, you find yourself gazing at a menu that promises you can search for printers, people, and stuff on the Internet. Some search or indexing programs plop themselves on that menu as well.

Here's what happens when you try these searches:

- ✔ **On the Internet:** This opens Internet Explorer with a search window open. For more on using this feature, see Chapter 16.

- ✔ **For Printers:** This opens a dialog box (Figure 8-6) where you can enter a printer name to look for. Don't know the name? Try clicking the Features tab and selecting your requirements — such as color or double-sided printing. Unless you're on a truly huge network, you're better off clicking the Start button, choosing Printers from the Settings menu, and checking the Printers shown there.

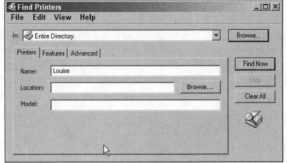

Figure 8-6: On a big network with many, many printers, you can search for one you want using this dialog box.

✔ **For People:** Alas, this feature won't help you find Mr./Ms. Right (or even Mr./Ms. Right Now) but it does offer a whole raft of search options for people you already know something about.

Select one of the Look In choices. Except for the Address Book option, all the other search locations are on the Internet. Enter the information you have and click Find Now.

Figure 8-7 shows the results when Sharon went looking for herself. If you don't find what you're looking for, try another choice in the Look In box. Or go to the search site's Web Page by clicking the Web Site button, where you can usually make adjustments that are more precise to your search criteria.

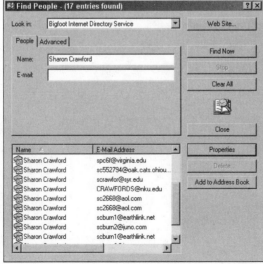

Figure 8-7: Sometimes a search turns up nothing, sometimes more answers than you know what to do with.

No Time to Search?

For files and folders you've used recently, there's no faster way to find them than in the Open dialog box. Start a Windows 2000 program (a program that comes with Windows 2000 or was updated especially for Windows 2000). Click the File menu and then Open. This opens the dialog box shown in Figure 8-8.

Figure 8-8:
The box for opening files includes icons that are short-cuts to lists of recently used files and folders.

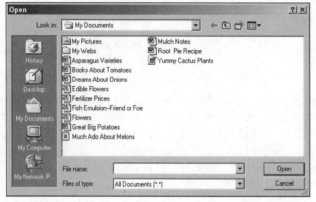

Click the History icon on the left side of the box to see a list of all the places you've visited recently. This list includes folders you've opened, files you've used, and Web sites you've visited on the Internet. The My Documents icon opens the My Documents folder. Double-click any filename to open it.

Chapter 9

Sharing It All on the Network

. . . .

In This Chapter

▶ Defining a network

▶ Finding other computers on the network

▶ Finding files and folders on other computers

▶ Making visiting easy

▶ Giving permission to others to look at your files

▶ Adding and using network printers

. . . .

A network is simply a bunch of computers and a few printers connected by cables or phone connections. When the network works right, everybody shares information quickly and easily, tossing computerized data back and forth like Frisbee-slingers in the park.

You use a network whenever you visit a bank's Automated Teller Machine (ATM). The keypad-bearing ATM is a very simple computer that sends your account number, password, and request for money to the bank's Big Computer downtown. The Big Computer knows all about you and tells the ATM that giving you the cash is okay (or not) — even if you've never visited that particular ATM before.

Networks of personal computers work much like the ATMs — except the software is more complicated than an ATM's keypad, the computers are more complicated than ATM terminals, and, unfortunately, the computers never slip you any cash.

If you connect two machines at home so they can both use the same printer, you've made a network. Networks connect thousands of computers in hundreds of locations on multiple continents. But size rarely matters from the network user's point of view: Your work is likely to take you to just a few places on the network, over and over. It's like driving a car: The car can take you anywhere, but most of your driving is from home to work to Bronco Billy's Pizza Palace.

This chapter explains how to share information on a network. It shows how to grab information from other computers, as well as how to let other people grab files off your own computer. It explains how to send stuff to the printer, even if the printer doesn't plug directly into your own computer. Plus the chapter tosses in a few tips on how to muddle your way through if the Network Administrator *still* hasn't returned from the deli down the street.

What's an Intranet?

An *intranet* — though it sounds complicated — is actually easier to use than the usual, run-of-the-mill computer network. An intranet is simply a company's network that includes *Web pages* — those funky World Wide Web things all the trendy people murmur about at coffee shops. (If you've never seen an intranet Web page, check out Figure 9-1.)

Figure 9-1:
An intranet Web page is just like the ones shown on the Internet.

Like magazine pages, Web pages display pictures, charts, text, and other fancy visual doodads that make them easier to see and use. However, Web pages also contain secret entries: special *links* to other Web pages. Move your mouse pointer over the Web page until the arrow turns into a hand, like the one shown in the left margin.

Click the mouse, and a new page leaps to the screen, bringing up a new Web page that relates to whatever subject you clicked on.

Internet Web pages are designed for the whole world to access. When you see the cryptic words `www.vw.com` in a magazine's glossy Volkswagen ad, you're looking at the company's Internet address. By heading there, you can see the Volkswagen Internet page and peruse the history of VW vans.

Intranet Web pages, by contrast, are designed for internal use inside a corporation. They're more like corporate newsletters, set up on the network to give information on company picnics, holidays, and impending layoffs.

- ✔ Yes, it's easy to click on those little Web links, over and over again, moving from Web page to Web page, just like pushing the remote control on the TV set. (Does the term *Web surfing* come to mind?)

- ✔ On a Windows 2000 network, you navigate both intranet and Internet Web pages by opening Internet Explorer (or any other Web browser).

- ✔ Trek over to Chapter 16 for more on Internet Explorer, Web pages, and Web surfing.

How Do I Know What Computers I Can Access on a Network?

Some kind soul may *tell* you where to find things on your network. It's much more likely you'll have to grab a torch and go spelunking on your own with My Network Places, described in the next section.

If you're worried about getting into trouble, the rule is simple: Windows 2000 rarely lets you peek into networked areas where you're not supposed to. In fact, it's so security conscious that you may not be able to see things that you should be able to see! (That's when you call on the Network Administrator.)

- ✔ If you double-click on a "restricted" folder or file that's not open to you, you just see an "access denied" message. No harm done.

- ✔ If you're supposed to be able to read a folder on someone else's computer and you can't, just casually tell the Network Administrator, "Pardon me bloke, but I don't seem to have permission to access folder X on computer Y. Could you check into that? There's a good chap." If you have a lorgnette handy, it may help to wave it around.

- ✔ If you do accidentally find yourself in a folder where you obviously don't belong — for example, the folder of employee evaluations on your supervisor's computer — that should also be brought to the Network Administrator's attention.

What Are My Network Places?

My Network
Places

The absolute fastest way to see what's connected to your computer is to head for the Desktop and double-click on the My Network Places icon.

A window pops open showing a couple of icons (see Figure 9-2) — including one labeled Entire Network and one labeled Add Network Place. To connect to other places on the network, double-click Add Network Place.

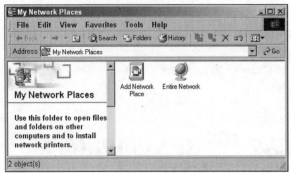

Figure 9-2:
To connect
to a shared
disk or
folder,
click Add
Network
Place.

✔ If you see other icons in the My Network Places window, it means that some kind person (perhaps the Network Administrator) already set up shortcuts to other places on the network.

✔ Networks being what they are, it's hard to predict what you'll see in your particular Network Places. Just about everybody's network is set up differently. But there's absolutely no rule against looking around. (If you're just curious, start spelunking by clicking Entire Network.)

When I look at the Entire Network, what am I looking at?

When you double-click on the Entire Network icon, and keep clicking, eventually you'll see all the objects that make up your network. But you'll only be able to poke around in disks and folders that have been *shared*. A shared folder or disk is just one that has been set up so that people from other computers can see and use it.

When an entire disk is shared, for example, other people have permission to come into that computer and stroll around that particular hard disk, pinching peaches and thumping melons.

The level of security all depends on how your network is set up. Some networks are quite open, with only a few folders that are not public. Other networks, where security is a big issue, have strict limits on what you can see.

Figure 9-3 shows a good-natured computer that's sharing all its hard disks and a printer. Figure 9-4 shows a much more paranoid model with basically nothing shared.

Figure 9-3:
This computer has nothing to hide (although the labels on the drives could be a little more informative).

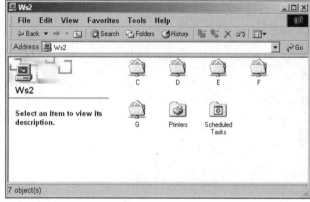

Figure 9-4:
This computer has nothing to offer a visitor.

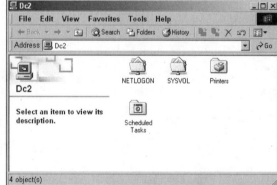

✔ Figure 9-4's NETLOGON and SYSVOL folders are part of Network Administration and are either empty or without interest to normal people like yourself.

✔ Likewise, that computer's Printers folder won't have anything in it that you don't see in your own Printers folder.

Adding a Network Place

To make a file (or folder) on another computer easily available, just double-click on My Network Places, then double-click Add Network Place. This starts the Add Network Place Wizard (see Figure 9-5). If you know the location of the place you want to add, type it in the text box. If you're not completely sure, click the Browse button.

In the Browse For Folder window (see Figure 9-6) find the folder or drive you want and then click OK. You get a chance to give the folder a different name (the name will be different only on your machine), and then click Finish. This puts the folder you want in the My Network Places window so you can connect to it any time with just a double-click.

Mapping a network drive

When you open the My Computer icon, you see a list of the hard disks on your computer (as well as a few other goodies, depending on what's installed). If you want, Windows 2000 can make any other computer's shared drives or folders act as if they were drives on *your* computer.

For example, if Windows 2000 takes Gerald's C drive and displays that drive as your own computer's G drive, it has *mapped* Gerald's drive onto your computer.

A mapped drive is even better than a shortcut in one important respect: Many older programs don't recognize newfangled stuff like My Network Places; they flat out refuse to open or save files to anywhere other than your own computer.

Mapping the drive tricks those programs into cooperating because they think they're working exclusively with your own computer — even though it's *really* Gerald's.

Here's how it works:

1. **Right-click My Computer and select Map Network Drive.**

   This opens the Map Network Drive box (see Figure 9-7).

Figure 9-7:
Getting
ready to
map a drive
or folder.

Windows 2000 is ready to map a drive for you. It chooses the next available drive letter on your computer — in this case, F. But you can use the drop-down box and select another letter if you want to.

Here's the scoop on the other options in this box:

Drive: This is the letter that the new drive will be assigned on your computer. It's usually the next one in the alphabet after your current ones.

Reconnect At Logon: Check this box and every time you log onto your computer, the connection is made to the computer where this drive physically resides. If you remove the check from the box, the connection isn't made until you actually go to use the drive.

Connect Using A Different User Name: Use this only if you need to have the drive connect in a name other than your logon name. This sometimes happens in a multi-domain environment, or other special circumstances. When it's necessary, you enter the other user name and are then prompted for that user's password. After you provide it, the drive is mapped. Generally, however, you leave this option alone.

Create A Shortcut To A Web Folder Or FTP Site: You'd use this if you want to create a new Network Place. It works much like the mapping function except that the shortcut is placed in My Network Places instead of My Computer.

2. **Click the Browse button and rummage around until you find the other computer's drive or folder that you want to show as one of your own drives. Click to highlight the drive or folder and click OK.**

   For example, click on Judy's computers (D) and find the folder where she keeps her World Wrestling Federation fan letters (in the Hunk-o-Rama folder). (See Figure 9-8.)

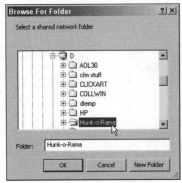

Figure 9-8: Find the drive or folder you want to show as your own.

3. **Back at the Map Network Drive box, click Finish.**

   The mapped drive or folder opens on your desktop.

   Open My Computer and take a look after you're through. See the Hunk-o-Rama icon in Figure 9-9? That's how Judy's folder ends up looking when it's mapped to your computer.

Figure 9-9:
After being mapped, the drive on the other computer is listed as if it were your own computer's disk drive.

- ✔ It didn't work? Maybe you're trying to map something that hasn't been shared — and you'll have to ask the Network Administrator to do that.

- ✔ Folders can be harder to map than drives, because they take a little more effort to share. That means you must tap the Network Administrator on the shoulder.

- ✔ The key word is "Network Administrator," discussed in the next section.

- ✔ Actually, don't bother to raise your hand. A *hard disk,* a *hard drive,* and a *disk drive* are three different words that describe the same thing: A computer device for storing files. The terms can be used interchangeably, although the term "networked drives" usually appears more often than "networked disks."

Make the Administrator Do It

The administrator of the network can share another computer's folder or files *for* you. In fact, that may have already happened. Figure 9-10 shows a computer with one folder shared: the Fascinating Fennel Facts folder.

Figure 9-10:
The administrator has made one fascinating folder available.

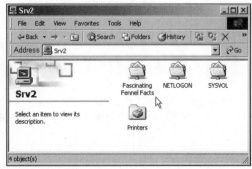

The Network Administrator can map drives for you, too. This isn't a bad approach, providing the administrator is actually approachable. And, best of all, if something goes wrong, you don't take the rap for it.

Running a Program That Lives on Someone Else's Computer

Two main ways exist to run a program that doesn't live on your own computer's hard disk.

If you're lucky, the administrator put the program's icon on your computer, and then set up a big server computer to run that program over the network. When you double-click on the program's icon, the program leaps to the screen, ready for some quick, rough-and-tumble action.

Administrators usually do this with things like the e-mail server program or a company-wide database server. Sometimes they're big programs like Microsoft Access or CorelDRAW!. Either way, if the program doesn't work, you need to ask for help; that stuff's not in your job description.

The second way to run a distant program is to head for My Network Places or a mapped drive, find the program's icon, and double-click on it. Sometimes the program runs, and, unfortunately, sometimes it doesn't. See, Windows 2000 is security conscious; it's full of bars and windows that keep out evil-minded intruders as well as cat-loving people who simply want to get their work done.

If your pointing and clicking doesn't bring your program into action, you may need to bring a Network Administrator into the fray.

There's no disgrace in asking for help on a network. No need to think "I should know this by now!" Maybe you should, just as we all should be feasting on organic sprouts, thinking only pure thoughts, and running five miles every day. But the fact is, as mere humans, we forget and do different things. (So do Network Administrators, though it's best to pretend that this isn't so.)

How Do I Share Stuff on My Computer?

Sharing on a network is not much different than sharing was when you were a kid. You could share voluntarily or Mom would *persuade* you to share.

Sad to say, your mom is probably not running your network. So the persuasion has turned into administrator fiat.

But the rules for sharing differ, depending on whether *you* made the file (or folder) or whether somebody else created it.

Generally, if you *didn't* create the file or folder, you can still read it and change it. However, you can't delete that file or folder, or change the rules about who *else* can play with it.

But, if you *did* create it, you can make all sorts of interesting rules about who gets to poke and prod it.

✔ When you make a new folder or a file, you are designated — as far as the network's concerned — as the owner of the new object.

✔ As the owner, you have full control over the object. You can make it available to everyone or keep it completely private. By default, the administrator has permission to use the object, but, as the owner, you can remove that permission.

✔ An administrator *can* force the issue by "taking ownership" of the file or folder in question. But it can't be done without your knowledge. If the administrator takes ownership, he or she can't give it back. So, if your files no longer show you as the owner, you know what happened.

✔ Yes, the network can be like a giant chess game, although it usually moves a little faster.

✔ Setting permissions for your files is covered in the next sections.

Graciously granting permissions

Now you have a group, but you still have to give the members of the group some purpose in life. In this example, the Hush-Hush Project team members are all going to be using a folder on your computer. The folder contains files and probably other folders. In the following steps, you can see how to give access permission to the project team.

1. **Right-click My Computer and select Explore. Find the folder you want to let the team use.**

   Or, if you want, create a new folder to let the team use — see Chapter 13 for the lowdown on creating folders.

2. **Right-click on the folder and choose Properties from the menu to open the Properties box.**

3. **Click on the Sharing tab and then the Share This Folder button (see Figure 9-11).**

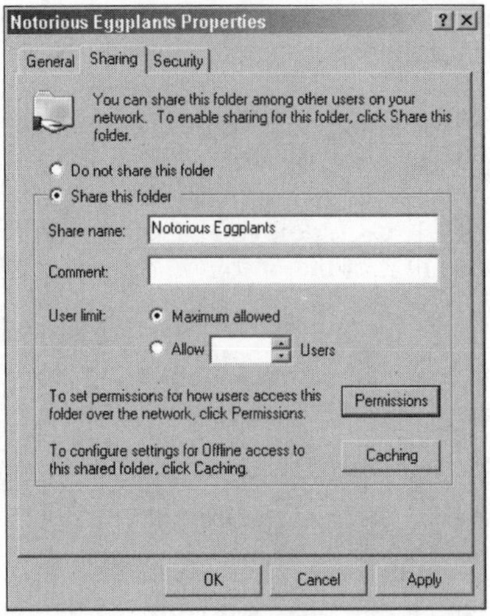

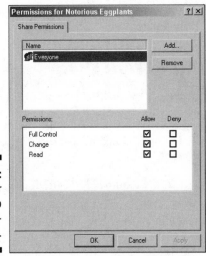

Figure 9-11:
The
Properties
dialog box
lets you
share fold-
ers and set
permissions
for others to
access files
and folders.

4. **Click the Permissions button.**

   Now you're at a window that looks similar to Figure 9-12. You can see that a whole bunch of people have access to the Notorious Eggplant Files — in fact, Everyone. The idea is that you don't want anyone except the Hush-Hush Team (and you, of course) to be able to use the folder. So you need to add the people you want and remove the ones you don't want.

Figure 9-12:
This folder
is set up to
give every-
one access.

5. **Highlight the group you want to dump and click on the Remove button. Then do the same for any others you want to exclude.**

   In this case, highlight Everyone and click on Remove.

6. **Click the Add button. Select your group from the list shown then click Add. When your group appears in the window at the bottom of the box (see Figure 9-13), click the OK button.**

   Because local groups — the kind you just made — are shown only on the computer where they're made, you may have to select your own computer's name from the Look In box.

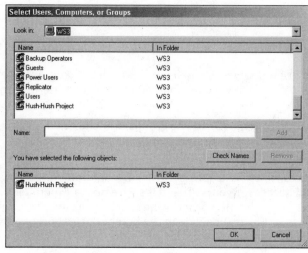

Figure 9-13:
Add your project team to the list of those who have permission to get at the folder.

7. **Back in the Share Permissions tab of the Permissions For dialog box, check the kind of permissions you want to allow the group. Then click OK twice.**

   You have many types of access, but *Full Control* is the one you should give to everybody. This means everyone can read, write, change, and add files. If you can't trust someone in your group to have Full Control, you have a problem that can't be solved by setting access rules. Under *very special and limited* circumstances, you can specify access as *Read* (the person or group can read the files but not change them in any way).

   ✔ If you want to assign yourself more permissions than the members of the group, add yourself to the Permissions list *separate* from the group.

   ✔ After you make these settings, anyone who is not in your group who tries to open the Notorious Eggplants folder will see the rude message in Figure 9-14.

Figure 9-14:
Once
you've set
permissions,
those with-
out access
rights will
see a rude
message
if they try
to poke a
nose in.

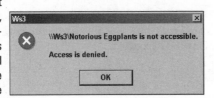

- ✔ You can grant permissions to a folder without making a workgroup of your own. Just right-click the folder and choose Properties from the menu.

- ✔ You can add or remove existing groups or members of groups to the list of people who have access, and you can pick out the kind of access granted to each person or group.

- ✔ Feel free to experiment with permissions, but don't forget to always leave full access for yourself. And it's wise not to experiment with per-missions on folders that other people actually have to use. You can drive the person in the next cubicle to the point of neighborly cubicide.

The Printers Are on the Network!

If you see your new computer and observe that no printer is attached, you may (being a reasonable person) assume that using a network printer is going to complicate your life. But even reasonable people are wrong now and again.

Generally speaking, only one difference exists between using a network printer and a printer that's directly attached to your own computer: With a network printer, you usually have to get up off your chair to pick up your printed pages. Admittedly, this situation isn't as nice as having those pages slip directly into your hands, but it's not much more complicated.

Looking for printers on the network

If no printer is directly plugged into your computer, you can easily find out what printers you can use.

1. **Click on the taskbar's Start button.**

2. **Choose Printers from the Settings menu.**

   A window appears listing one or more printers, plus the Add Printer icon.

That's it. The printers listed in the window are the ones your computer can send information to.

If the printers all have dumb, incomprehensible names, right-click on them in turn, choosing Properties from the menu each time. As shown in Figure 9-15, this brings up a box with a little information about the type of printer and its location.

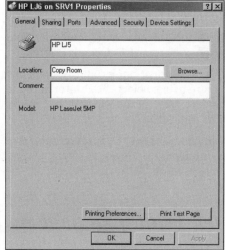

Figure 9-15:
Right-click on a printer icon and choose Properties from the menu to see information about it.

Picking a favorite printer for everyday use

If you're lucky enough to have a whole bunch of printers you can use, you need to set one of them as the default printer. That designation just means that all your Windows print jobs go to that printer unless you intervene.

Right-click on the printer you want to use most of the time and then click on Set As Default Printer (see Figure 9-16). A check mark in front of Set As Default Printer means the printer has already been made the default printer.

Figure 9-16:
The check
mark means
that this
printer is the
one your
Windows
programs
use unless
you make a
change.

✔ Only one printer at a time can be the default printer for your computer.
   To change which printer is the one used by default, just right-click on
   the one you want and then click on Set As Default Printer.

✔ Wanna use a different printer for just one print job? Look at the File
   menu in the program you're using. Select the Printer Setup item if one
   exists. Otherwise, just select Print. In the window that opens, look for a
   drop-down list of printers and select the one you want.

✔ Next time you use that program, check the Printer Setup to see what
   printer is chosen. Some applications are smart enough to go back to the
   default printer, and others are not. Sigh.

Adding a network printer to your machine

If a new printer is placed on the network and shared with everyone, you'll be
able to use it — but only after you tell your computer about it. To add a networked printer to your Printers folder, follow these steps.

1. **Click on the taskbar's Start button, and slide the mouse up to Settings
   and over to Printers. Click on Printers.**

2. **In the Printers folder, double-click on Add Printer.**

   A helpful wizard program opens (see Figure 9-17).

3. **Click Next. Check the Network Printer box to tell the wizard that the
   printer you want to use is on the network.**

4. **On the wizard's next page, you can instruct the wizard to find a
   printer in the (Active) Directory. Or choose the second option to type
   the printer name or browse for a printer. Click Next.**

Figure 9-17:
The Add
Printer
Wizard does
all the work
of installing
a new
networked
printer.
(And about
time too.)

5. **If you chose to search the directory, click Find Now. The wizard return a list of printers available to you. If you chose to browse for a printer, you also see a list of shared printers in the Browse for Printers box.**

6. **Highlight the printer you want to add and click Next.**

7. **If you want the printer to be the default printer (the one your programs will use automatically), click Yes. Click Next again.**

8. **The final wizard window summarizes the selections you made. If they're OK, click Finish. If the settings need adjustment, click the Back button.**

Even if a printer actually exists, you may not be able to see it on the network because you haven't been granted access to it. The administrator is the only one who can fix that for you. But if you can see it, you probably have the right to use it, so go ahead and try.

Chapter 10

Shuffling Words, Pictures, and Sounds from One Place to Another

· ·

In This Chapter

▶ Understanding cutting, copying, and pasting

▶ Highlighting what you need

▶ Cutting, copying, deleting, and pasting what you highlighted

▶ Making the best use of the Clipboard and ClipBook Viewer

▶ Putting scraps on the Desktop

▶ Discovering Object Linking and Embedding

▶ Controlling Print Manager

· ·

*U*ntil Windows came along, IBM-compatible computers lived in a dismal DOS world where they had a terrible time sharing anything. The DOS programs were rigid, egotistical things, with no sense of community. Information created by one DOS program couldn't always be shared with another program. Older versions of these programs passed down this selfish system to newer versions, enforcing the segregation with proprietary file formats and compatibility tests.

To counter this bad trip, the Windows programmers created a communal Windows workplace where all the programs could groove together peacefully. In the harmonious tribal village of Windows, programs share their information openly to make a more beautiful environment for all.

In the Windows co-op, all the windows can beam their vibes to each other freely, without fear of rejection. Work created by one Windows program is accepted totally and lovingly by any other Windows program. Windows programs treat each other equally, even if one program is wearing some pretty freaky threads or, in some gatherings, no threads at all.

How does it work? When two programs are on the screen, you can simply copy or move information from one window to another without fear of rejection, humiliation, or, worst of all, corporate attorneys.

This chapter shows you how easily you can move those good vibes from one window to another.

Examining the Cut-and-Paste Concept (And Copy, Too)

All Windows programs take a tip from the kindergartners and make cut and paste an integral part of their operations. Information can be electronically cut from one window and pasted into another window with little fuss and none of those little pots of mucilage.

Just about any part of a window is up for grabs. You can highlight an exceptionally well-written paragraph in your word processing program, for example, or a spreadsheet that tracks the value of your Indian-head pennies. After highlighting the desired information, you press a button to copy or cut it from its window.

At the press of the button, the information heads for a special place in Windows 2000 Professional called the Clipboard. From there, you can paste it into any other open window.

The beauty of Windows 2000 Professional is that with all those windows on-screen at the same time, you can easily grab bits and pieces from any of them and paste all the parts into a new window.

- ✔ Windows programs are designed to work together, so taking information from one window and putting it into another window is easy. Sticking a map onto your party fliers, for example, is really easy.

- ✔ Cutting and pasting works well for the big stuff, like sticking big charts into memos. But don't overlook it for the small stuff, too. For example, copying someone's name and address from your address book program is quicker than typing it by hand at the top of your letter. Or, to avoid typographical errors, you can copy an Internet address into Internet Explorer, which is especially important if you want to go to the Web site for a certain famous Welsh village: `llanfairpwllgwyngyllgogeryc wyrndrobwllllantysiliogogogoch.co.uk/`

- ✔ Cutting and pasting is different from that weird Object Linking and Embedding stuff (OLE) you may have heard about. That more powerful (and, naturally, more confusing) OLE stuff gets its own section later in this chapter.

✔ When you cut or copy some information, it immediately transfers to a special Windows program called ClipBook Viewer. From the Clipboard, you can paste it into other windows. You don't have to *see* the Clipboard for this to happen, but if you want to, see the section later in this chapter on how to track down the ClipBook Viewer and lure it out into the open.

Highlighting the Important Stuff

Before you can grab information from a window, you have to tell the window exactly what parts you want to grab. The easiest way to tell it is to highlight the information with a mouse.

You can highlight a single letter, an entire novel, or anything in between. You can highlight pictures of water lilies. You can even highlight sounds so that you can paste sneezes into other files (see the "Looking at Cool Object Linking and Embedding Stuff" section later in this chapter).

In most cases, highlighting involves one swift trick with the mouse: Put the mouse arrow or cursor at the beginning of the information you want and hold down the mouse button. Then move the mouse to the end of the information and release the button. That's it! All the stuff lying between your mouse moves is highlighted. The information turns a different color so that you can see what you grabbed. An example of highlighted text is shown in Figure 10-1.

Figure 10-1: Highlighted text turns a different color for easy visibility.

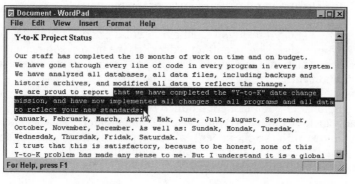

If you're mouseless, use the arrow keys to put the cursor at the beginning of the stuff you want to grab. Then hold down the Shift key and press the arrow keys until the cursor is at the end of what you want to grab. You see the stuff on-screen become highlighted as you move the arrow keys. This trick works with almost every Windows 2000 program. (If you're after text, hold down the Ctrl key and the text is highlighted word by word.)

Some programs have a few shortcuts for highlighting parts of their information:

✔ To highlight a single word in Notepad, WordPad, or most text boxes, point at it with the mouse and double-click. The word turns black, meaning that it's highlighted. (In WordPad, you can hold down the button on its second click and then, by moving the mouse around, you can quickly highlight additional text word by word.)

✔ To highlight a single line in WordPad, click next to it in the left margin. Keep holding down the mouse button and move the mouse up or down to highlight additional text line by line.

✔ To highlight a paragraph in WordPad, double-click next to it in the left margin. Keep holding down the mouse button on the second click and move the mouse to highlight additional text paragraph by paragraph.

✔ To highlight an entire document in WordPad, hold down the Ctrl key and click anywhere in the left margin. (To highlight the entire document in Notepad, press and release the Alt key and then press E and then A. So much for consistency between Windows 2000 programs. . . .)

✔ To highlight a portion of text in just about any Windows 2000 program, click on the text's beginning, hold down the Shift key, and click on the end of the desired text. Everything between those two points becomes highlighted.

✔ To highlight part of a picture or drawing while in Paint, click on the Select tool — the little tool button with the dotted lines in a square. After clicking on the Select tool, hold down the mouse button and slide the cursor over the desired part of the picture.

After you highlight text, you must either cut it or copy it immediately. If you do anything else, like absentmindedly click the mouse someplace else in your document, all your highlighted text reverts to normal, just like Cinderella after midnight.

Be careful after you highlight a bunch of text. If you press any key — the spacebar, for example — Windows 2000 immediately replaces your highlighted text with the character that you type — in this case, a space. To reverse that calamity and bring your highlighted text back to life, hold down Alt and press the Backspace key.

Deleting, Cutting, or Copying What You Highlighted

After you highlight some information (which is described in the preceding section, in case you just entered the classroom), you're ready to start playing with it. You can delete it, cut it, or copy it. Each option means a completely different thing.

Deleting the information

Deleting the information just wipes it out. Zap! It just disappears from the window. To delete highlighted information, press the Delete or Backspace key.

- ✔ If you accidentally delete the wrong thing — panic. Then hold down the Ctrl key and press the letter Z. Your deletion is graciously undone. Any deleted information pops back up on-screen. Whew!

- ✔ Holding down the Alt key and pressing the Backspace key also undoes your last mistake. (Unless you've just said something dumb at a party. Then use Ctrl+Z.)

Cutting the information

Cutting the highlighted information wipes it off the screen, just as the Delete command does, but with a big difference: When the information is removed from the window, it is copied to a special Windows 2000 storage tank called the Clipboard.

When you're looking at the screen, cutting and deleting look identical. In fact, the first few times you try to cut something, you feel panicky, thinking that you may have accidentally deleted it instead. (This feeling never really goes away, either.)

To cut highlighted stuff, hold down the Ctrl key and press the X key. (Get it? That's an X, as in you're crossing, or X-ing, something out.) Whoosh! The highlighted text disappears from the window, scoots through the under-ground tubes of Windows 2000, and waits on the Clipboard for further action.

- ✔ One way to tell whether your Cut command actually worked is to paste the information back into your document. If it appears, you know that the command worked, and you can cut it out again right away. If it doesn't appear, you know that something has gone dreadfully wrong. (For the Paste command, discussed a little later, hold down the Ctrl key and press the V key.)

✔ **Little known fact department:** You can also cut highlighted stuff by holding down Shift and pressing the Del key. To Paste stuff, you can hold down Shift and press Insert. Some people find this "Delete" and "Insert" metaphor a little easier to remember.

Copying the information

Compared with cutting or deleting, copying information is quite anticlimactic. When you cut or delete, the information disappears from the screen. But, when you copy information to the Clipboard, the highlighted information doesn't move from the window. In fact, it looks as if nothing has happened, so you repeat the Copy command a few times before giving up and hoping it worked.

To copy highlighted information, hold down the Ctrl key and press the C key. Although nothing seems to happen, that information really does head for the Clipboard.

Finding out more about cutting, copying, and deleting

Want to know more about cutting, copying, and deleting? Read on (you really should read this stuff):

✔ Windows 2000 often puts toolbars across the tops of its programs. Figure 10-2 shows the toolbar buttons that stand for cutting, copying, and pasting things.

✔ If you prefer to use menus, the Cut, Copy, and Paste commands tumble down after you choose the word Edit on any menu bar.

✔ If you're using the Print Screen key trick to copy a window or the entire screen to the Clipboard, one important component is left out: The mouse arrow is not included in the picture, even if it was in plain sight when you took the picture. Are you asking yourself how all the little arrows got in this book's pictures? Well, it's magic!

✔ Sometimes you may have difficulty figuring out whether the Cut or Copy commands are really working. To know for sure, you can keep the ClipBook Viewer showing at the bottom of the screen. Then you can watch the images appear on it when you press the buttons.

✔ Don't be confused when you open ClipBook Viewer and see the local ClipBook window plus another window labeled ClipBook Viewer. First, take a deep breath and read the section a little later in this chapter called "ClipBook Viewer — Enemy or Foe?"

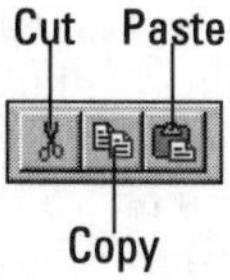

Figure 10-2:
From left to right, clicking on these toolbar buttons cuts, copies, or pastes information.

Cut   Paste

Copy

Pasting Information into Another Window

After you cut or copy information to the special Windows Clipboard storage tank, it's ready for travel. You can paste that information into just about any other window.

Pasting is relatively straightforward compared with highlighting, copying, or cutting: Click the mouse anywhere in the destination window and click on the spot where you want the stuff to appear. Then hold down the Ctrl key and press the V key. Presto! Anything that's sitting on the Clipboard immediately leaps into that window.

 ✔ Another way to paste stuff is to hold down the Shift key and press Insert. That combination does the same thing as Ctrl+V.

 ✔ You also can choose the Paste command from a window's menu bar. Choose the word Edit and then choose the word Paste. But don't choose the words Paste Special. That command is for more advanced pasting like the Object Linking and Embedding stuff, which gets its own section later in this chapter.

 ✔ Some programs have toolbars along their top. Clicking on the Paste button, shown in Figure 10-2, pastes the Clipboard's current contents into your document.

 ✔ The Paste command inserts a copy of the information that's sitting on the Clipboard. The information stays on the Clipboard, so you can keep pasting it into other windows if you want. In fact, the Clipboard's contents stay the same until a new Cut or Copy command replaces them with new information.

Using the ClipBook Viewer

Cutting and pasting has always been a part of Windows. And all along, when anything was cut or copied, it was temporarily stored in a special Windows space called the Clipboard. Windows 2000 employs a special program to let you save stuff that's on the Clipboard, share it with others on your network, and perform several other equally unlikely tricks. The program is called ClipBook Viewer and as proof that it's quite special, there's a special trick *you* have to do in order to see it.

To see ClipBook Viewer, click on the Start button and click on Run. In the Open box, carefully type in **clipbrd** then click the OK button. Inside the ClipBook Viewer is the Clipboard, where you can see whatever was most recently cut or copied (see Figure 10-3).

Figure 10-3: This Clipboard contains a recently copied picture of a couple of cool cats.

  ✔ Inside the ClipBook Viewer window lives Clipboard plus another window called Local ClipBook. They're probably not named that way just to be confusing, but confusing it is.

  ✔ Sometimes the Clipboard (inside ClipBook Viewer) can't show you exactly what you've copied. For example, if you copy a sound from the Windows 2000 Sound Recorder, you see only a picture of the Sound Recorder's icon. And, at the risk of getting metaphysical, what does a sound look like anyway?

✔ The Clipboard functions automatically and transparently. Unless you make a special effort, you don't even know it's there. (That's why ClipBook Viewer is handy — it lets you see what the Clipboard is up to.)

The *Clipboard* is a special area inside memory where Windows 2000 keeps track of information that was cut or copied. *ClipBook Viewer* is a program that lets you see the information that's currently on the Clipboard.

✔ The ClipBook Viewer usually contains two windows: the Local ClipBook window and the Clipboard. The Clipboard contains immediately cut or copied information, and the Local ClipBook window lets you save assorted Clipboard tidbits and share them with other computers on the network. (That's covered in the next section.)

✔ To better track what's being cut and pasted, some people leave ClipBook Viewer sitting open at the bottom of the screen. Then they can actually see what they've cut or copied.

✔ Most of the time, the Clipboard is used just for temporary operations — a quick cut here, a quick paste there, and on to the next job. But ClipBook Viewer lets you save the Clipboard's contents for later use. Choose File from the menu bar and then choose Save As from the pull-down menu. Type in a filename and click on the OK command button (or just press Enter).

✔ The Clipboard can hold only one thing at a time. Each time you cut or copy something else, you replace the Clipboard's contents with something new. If you want to collect a bunch of clips for later pasting, use the Save As option described in the preceding paragraph. The Clipboard also starts up empty each time you start Windows 2000.

✔ If you're using Office 2000, don't bother with the Clipboard. The Office 2000 programs have an automatic collect and paste feature that allows you to have up to a dozen items on a floating clipboard.

✔ Want a permanent link to the ClipBook Viewer? Click the Start button, then click Search. In the Search for Files and Folders, tell the program to search for a program named clipbrd. When the file appears in the Search Results window (see Figure 10-4), right-click the file named clipbrd (found in the WINNT\system32 folder) and drag it to your Desktop and drop it. After you drop it, select Create Shortcut Here from the menu that pops up. Now you have an express route to ClipBook Viewer — just double-click the icon (Figure 10-5) whenever you want to see it.

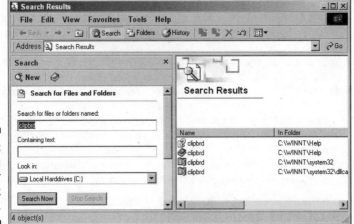

Figure 10-4:
Searching
around for
the ClipBook
Viewer.

Figure 10-5:
Here's a
shortcut to
the ClipBook
Viewer.

 ✔ If some programs and settings don't seem exactly as they're described in this book, it's for a special reason: Your Network Administrator has probably been fiddling with your computer's settings. For example, your Network Administrator can remove ClipBook Viewer — or practically any other function — for reasons unknown to most mortals. If in doubt, ask 'em.

ClipBook Viewer: Enemy or Foe?

When you open ClipBook Viewer, as described in the preceding section, it contains your Clipboard's window and a window called Local ClipBook.

Although ClipBook Viewer lets you see the information that you're cutting and pasting on your own computer, ClipBook Viewer shares that information with other people on your network. Anything you copy to the Clipboard can be copied to the ClipBook and passed around to other network users like an hors d'oeuvre with a fancy toothpick (providing you're willing to share, of course). More likely, ClipBooks on other machines may offer information you want to see. To see whether any fascinating reading (or eating) is available on other computers, follow these steps:

1. **Click the Start menu, and then click Run.**

2. **In the Run box, type** clipbrd **and then click the OK button.**

   See the preceding section for a handy tip on creating a shortcut to the ClipBook Viewer.

3. **Click the File menu and select Connect.**

   A window opens with a list of computers.

4. **Double-click on the one that looks the most appetizing.**

   The ClipBook on the computer in question opens and shows you a list of what's available (see Figure 10-6).

Figure 10-6:
ClipBook
Viewer lets
you use
information
on the
ClipBooks of
other com-
puters on
the network.

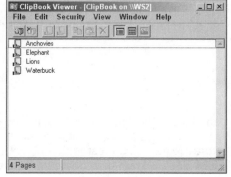

5. **Double-click on your choice, and you can see what's inside.**

   ✔ ClipBook may not be available at all on your network because there are other, more slick ways to share information (if your Network Administrator has installed them). You may have local newsgroups or something called groupware. If so, your network administrator will tell you all about them.

   ✔ The list of items on another computer's ClipBook can be shown as a table of contents or a bunch of little pictures (called *Thumbnails*). Choose either look from the View menu. Or highlight a particular item and select Full Page from the View menu.

Looking at Cool Object Linking and Embedding Stuff

Because the concepts of cutting and pasting are so refreshingly simple, Microsoft complicated them considerably with something called Object

Linking and Embedding, known as OLE. It sounds complicated, so we start with the simple part: the object.

The *object* is merely the information you want to paste into a window. It can be a sentence, a road map, a sneeze sound, or anything else that you can cut or copy from a window.

Normally, when you paste an object into a window, you're pasting the same kind of information. For example, you paste text into a word processor and pictures into the Windows 2000 Paint program. But what if you want to paste a sound into WordPad, the Windows 2000 word processor?

That's where Object Linking and Embedding comes in, offering subtle changes to the paste concept. You'll probably never use them, but they can be fun to fiddle around with on cloudy days. Beware, however: OLE awareness is the first step down those ever-spiraling stairs toward computer-nerd certification.

Embedding

On the surface, embedding an object looks just like pasting it. The object shows up in the window. Big deal. But, when you embed an object, you're also embedding the name of the program that created that object. When you double-click on the object, poof! The program that created it jumps to the top of the screen, ready to edit whatever the object is.

For example, you can embed a spreadsheet chart showing your current net worth in a letter you're writing to an old high-school friend. Then, if the stock market changes before you mail the letter, you can easily update the letter's chart. Just look at the letter in your word processor and double-click on the chart. The spreadsheet that created the chart pops up, ready for you to make the changes. After you finish, you close the spreadsheet. The spreadsheet disappears, leaving the updated chart in your letter.

Embedding is really pretty handy. You don't have to remember the chart's filename. You don't even have to call up your spreadsheet. Windows 2000 does all that grunt work automatically. Just double-click on the chart, make the changes after your spreadsheet appears, and then quit the spreadsheet to return to the letter.

As with most things in Windows 2000, the OLE concept is easier to use than its name implies.

Linking

Linking looks just like embedding or pasting. Your chart appears in your letter, just as before. But here's where things get weird: You're not really pasting the chart. You're pasting the chart's filename.

The word processor runs over to the file containing the chart, sees what the chart looks like, and then puts a copy of it in the letter.

What's the point? Well, unlike with pasting or embedding, you're keeping only one copy of the chart around. When you call up the chart in your spreadsheet and change it, those changes are automatically reflected in your word processor the next time you load that letter. With only one real version of the object lying around, every copy is always the right version.

- ✔ Not all Windows 2000 programs can handle Object Linking and Embedding. In fact, of the programs that come in the Windows 2000 box, only WordPad is really OLE savvy.

- ✔ Object Linking and Embedding can get pretty complex, so the vast majority of Windows 2000 users simply acknowledge that their computer can do that stuff and let the technicians play with it.

Should you paste, embed, or link your important objects? Here's what to do:

- ✔ Use Paste for objects you never want to change.

- ✔ Embed objects if you want to be able to easily edit them at a later date.

- ✔ Choose the Link option if you want several programs to share the same version of a single object.

Windows 2000 Professional tries really, really hard to make Object Linking and Embedding work across networks so, for example, you can send a message with an embedded Excel worksheet to someone who doesn't have Excel on his computer. Sometimes this can be made to work and sometimes it can't. But in either case, you need the help of an expert.

Leaving Scraps on the Desktop Deliberately

The Clipboard's a handy way to copy information from one place to another, but it has a major limitation: Every time you copy something new to the Clipboard, it replaces what was copied there before. What if you want to copy a bunch of things from a document?

If you were cutting and pasting over a real desktop, you could leave little scraps lying everywhere, ready for later use. The same scraps concept works with Windows 2000: You can move information from window to window, using the Desktop as a temporary storage area for your scraps of information.

For example, suppose you have some paragraphs in a WordPad document you want to copy to some other places. Highlight the first paragraph, drag it out of the WordPad window, and drop it onto the Desktop. Poof! A small Scrap icon appears on your Desktop (see Figure 10-7). See another interesting paragraph? Drag it onto the Desktop, as well: Another Scrap icon appears.

Figure 10-7:
Scraps on
the desktop
look a lot
like . . . well,
scraps.

Eventually, copies of your report's best paragraphs are sitting in little scraps on your Desktop. To move any of the scraps into another document, just drag them into that other document's window and let go.

You can dump any remaining, unused scraps into the Recycle Bin, or simply leave them on the Desktop, adding a nice, comfortable layer of clutter.

To make a scrap, highlight the information you want to move, usually by running the mouse pointer over it while holding down the mouse button. Then, point at the highlighted information and, while holding down the mouse button, point at the Desktop. Let go of the mouse button, and a scrap containing that information appears on the Desktop.

If you're using Office 2000, don't bother with scraps. The Office 2000 programs have an automatic collect and paste feature that allows you to have up to a dozen items on a floating clipboard.

Controlling the Printer

Many of the Windows 2000 features work in the background. You know that they're there only if something is wrong and weird messages start flying around. The Windows 2000 print program is one of those programs.

When you choose the Print command in a program, you may see the little Windows 2000 printer icon appear at the bottom corner of your screen. After your printer stops spitting out pages, the little printer icon disappears.

If everything is running smoothly, the printer icon looks like this in the corner of your taskbar:

Your printer can print only one thing at a time. If you try to print a second memo before the first one is finished, Windows 2000 jumps in to help. It intercepts all the requests and lines them up in order, just like a harried diner cook.

To check up on what is being sent to the printer, double-click on the taskbar's little printer icon, and you see the print program in all its glory, as shown in Figure 10-8.

Figure 10-8:
Double-click
on the
taskbar's
printer icon
to see what
files are
about to be
printed.

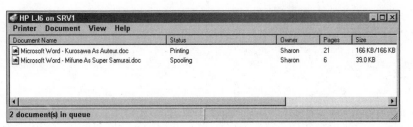

✔ After the printer is through with the Kurosawa document, it moves to the second file in the lineup, which, in this case, is Mifune As Super Samurai.

✔ Changing the order of the files as they're about to be printed is easy. For example, to scoot the Mifune document ahead of Kurosawa, click on its name and hold down the mouse button. Then drag the file up so it cuts in front of Kurosawa. Release the button, and Print Manager changes the printing order. (The printing order is called a *queue,* pronounced Q.)

✔ To cancel a print job, click on the filename you don't like with your right mouse button and then choose Cancel Printing from the menu that pops up.

✔ If the boss is walking by the printer while you're printing your party flier, choose Document from the menu and select Pause Printing from the menu that drops down. The printer stops. After the boss is out of sight, click on Pause Printing again to continue. Unfortunately, many laser printers have their own memory, so they'll continue printing a few more pages.

✔ Once a print job starts actually printing , you can't move another print job ahead of it. Also, it's almost impossible to cancel a job that's already in the process of printing. The best you can hope for is to pause it.

✔ If you're on a network, you may have no control over the order in which files are printed, which printer is used, or whether or not you can pause a print job. It all depends — and you're probably tired of hearing this — on how the network is set up. Yawn.

✔ If your printer is not hooked up, Windows 2000 will probably try to send your file to the printer anyway. When it doesn't get a response, it sends you a message that your printer isn't ready. Plug the printer in, turn it on, and try again. Or hit Chapter 19 for more printer troubleshooting tips.

Chapter 11

Switch Flipping in the Control Panel

- -

In This Chapter

▶ Exploring the Control Panel

▶ Customizing the display

▶ Do-it-yourself Desktop with Active Desktop

▶ Folders and their options

▶ Dialing out

▶ Changing to a different printer

▶ Staying on schedule

▶ Hoppin' 'n' jivin' with multimedia sounds

▶ Installing or removing programs

▶ Avoiding dangerous and unfriendly icons

- -

*I*n a way, working with Windows 2000 is like remodeling a bathroom. You can spend time on the practical things, like calculating the optimum dimensions for piping or choosing the proper brand of caulking to seal the sink and tub. Or you can spend your time on the more fun options, like adding an oak toilet paper holder or a rattan cover for the Kleenex box.

You can remodel Windows 2000, too, and in just as many ways. On the eminently practical side, head for the Windows 2000 Control Panel, call up the Mouse icon, and spend hours optimizing the way Windows 2000 recognizes your mouse clicks.

Or check out the Control Panel's more refined options: Change the color of the title bars to teal, for example, or cover the Windows 2000 Desktop with daisy patterns or argyle wallpaper.

This chapter shows you how to turn Windows 2000 into that program you've always dreamed of owning someday. (Although you still can't have bay windows. . . .)

Finding the Control Panel

The Control Panel is the cupboard that holds most of the Windows 2000 switches. Flip open the Control Panel and you can waste a few hours scratching your head over all the Windows 2000 options.

To find the Control Panel, click on the Start button, choose Settings, and click on Control Panel. The Control Panel window pops up, as shown in Figure 11-1. (Because different computers often contain different parts, your Control Panel may look a little different than the one in the picture.) Each icon in the Control Panel's window represents a switch that controls part of the computer.

Figure 11-1: Double-click on an icon in the Control Panel to reveal hidden switches controlling that particular icon's subject.

Everybody's Control Panel looks different because everybody (and everybody's corporation) can afford different computer toys. For example, some modem hounds have special icons that control the way their modems collect mail from all their electronic mailboxes. Others have icons that help them agonize over settings for their networks or sound cards. Table 11-1 looks at some of the icons you may come across in your copy of Windows 2000.

For a quick way to access your Control Panel, double-click on the My Computer icon (it's usually hiding in the upper-left corner of your Desktop). You find a Control Panel folder inside, waiting for you to open it with a double-click.

All those icons in the Control Panel can be persuaded to pop off your Start menu with just a little encouragement. Right-click on a blank spot on the Taskbar and choose Properties on the menu that pops up. Click on the Advanced tab, then check the box next to Expand Control Panel in the list under Start Menu Settings. Last but not least, click OK. Now, if you click on the Start button and choose Settings and then Control Panel, all those icons come rolling out (see Figure 11-2).

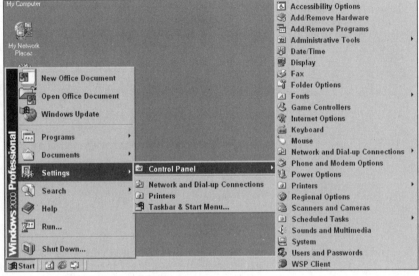

Figure 11-2: All the icons inside the Control Panel can be persuaded to come out and play on the Start menu.

Your Control Panel may have more icons than the ones described in Table 11-1. Some programs and some hardware plop an icon of their own in the Control Panel when they install.

Table 11-1	Deciphering the Control Panel Icons
This Icon	*Does This*
Accessibility Options	Windows 2000 can be customized to work more easily for people with physical limitations. The screen can be made more readable, for example, or the numeric keypad can be converted into a makeshift mouse (which is also handy for laptop users).
Add/Remove Hardware	Double-clicking on this icon actually starts up the Add/Remove Hardware Wizard, which can help you add, remove, unplug, and troubleshoot your hardware. Its presence doesn't guarantee that you'll never have a hardware problem you can't solve (that's what computer gurus are for, after all), but it puts you a giant step closer to plug and play than Windows NT ever did.

(continued)

Table 11-1 *(continued)*

This Icon	*Does This*
Add/Remove Programs	Are you eager to install that new (insert name of expensive software here)? Double-click here to make Windows 2000 automatically install your new software. Use this icon to tell Windows 2000 to add on any optional components, too, like the Freecell card game. (You may need to consult the Network Administrator first, though.)
Administrative Tools	Don't touch this icon unless you're planing to be elected System Administrator for a Day (our worst nightmare!). This is where you find tools that let you manage some of the higher-order functions of your computer, monitor its performance, and more. Our advice: If you don't know what you're doing here, keep away.
Date/Time	This area lets you change your computer's date, time, and time-zone settings.
Display	Double-click on the Display icon to change your screen's wallpaper, color scheme, number of available colors, resolution, screensaver, and other display-oriented settings. (Or, right-click on a blank part of your Desktop and choose Properties from the pop-up menu; both methods work.)
Fax	We've included a whole chapter about how to make the Fax icon do your bidding, so check out Chapter 14.
Folder Options	Using this icon, you can customize the display of files and folders, change file associations, and more. Much more on this later in the chapter.
Fonts	Windows 2000 comes with fonts like Arial and Courier. If you head back to the software store and buy more, like Lucida-Blackletter, install them by double-clicking on this icon. (**Nerdly Note:** This icon is actually a *shortcut* to the real Fonts setting area. We cover shortcuts in Chapters 4 and 12.)
Game Controllers	If you're fiddling with this icon at the office, chances are you're not doing what you're supposed to be doing. This is where you can add, remove, or configure game controller hardware such as joysticks and gamepads.

This Icon	*Does This*
Internet Options	Don't mess with this icon until you've had a chance to read up on Internet Explorer in Chapter 16. Even then, you may want to leave the settings alone.
Keyboard	Here you can change how long the keyboard takes to repeat a letter when you hold down a key. Yawn. Rarely used. Or, if you pack up the computer and move to Sweden, double-click here to switch to the Swedish language format (or Belgian, Finnish, Icelandic, and a bunch of other countries' formats). Finally, here's where you tell Windows 2000 whether you upgraded to a newer 101- or 102-key keyboard.
Mouse	Make that mouse scoot faster across the screen, change it from right-handed to left-handed, fine-tune your double-click, choose between brands, and change all sorts of mouse-related behaviors.
Network and Dial-up Connections	Save this one for the office network guru. You aren't missing much, just the mechanics of linking computers so that people can swap information.
Phone and Modem Options	Before you can talk to other computers over the phone lines, you need a modem. Double-click here, and Windows 2000 tries to figure out what sort of modem you have so that it can start bossing it around. If you're working in an office, check with the Network Administrator first — you don't want to fiddle with any settings that are already in place.
Power Options	This icon can help you be an earth-friendly computer user by taking advantage of energy-saving settings for your computer. If you'd like to turn your monitor off when it's not being used, for example, this is the place to do it.
Printers	This is a shortcut to the Printers folder.
Regional Options	Used mostly by laptoppers with lots of Frequent Flyer miles, this area changes the way Windows 2000 displays and sorts numbers, currency, the date, and the time. (If you change time zones, just click on the date/time display on the bottom-right corner of the taskbar, a process described later in this chapter.)

(continued)

Table 11-1 *(continued)*

This Icon	Does This
Scanners and Cameras	You won't need to touch this icon unless you're lucky enough to have a scanner or digital camera to use with your computer. If you do have one or more of these devices, this is where you can install, remove, or troubleshoot the software that lets your snazzy toy communicate with your computer.
Scheduled Tasks	This icon is the digital equivalent of tying a string around your finger — except it's even better since it not only reminds you of a task, it actually goes ahead and does whatever you've told it to do. (However, it won't go out and pick up the pizza — and anyone who says it will is just pulling your leg.)
Sounds and Multimedia	This area is the most fun! Make Windows 2000 play different sounds for different events. For example, hear a cool Pink Floyd riff whenever a Windows 2000 error message pops up on-screen. Windows 2000 comes with a few sounds, but you have to record Pink Floyd yourself, unfortunately. Grab a microphone, fire up Sound Recorder and check out the ultra-hip *MP3 For Dummies* for hard drive recording tips.
System	As boring as a mechanic's manual for '74 Pontiacs, this icon lets the Network Administrator tweak incredibly detailed parts of your computer's life. Stay away from it.
Users and Passwords	Here's where you can taste true power. Use this icon to grant or deny other people access to your computer and to change passwords and other security-related settings — if you dare.

Customizing the Display

Display

The most-often-used part of the Control Panel is probably the Display icon, which looks like the picture in the margin. When you open this door, you can change the wallpaper, screen saver, and other visual aspects of the Windows 2000 Desktop (see Figure 11-3).

Unlike some switches in the Control Panel, the Display icon doesn't control anything too dangerous. Feel free to fiddle around with all the settings. You can't cause any major harm. If you do want to play, however, be sure to write down any original settings. Then you can always return to normal if something looks odd.

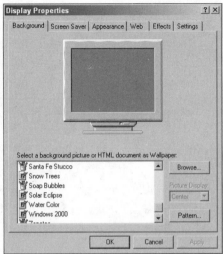

Figure 11-3:
The Display icon brings up a dialog box that lets you change your Desktop's colors and other display-oriented options.

Basically, just don't change both the color of your text and the color of your background to white, like some poor fellow in Minnesota once did. That makes it much too hard to see what you're doing.

You don't have to root through the Start button and the Control Panel to get to the Display icon's contents. Instead, just click on a blank part of your Desktop using your right mouse button. After the menu pops up out of nowhere, click on Properties. That bypasses the Control Panel and takes you straight to the Display settings area.

The display's background (hanging new wallpaper)

When Windows 2000 first installs itself, it paints a dull green-blue background across the screen and then starts sprinkling windows and icons over it. Windows 2000 has to choose that dull color in the beginning, or nobody would think it's a serious business application.

However, Microsoft snuck other backgrounds, known as wallpaper, into the Windows 2000 box. Those pieces of wallpaper are hiding on the hard disk, just waiting for you to install them. Different wallpaper can reflect different moods. For example, you can turn the window's background into a pattern of flowers or trees or soap bubbles. You can use a scanned photo of your choice for a cheery day (see Figure 11-4). Or you can create your own wallpaper in Paint, the Windows 2000 graphics program, and hang your new wallpaper yourself.

Figure 11-4:
Windows
wallpaper,
the
backdrop
beneath
all the
windows
and icons,
can match
your mood
for the day.

To change the wallpaper, do the following:

1. **Double-click on the Display icon from the Control Panel**.

   Or you can click on a blank spot of your Desktop with your right mouse button and choose Properties from the menu that appears.

   A rather large dialog box appears (refer to Figure 11-3).

2. **Find the list of wallpaper choices and click on one of the names.**

   Wham! Windows 2000 displays a small preview of how your selection would look as wallpaper (see Figure 11-5).

3. **To see more names on the list, click on the little arrows on the bar next to the names.**

   If you aren't using a mouse, you can select a listed item by using the arrow keys to highlight the item you want and then pressing Enter. In a long list, you can find a certain name more quickly by pressing the name's first letter.

4. **After you see the name of the wallpaper you want, select it and then click the Apply button to make Windows 2000 install it.**

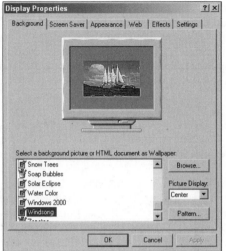

Figure 11-5:
Windows 2000 displays a small preview of how your selection will look as wallpaper.

5. **Like the way your new wallpaper looks on-screen? Then click the OK button. If you don't like the way it looks, go back to Step 4 and choose a new one.**

   The dialog box disappears, and you are back at your Desktop (with the new wallpaper displayed proudly in the background).

✓ Wallpaper can be tiled across the screen, centered, or stretched to fit the whole screen. Small pictures look best when tiled, or painted repeatedly across the screen. Larger pictures look best if they're centered. The Stretch option works best with pictures that are in the same proportion as your screen. Click the little downward-pointing arrow below the words Picture Display button to select your preference. Or try all three and then choose the one you like best.

✓ Wallpaper files can be almost any sort of graphic file — including files with the extensions bmp, jpg, gif, dib, png, and htm.

✓ See a pretty picture you like while browsing on the World Wide Web with Internet Explorer? Then click on the picture with your right mouse button and choose Set as Wallpaper from the pop-up menu. (You may need to save the file onto your hard disk first.)

✓ Windows 2000 lists wallpaper that's stored directly in the Windows 2000 folder and any bitmap files that are in the My Pictures folder inside the My Documents folder that roosts on your Desktop. If you create some potential wallpaper in Paint, save the file to the My Pictures folder and the file will appear in the list of available wallpaper. If this concept seems strange, foreign, confusing, or all three, check out Chapter 12 for more information about folders and moving files between them.

Wallpaper looks like a lot of fun, but it may be too much fun if your computer is running big programs and trying to display complicated wallpaper at the same time. Large chunks of wallpaper can use up a great deal of the computer's memory, consistently slowing Windows 2000 down. If you find yourself running out of memory, change the wallpaper to the (None) option. The screen won't look as pretty, but Windows 2000 may work better.

Small files that are tiled or stretched across the screen take up much less memory than large files that are centered on-screen. If Windows 2000 seems slow or it sends you furtive messages saying it's running out of memory, try tiling or stretching some smaller bits of wallpaper.

- ✔ The Pattern option sprinkles tiny patterns across the screen, providing a low-budget alternative to wallpaper. To add or change those sprinkles, click on the Pattern button to bring up a list of pattern names (refer to Figure 11-3). Choose from the patterns Microsoft provides; or if you're desperate for something to do, click on the Edit Pattern button to create your own little patterns.

- ✔ Patterns are a poor-man's wallpaper. They're only one color, and they don't vary much. If Windows 2000 keeps complaining about needing more memory, dump your wallpaper and switch to patterns. They don't eat up nearly as much memory. (They're pretty ugly, though.) And remember, your best bet is to buy as much memory as possible — especially because memory costs so little.

- ✔ To see patterns across the back of the Desktop, you need to change the wallpaper option to (None); otherwise, the patterns won't show up.

The display's screen saver

In the dinosaur days of computing, computer monitors were permanently damaged when an oft-used program burned its image onto the screen. The program's faint outlines showed up even if the monitor was turned off.

To prevent this burn-in, people installed screen savers to jump in when a computer hadn't been used for a while. The screen saver would either blank the screen or fill it with wavy lines to keep the program's display from etching itself into the screen.

Today's monitors don't really have this problem, but people use screen savers anyway — mainly because they look cool.

Windows comes with several screen savers built in, although none of them is activated at first. To set one up, do the following:

1. **Click on the Screen Saver tab along the top of the Display Properties dialog box (refer to Figure 11-3).**

2. **Then click on the downward-pointing arrow in the Screen Saver box.**

3. **Select the screen saver you want.**

   Immediately after choosing a screen saver, click on the Preview command button to see what the screen saver looks like. Wiggle the mouse or press the spacebar to come back to Windows 2000.

4. **Click OK to save your new screen saver settings.**

✔ Fiddlers can click on Settings for more options. For example, you can control the colors and animation speed.

✔ If you click on the Password protected box, your workstation locks up when the screen saver kicks in. You unlock it by typing your password (the one you use to log on with). If you forget your password, you have to make your feeble excuses to the Network Administrator and get that oh-so-jolly soul to unlock it.

✔ Click on the up or down arrows next to Wait to tell the screen saver when to kick in. If you set the option to 5, for example, Windows 2000 waits until you haven't touched the mouse or keyboard for five minutes before letting the screen saver out of its cage.

The display's appearance (getting better colors)

The time has come to put your fancy color monitor and video card to some good use. You can make Windows 2000 appear in any color you want by clicking on the tab marked Appearance, found along the top of the Display Properties box.

You can find the Display Properties box (shown back in Figure 11-3) by either double-clicking on the Control Panel's Display icon or right-clicking on a blank part of the Desktop and choosing Properties from the pop-up menu.

Clicking on the Appearance tab enables you to choose among several Microsoft-designed color schemes or to create your own. (Tell your boss that a more pleasant color scheme will enhance your productivity.) Figure 11-6 shows the Appearance tab.

Figure 11-6:
Windows
2000 lets
you
personalize
your
computer by
choosing
different
color
schemes.

To choose among previously designed color schemes, do the following:

1. **Click on the arrow next to the box beneath Scheme.**

2. **After the list drops down, click on the name of the scheme you want to try out.**

   Each time you select a new color scheme, the sample window shows you how the colors will look.

3. **Click OK to save your new Scheme settings.**

If you want to change one of the color schemes slightly, go for it: Click on the box beneath Item to see a list of areas you can fiddle with. For example, to change the font Windows 2000 uses for icon titles, choose Icon from the list and select a different font from the ones listed in the Font box.

And, if you want even more choices, you can mix your own colors by selecting Other from the Color menu and clicking on the Define Custom Colors command button.

Feel free to play around with the colors by trying out different schemes or designing your own combinations. Playing with the colors is an easy way to see what names Windows 2000 uses for its different components. It's also a fun way to work with dialog boxes. But if you goof something awful, and all the letters suddenly disappear, click on the Cancel button. (It's in the middle of the three buttons along the bottom.)

- ✔ Color schemes don't refer to color alone; they can change the appearance of Windows 2000 in other ways. For example, the Icon Spacing (Horizontal) setting listed in the Item box determines how closely your icons sit next to each other. Also in the Item box, the Scrollbar setting determines the width of the scroll bars and their elevator-like buttons you click on to move around in a document.

- ✔ Created an outstanding new color scheme? Then click on the Save As button and type in a new name for your creation. If you ever grow weary of your creative new color scheme, you can always return to the Windows 2000 original colors by selecting Windows Standard from the Scheme box.

- ✔ Windows 2000 continues to display your newly chosen colors until you head back to the Appearance tab and change them again.

- ✔ All this talk of "dialog boxes," "command buttons," and "funny arrow things" got you down? Then head to Chapter 6 for a field guide to figuring out these assorted Windows 2000 doodads.

The display's appearance, continued (playing with the Active Desktop)

The Active Desktop feature of Windows 2000 enables you to customize your Desktop area far beyond your wildest dreams; instead of just hanging new wallpaper, choosing a different screen saver, or getting better colors, you can make your Desktop display a Web page of your choice. That way, if you want to keep track of your stock portfolio or catch up on what's happening on your favorite soap opera while you're working, you can (provided you're sneaky enough). Windows 2000 will even update the contents of the Web page on your Active Desktop if you want it to.

To turn on the Active Desktop feature and display your favorite Web page on your Desktop, do the following:

1. **Click on the Web tab along the top of the Display Properties dialog box (refer to Figure 11-3).**

2. **Click the mouse button once to place a check in the box labeled Show Web Content On My Active Desktop.**

3. **To display your current home page on your Active Desktop, place a check in the box labeled My Current Home Page and click OK.**

   Now check out your Desktop to see a box containing your home page. Maximize it if you want so that everyone can see exactly what you've got up there. (You have to point at the top of the page for a second or two before the title bar will appear.)

4. **If you'd rather display a different Web page on your Desktop, click New and then type the Web address (URL) of the new page into the Location box on the New Active Desktop Item screen.**

5. **Click OK to see a dialog box confirming the new addition to your Active Desktop, then click OK again and you're all set.**

Go admire your newly adorned Desktop!

If you get sick of displaying Web content on your Desktop, here's how to turn off the Active Desktop feature:

1. **Click on the Web tab along the top of the Display Properties dialog box (refer to Figure 11-3).**

2. **Click your mouse button once to clear the checkbox labeled Show Web Content On My Active Desktop.**

3. **Click OK to revert to your normal Desktop.**

If these steps seem overly complicated, here are some shortcuts you can use to manage your Active Desktop. To turn the Active Desktop feature on, right-click on a blank area of your Desktop, then select Active Desktop and Show Web Content from the menus that pop up. Now, if you right-click on a blank area of your Desktop again, you see some additional menu options. Here's what they do:

- ✔ **Show Web Content** toggles the Active Desktop feature on and off. If you see a check next to this option, the Active Desktop is on; if not, it's off.

- ✔ **Show Desktop Icons** displays the icons on the left-hand side of your Desktop. If you turn this option off, you may find yourself lost since you'll no longer see the familiar Desktop icons — such as My Computer and Recycle Bin — so we recommend leaving it alone.

- ✔ **Lock Desktop Items** secures the size and location of Active Desktop items. This option locks your Desktop icons in place so you can't mess up your Active Desktop by accident. If you're afraid you might, turn this option on.

- ✔ **Synchronize** updates the content of the Web page you've chosen to display on your Active Desktop, so if you want to stay absolutely current, give this option a try.

Special effects

Although they may seem as useful as a cherry on top of a banana split, some of the items on the Effects tab of the Control Panel's Display icon can actually be helpful. Here's what you need to know about changing Desktop icons and the other visual effects that this tab offers you.

To change a Desktop icon, follow these steps:

1. **Highlight the icon you want to change and click Change Icon.**

2. **Choose an icon from the current file by scrolling up and down the list of available icons and clicking on the one you want, or click Browse to select another icon file altogether.**

3. **Click OK to save your new Desktop icon.**

If you decide that you absolutely hate the new icon you've selected, you can always click the Default Icon button, which puts you back where you were before you started fooling around with the icons.

The Effects tab also offers you the following visual effects, which are intended to make the movements of Windows 2000 a little easier to see:

- ✔ **Use transition effects for menus and tooltips.** This option animates menu and file commands so that the appearance of the screen changes when you're using menus, opening and closing windows, and so forth. By default, this option is on. If you think your Desktop is just a little too active, turn it off.

- ✔ **Smooth edges of screen fonts.** This option is supposed to make the type on the screen more legible, but you probably won't see any difference either way.

- ✔ **Use large icons.** Large icons are nice for people with impaired vision. They're also nice if you have your monitor set to a high resolution (see the Display settings section that follows), which makes your icons really, really tiny.

- ✔ **Show icons using all possible colors.** This option does exactly what its name implies; it uses all the colors supported by your current display and color palette settings to make the icons as visible as possible. It is turned on by default, and your screen may look funny if you turn it off.

- ✔ **Show window contents while dragging.** If you turn this option off, all you see when dragging a window from one place to another is its bare outline.

- ✔ **Hide keyboard navigation indicators until I use the Alt key.** This is on by default and probably should stay that way unless you really want to see File, Edit, View and other underlines in the menus.

Display settings (playing with new video modes)

Just as Windows 2000 can print to hundreds of different brands of printers, it can accommodate zillions of different monitors, too. It can even display different video modes on the same monitor.

For example, Windows 2000 can display different amounts of color on-screen, or it can slightly shrink the size of everything, packing more information onto the screen. The number of colors and the size of the information on-screen comprise a video mode, or video resolution.

Some Windows 2000 programs only work in a specific video mode, and those programs casually ask you to switch to that mode. Huh?

Here's what's happening: Monitors plug into a special place on the back of the computer. That special place is an outlet on a video card — the gizmo that translates your computer's language into something you can see on the monitor. That card handles all the video-mode switches. By making the card switch between modes, you can send more or fewer colors to your monitor or pack more or less information onto the screen.

To make a video card switch to a different video mode, do the following:

1. **Head for the Control Panel's Display icon and give it a double-click.**

2. **Then click on the Settings tab — one of the tabs along the top of the Display Properties dialog box (refer to Figure 11-3).**

   Can't find the Display Properties dialog box? Click on a blank part of your Desktop by using the right mouse button and choose Properties from the menu that springs up.

As shown in Figure 11-7, the Display Properties Settings tab lets you select the colors and resolution you want Windows 2000 to display on-screen.

Figure 11-7:
The Settings tab of the Display Properties box lets you select the colors and resolution you want to display on-screen.

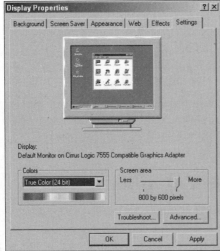

To change the number of colors Windows 2000 currently displays on the screen, do the following:

1. **Click on the arrow next to the Colors box.**

2. **Choose the desired number of colors from the drop-down menu.**

3. **Click on the Apply button to see if your monitor can handle the load.**

   Windows 2000 produces a dialog box explaining what is about to happen to your computer. It displays those colors for 15 seconds, and then returns to the previous number of colors.

4. **If the test looks okay, click Yes to keep the settings you just tried out. Doesn't look okay? Click No and your monitor settings revert to the ones you started with.**

To change the amount of space you have on your Desktop for displaying programs, follow these steps:

1. **Slide the lever in the Screen Area box.**

   Sliding the lever to the side marked More lets you fit more information onto the screen; sliding to the Less side fits less information on the screen, but makes the windows larger and easier to see.

2. **Click on the Apply button to make sure that your monitor and card can handle the new settings.**

   Windows 2000 produces a dialog box telling you what to do next. Clicking OK displays the new spacing for 15 seconds, and then returns to the way it was before.

3. **If the test looks fine, click OK to close the Display Properties box.**

Windows 2000 subsequently gives you a chance to back out, thank goodness, if you choose a video mode your computer can't handle.

The number of screen colors plus the screen area equals the capacity of your video equipment. This means that when you increase the screen area, the number of possible colors may go down. And when you move the colors up to their highest setting, the top screen area may get smaller. For more information about this monitor/card/resolution stuff, troop over to Chapter 2 and read the section about computer parts.

Don't go wandering into the area behind the Advanced button. If you do (despite our advice), especially steer clear of the Refresh Frequency. This is one place you can actually do some damage because choosing an incorrect setting can turn your monitor into toast. Don't make changes here.

✔ Earlier versions of Windows made users shut down Windows while changing resolution. Windows 2000 isn't nearly as rude. You can change resolution while all your programs are still running. (Make sure that you save your work anyway, however. Who really trusts their computer to be polite these days?)

✔ New video cards usually come with a disk that contains special information called a driver. If Windows 2000 doesn't recognize your breed of video card, it may ask you to insert this disk when you're changing video modes.

✔ If you'll be looking at pictures stored through Kodak's PhotoCD technology, you'll probably want Windows 2000 to display as many colors as possible — often 65,000 (16-bit) or 1.6 million (24-bit). Switch back to fewer colors after you're done, however, if Windows 2000 starts running too slowly.

✔ If Windows 2000 acts goofy with your video card or monitor — or you recently installed new ones — head for the "Adding New Hardware" section later in this chapter. Windows 2000 probably needs to be formally introduced to your new equipment before it will talk to it.

Folders and Their Options

Folder Options

Windows 2000 offers you a slew of options for how to display folders' contents and much more. Check out the Folder Options icon in the Control Panel and you'll see what we mean. To open the Folder Options icon and examine what it offers, follow these steps:

1. **Double-click on the Folder Options icon in the Control Panel.**

2. **Click the View tab to open the page shown in Figure 11-8.**

Three options on the View tab really come in handy; the rest are too esoteric for most of us. Here's the lowdown on the useful ones:

✔ **Remember each folder's view settings.** This option is another time- and labor-saver since it eliminates the need to keep fiddling with the settings — once you set a folder the way you want it to look, it stays that way.

✔ **Show My Documents on the Desktop.** All this option does is place an icon for the My Documents folder on your Desktop. This doesn't sound like much, but considering that the My Documents folder is where most documents (not to mention picture files) are automatically stored, it's handy.

✔ **Show pop-up description for folder and desktop items.** This option is what makes those little descriptive boxes pop up every time your mouse pauses for breath. These are usually useful, but when you get tired of seeing the boxes, you can turn them off here.

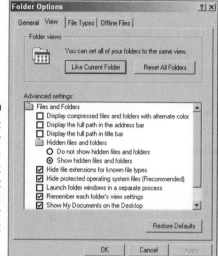

Figure 11-8:
The Folder
Options
dialog box
lets you set
up folders
just the way
you want
them.

Use the Reset All Folders button to go back to the settings that were in effect when Windows 2000 was installed.

Understanding the Fuss about Fonts

In the first few versions of Windows, the *fonts,* or sets of letters, numbers, and other characters, produced individual letters and numbers that looked kind of jagged. A capital A, for example, didn't have smooth, diagonal lines. Instead, the sides had rough ridges that stuck out. They usually looked fine on the printer but pretty awful on-screen, especially if the headlines were in large letters.

A few years later, Windows introduced a font technology called TrueType fonts to eliminate the jaggies and make the screen match more closely what comes out of the printer. In 1995, the TrueType fonts were modified into TrueType Open fonts, which are even sharper and clearer. The technology is still around in Windows 2000.

Fonts

Double-click on the Control Panel's Fonts icon to see what fonts come with Windows 2000, to install additional fonts, or to delete the ugly ones you don't like anymore.

Double-click on any of the Font icons, and you see what that particular font looks like. For example, a double-click on the icon marked Arial Italic brings up an eye chart displaying how that font would look on the printed page, as shown in Figure 11-9.

Figure 11-9:
Double-click
on a Font
icon to see
what it
looks like.

✔ Icons marked with the letter O are TrueType Open fonts, so they always look better than the fonts marked with the letter A.

✔ *Note:* You'll probably never need to fiddle with the Fonts icon. Just know that it's there in case you ever want to get fancy and install more fonts on your computer.

Fonts can eat up a great deal of hard disk space. If you installed some fonts that you no longer use, delete them using the following steps:

1. **Double-click on the Control Panel's Fonts icon.**

2. **Right-click on the name of the font you no longer use.**

3. **Then choose Delete from the pop-up menu.**

   A box appears, asking whether you're sure that you want to remove that font.

4. **Click the Yes button if you really want to give it the purge.**

   Changed your mind? Click the No button instead.

To be on the safe side, don't delete any fonts that come with Windows 2000; only delete fonts that you installed yourself. Windows programs often borrow Windows 2000 fonts for menus; if you delete those fonts, your menus mysteriously vanish.

Making Windows 2000 Recognize Your Double-Click

Clicking twice on a mouse button is called a double-click; you do a great deal of double-clicking in Windows 2000. But sometimes you can't click fast enough to suit Windows 2000. It thinks your double-clicks are just two single-clicks. If you have this problem, head for the Control Panel's Mouse icon.

Mouse

When you double-click on the Mouse icon, the Mouse Properties dialog box pops up. If your mouse dialog box doesn't look like the one in Figure 11-10, the company that made your mouse slipped its own software into the Control Panel. The following instructions may not work for you, but you can generally access the same types of options for any mouse. If your menu looks weird, try pressing F1 for help.

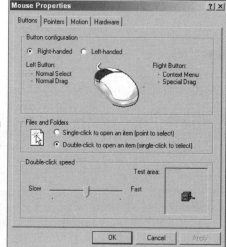

Figure 11-10: Double-click on the Test Area box to check your current settings.

To check the double-click speed, do the following:

1. **Double-click on the box marked Test Area.**

   Each time Windows 2000 recognizes your double-click, a little puppet with water buffalo horns pops out of the jack-in-the-box. Double-click again, and the puppet disappears.

2. **Slide the scroll box toward the words Fast or Slow until Windows 2000 successfully recognizes your double-click efforts.**

3. **Click on the OK command button after you're through, and you're back in business.**

✔ Or just skip the whole darn thing and go to a single-click. Just above the double-click area on the Mouse Properties box, click the option button labeled Single-Click To Open An Item — then you won't be troubled with the double-click any more.

✔ If you're left-handed, click on the little circle marked Left-handed, shown along the top of Figure 11-10, and click on the Apply button. Then you can hold the mouse in your left hand and yet still click with your index finger.

✔ Looking for some fun? Click on the Pointers tab, click on the arrow next to the Scheme box, and choose some of the different point schemes for your mouse pointers. Yep, the Serious Windows 2000 software lets you substitute dinosaur cartoons for your mouse pointer. Fun!

Phoning the Modem

Phone and
Modem Options

These days, a popular thing to do with your computer is to dial out — not for Chinese food, but to let your computer chat with another computer. To do this successfully, you may need to tell your computer where you're dialing from or tweak your modem settings. The Phone and Modem Options icon in the Control Panel is command central for all things phone- and modem-related in Windows 2000.

Double-click the icon and you see that it has three tabs, but you probably shouldn't go anywhere near that tab labeled Advanced, lest you get snared in a technotrap. Keeping that in mind, here's what you can do with the Dialing Rules and Modems tabs of the Phone and Modem Options dialog box.

The primary function of the Dialing Rules tab is to tell your computer where you are when you're trying to dial out. Multiple dialing locations are most useful for people who travel a lot, so if you fall into this category, or even if you dial out on your computer from both home and work, here's how to create a new dialing location:

1. **Double-click the Phone and Modem Options icon in the Control Panel.**

2. **Click on the Dialing Rules tab (if it's not already showing).**

3. **Click New.**

4. **Give the new location a name, preferably a logical one.**

5. **In the Country/region area, indicate the country/region you'll be dialing from and the area code of that country/region, if applicable.**

6. **In the Dialing Rules area, fill in any information that applies to your location.**

   If you have to dial a number to access an outside line, type that number into the appropriate box. Ditto if you have to dial a number to access an outside line for long distance calls. If you're using a phone line that has call waiting and you'd prefer to disable it while using the modem (usually a good idea), type the number used to accomplish this into the appropriate box.

7. **In the Dial Using area, indicate whether your location has Tone dialing (normal), or Pulse dialing (unusual).**

8. **Click OK (or Apply and then OK).**

   Your new location is ready to go.

The Modems tab of the Phone and Modem Options icon in the Control Panel lets you tweak the properties of the modem(s) in your computer. Click this tab and you see what ports the modems are on and much more.

Setting the Computer's Time and Date

Many computer users don't bother to set the computer's clock. They just look at their wristwatches to see when it's time to stop working. But they're missing out on an important computing feature: Computers stamp new files with the current date and time. If the computer doesn't know the correct date, it stamps files with the wrong date. Then how can you find the files you created yesterday? How about the ones from last week?

Also, Windows 2000 sometimes does some funny things to the computer's internal clock, so you may want to reset the date and time if you notice that the computer is living in the past.

To reset the computer's time or date, double-click on the Control Panel's Date/Time icon.

Date/Time

A double-click on the Date/Time icon brings a little calendar to the screen, shown in Figure 11-11. To change the date, just click on the correct date as listed on the on-screen calendar. If the date's off by a month or more, click on the little arrow next to the currently listed month. A list drops down, letting you select a different month. To change the year or the hour, click on the number you want to change and then click on the up or down arrows to make the number bigger or smaller. After the number is correct, click on the OK button for Windows 2000 to make the changes.

Figure 11-11:
To change
the time,
click on the
numbers
beneath the
clock; then
click on the
little arrows
next to the
numbers.

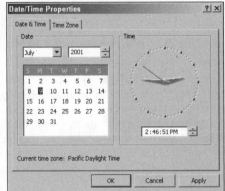

TIP

For an even quicker way to change your computer's time or date, double-click on the little clock Windows 2000 puts on the taskbar that lives along the edge of the screen. Windows 2000 brings up the Date/Time Properties box, just as if you waded through the Control Panel and double-clicked on the Date/Time icon.

Fiddling with the Printer

Most of the time, the printer works fine — especially after you turn it on and try printing again. In fact, most people never need to read this section. (And if you're working in a corporation, the network folks are in charge of fiddling with a malfunctioning printer.)

Printers

Occasionally, however, you may need to tweak some printer settings. You may need to install a new printer or remove an old one that died (so it doesn't keep cluttering up the list of printers). Either way, start by clicking on the Control Panel's Printers icon.

The Printers dialog box surfaces, as shown in Figure 11-12.

If you're installing a new printer, grab the Windows 2000 compact discs that came in the box; you may need them during the installation. To add a new printer, follow these steps:

1. Double-click on the Add Printer icon.

Déjà vu! You see the same Add Printer Wizard that appeared when you first installed Windows 2000.

2. **Click Next. Select the Local Printer or Network printer option.**

   If you're plugging the printer into the back of your own computer, select the Local Printer option. If you prefer to let Windows 2000 do the work and figure out what kind of printer you've got, make sure to put a checkmark in the box next to Automatically Detect My Printer.

   If you'll be using a computer on a network, jump to the section "Adding a Network Printer" later in this chapter.

3. **Click on the Next button and select LPT1 from the list.**

   Windows 2000 must keep up a reputation for being the best, so it offers zillions of options for printer ports. Just about every printer you may come across in your lifetime uses LPT1, however, so start by selecting that one.

4. **If you're a determined do-it-yourselfer and you haven't let Windows 2000 detect the printer for you, click on the Next button and then use the PgUp and PgDn keys to choose your printer's manufacturer and model number.**

   The Add Printer Wizard box lists the names of printer manufacturers on the left; click on the name of your printer's manufacturer. The right side of the box lists the models of printers that the manufacturer makes.

5. **After you see your printer listed, press Enter or double-click on the printer's name.**

   Windows 2000 asks you to stick the appropriate setup disks into a drive, and the drive makes some grinding noises. After a moment, you see the new printer listed in the box.

6. **Give the new printer a name and click Yes to have Windows-based programs use this printer as the default printer.**

   That's it. If you're like most people, your printer works like a charm.

Figure 11-12:
Double-
clicking on
the Add
Printer icon
tells
Windows
2000 about
your new
printer.

If you have more than one printer attached to your computer, choose your most-often-used printer as the default printer. That choice tells Windows 2000 to assume that it's printing to that often-used printer.

Also, if you feel generous enough to let other computers on your network use your printer, select the Shared As option after that page comes up toward the end of the installation process.

Adding a Network Printer

Installing a network printer so that you can use it is even easier than installing a printer connected directly to your computer. The setup is easy because Windows 2000 and the Network Administrator do all the heavy lifting.

1. **To add a network printer, double-click on the Printers folder in the Control Panel.**

2. **Double-click on the Add Printer icon to start up the Add Printer Wizard and click Next to get started.**

3. **Select Network Printer and then click Next.**

4. **The Add Printer Wizard wants to be told where to look for the new printer (see Figure 11-13). Always start with the easiest option — tell it to Find A Printer In The Directory. Click Next.**

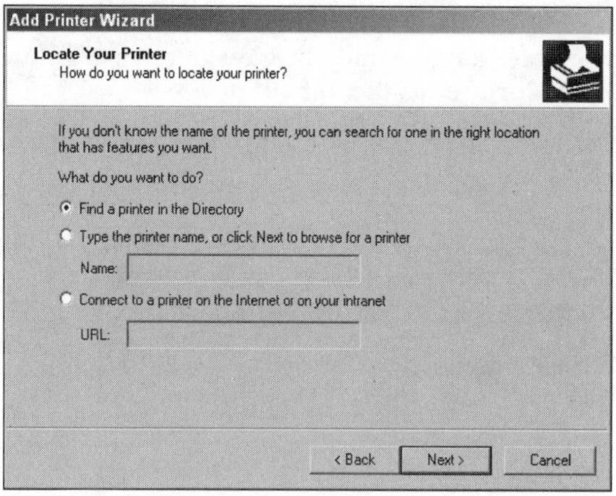

Figure 11-13: Tell the Add Printer Wizard where to look for your network printer.

> **Add Printer Wizard**
>
> **Locate Your Printer**
> How do you want to locate your printer?
>
> If you don't know the name of the printer, you can search for one in the right location that has features you want.
>
> What do you want to do?
>
> ⦿ Find a printer in the Directory
>
> ○ Type the printer name, or click Next to browse for a printer
>
> Name:
>
> ○ Connect to a printer on the Internet or on your intranet
>
> URL:
>
> [< Back] [Next >] [Cancel]

5. **In the Find Printers box, click Find Now and all the available printers show up (see Figure 11-14). Click the one you want and then click OK.**

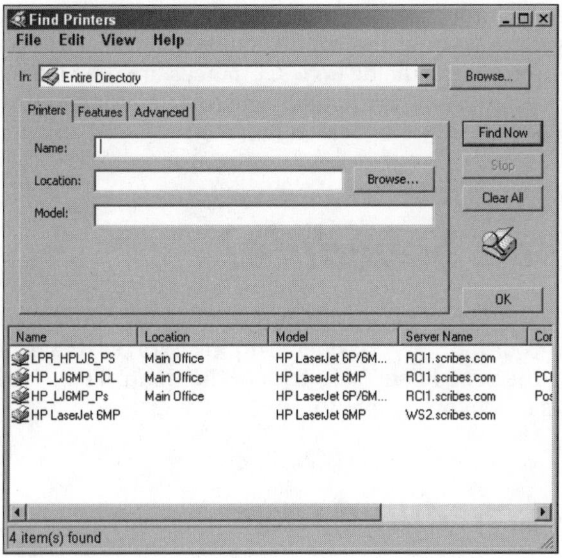

Figure 11-14:
The wizard
reports on
all the
printers to
be found.

6. **Tell Windows 2000 whether you want this printer to be your default printer. Click Next again.**

   The default printer is the one all your programs will use unless you tell 'em otherwise. See the end of Chapter 9 for a section on selecting which printer you'll use most of the time and how to make exceptions.

7. **The very last screen of the Add Printer Wizard summarizes the choices you made. If they look okay, click Finished. If you see something fishy, click the Back button and fix it.**

   ✔ To remove a printer you no longer use, call up the Control Panel, double-click on the Printer icon, and click on the icon for the printer you don't like anymore. Then press the Delete key on the keyboard. Windows 2000 asks if you're sure that you want to delete the printer before removing it from your options.

   ✔ You can change most of the printer options from within the program you're printing from. Click on Files in the program's menu bar and then click on Print Setup. From there, you can often access the same box of printer options as you find in the Control Panel.

   ✔ Some printers offer a variety of options. For example, you can print from different paper trays or print at different resolutions. To play with these options, click on the Printers icon with the right mouse button and choose Properties from the menu that pops up. Although different models of printers offer different options, most let you change paper size, fonts, and types of graphics.

> ✔ Working with printers can be more complicated than trying to retrieve a stray hamster from under the kitchen cupboards. Feel free to use any of the Help buttons in the dialog boxes. Chances are they'll offer some helpful advice, and some are actually customized for a particular brand of printer. Too bad they can't catch hamsters.

Is Everything on Schedule?

Scheduled
Tasks

If there's a task you'd like to have Windows 2000 do for you automatically, such as clean up your hard disk or open Outlook Express, that's no sweat. Just double-click the Scheduled Tasks icon in the Control Panel and you can see how easy it is to let your computer do the work.

Adding a scheduled task

Follow these steps to add a scheduled task to your system:

1. **Double-click the Add Scheduled Task icon to make Windows 2000 perform a designated task automatically at a specified time.**

   This starts up the Scheduled Task Wizard, which helps you tell your computer exactly what it needs to know in order to do what you want it to do.

2. **Click Next to continue.**

3. **Select the program you want Windows 2000 to run or click Browse to see more programs. Supply the information the wizard asks you for and your task is automated — automatically.**

   After you add the scheduled task, you see an icon for that task in the Scheduled Tasks window.

Modifying a scheduled task

Here's how to change a scheduled task's properties after you've added it:

1. **Locate the icon for the task whose properties you'd like to change in the Scheduled Tasks window and right-click on it.**

   Properties you can change include when the task is performed, the rules for when it doesn't perform (if the computer is being used or is running on batteries), and whether a password is required to run the task.

2. **Choose Properties from the menu that pops up.**

3. **Make your changes to the task's properties. When you're done, click Apply and then OK.**

   That's all there is to it.

Deleting a scheduled task

To delete a scheduled task, do the following:

1. **Locate the icon for the task whose properties you'd like to change in the Scheduled Tasks window and right-click on it.**

2. **Choose Delete from the menu that pops up.**

3. **Click Yes to confirm the deletion of this scheduled task.**

   After you've successfully deleted a scheduled task, its icon disappears from the Scheduled Tasks window.

Passwords

Users and
Passwords

If you want to restrict access to your computer, open the Users and Passwords icon in the Control Panel to see what options it offers you.

Here are the steps required to make relatively minimal use of this potentially powerful (and dangerous!) icon:

1. **Double-click the Users and Passwords icon in the Control Panel to open the Users and Passwords box.**

2. **To make users type in a password to use your computer, check the box labeled Users Must Enter A User Name And Password To Use This Computer.**

   After you enable this feature, you can start wielding your newfound power — by assigning (and later on, changing) passwords.

3. **To assign a password, highlight a user name, then click Change Password.**

4. **Type the user's password into the New Password and Confirm New Password boxes and click OK.**

Don't go completely hog-wild assigning user passwords unless you have a good reason to restrict access to your computer. If you do, you may find that you've forgotten which user had which password, and you may end up having to call the system administrator in to bail you out.

Stirring Things Up with Sound and Multimedia

The term multimedia means mixing two or more media — usually combining sound and pictures. A plain old television, for example, could be called a multimedia tool, especially if you're trying to impress somebody.

Windows 2000 can mix sound and pictures if you have a sound card: a gizmo costing from $20 to $200 that slips inside the computer and hooks up to a pair of speakers or a stereo.

Sounds and Multimedia

Macintosh computers have had sound for years. And for years, Mac owners have been able to assign sounds to system events. In lay language, that means having the computer make a barfing sound when it ejects a floppy disk. Windows 2000 doesn't normally let you assign sounds to the floppy disks, but you can assign noises to other events by double-clicking on the Control Panel's Sounds and Multimedia icon.

The Sounds and Multimedia Properties dialog box appears (see Figure 11-15). Windows 2000 automatically plays sounds for several system events. An event can be anything as simple as when a menu pops up or when you first log on to Windows 2000 in the morning.

Windows 2000 lists the events on the top of the box and lists the possible sounds directly below them in the box called Name. To assign a sound, click on the event first and then click on the sound you want to hear for that event. In Figure 11-15, for example, Windows 2000 is set up to make a barfing sound whenever it sends out an urgent dialog box with an exclamation point in it.

Figure 11-15:
Windows
2000 can
play back
different
sounds
when
different
things
happen
on your
computer.

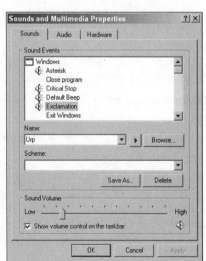

✔ Are you satisfied with your new choices of sounds? Then click on the box marked Save As, and change the words in the box to something else, like My Sound Settings. That way you can still change back to the more polite Windows 2000 Default sounds if you don't want houseguests to hear your computer barf. (You can change back to My Sound Effects after they leave.)

✔ To take advantage of this multimedia feature, you must buy and install a sound card. Then you have to tell Windows 2000 about your new card by clicking on the Control Panel's Add/Remove Hardware icon.

✔ To hear a sound before you assign it, click on its name and then click on the Preview button (the little black triangle next to the Browse button).

✔ You can record your own sounds through most sound cards. You can probably pick up a cheap microphone at Radio Shack; many of the cheaper sound cards don't include one.

✔ Be forewarned: Sound consumes a lot of disk space (especially when recorded in 16-bit stereo) so stick with short recordings — short and sweet B. B. King guitar riffs, for example, or the sound of a doorbell ringing work well.

✔ Is your sound card not working right? You may have to muddle through the other pages behind the Sounds and Multimedia icon, described in the dreary technical sidebar in this section.

Multimedia setup problems

Multimedia gadgetry inevitably brings a multitude of setup problems. Too many file formats and program settings exist for an easy ride. Although Windows 2000 tries to set up your computer's hardware automatically, the Control Panel's Sounds and Multimedia icon lets techno-fiddlers change some of the settings. Because different computers use different parts, the settings listed under the Sounds and Multimedia icon vary, but here's a general look at what they can do:

✔ **Audio:** This page controls your sound card's volume settings as well as its recording quality. The better the quality of the recording, the more hard disk space your recordings consume. A quicker way to adjust the volume is to click on the little speaker in the corner of the taskbar.

✔ **Speech:** If you have a speech recognition program — here's where you adjust it.

✔ **Hardware:** Here Windows 2000 lists all the multimedia devices attached to your computer (as well as a few devices you may want to add to your computer in the future). By clicking on a device and clicking on the Properties button, you can turn a device on or off.

Adding and Removing Programs

Add/Remove
Programs

With the Add/Remove Programs icon to the Control Panel, Windows 2000 is trying to trick you into thinking it's easier than ever to install or remove a program. Nope.

Here's how the installation programs work — if you're lucky:

1. **After you get a new program, look for a disk marked Install or Installation or Setup and stick the disk into any disk drive that it fits.**

   If the program came on a CD-ROM, put it into your CD-ROM drive.

2. **Next, double-click on the Control Panel's Add/Remove Programs icon.**

3. **Click on the Add New Programs button and tell the wizard whether you want to add a program from a CD-ROM or floppy disk or whether you'd like to get Windows features or updates over the Internet.**

   Windows 2000 searches all your disk drives for a disk containing an installation program. If it finds an installation program, it runs it, effectively installing the program. If it doesn't find one, it just gives up. What to do? Search for a file named SETUP.EXE on your floppy disk or CD-ROM, and double-click on that file.

   ✔ Most programs you buy at software stores come with installation programs, so Windows 2000 can install them without too much trouble. Some of the smaller shareware programs found on online services don't come with installation programs, unfortunately, so you have to install them yourself.

   ✔ Forced to install a DOS or Windows program yourself? Make a new folder somewhere on your hard disk and copy all the files from the program's disk to the new folder. Then to load the program, double-click on the program's icon from within that folder. Chapter 13 is filled with tips on creating folders, copying files, and sticking new programs on the Start menu.

   ✔ The Add/Remove Programs icon can uninstall programs, but only if those programs were designed with the uninstall feature in mind.

Finding Out Which Icons to Avoid

Unless you have a very pressing reason, avoid these icons in the Control Panel: Keyboard, Internet Options, Phone and Modem Options, Network and Dial-Up Connections, Regional Options, and System.

   ✔ The Keyboard icon doesn't do any major damage, but it doesn't do any major good, either. It controls how fast a key repeats if you hold it down. Big deal.

✔ Just as you don't need to climb a telephone pole to make a phone call, you probably won't need to use the Internet Options icon to surf the Web. Zip over to Chapter 16 for the basics on using the Internet features.

✔ ***Exception Department:*** If you don't want to bother the Network Administrator, feel free to double-click on the Phone and Modem Options icon when you need to adjust your modem's settings (or install a new modem). Windows 2000 usually does a surprisingly good job of automatically detecting your modem and setting it up for you.

✔ The Network and Dial-Up Connections icon controls how Windows 2000 talks to other computers through your office's network — those cables meandering from PC to PC. Talk to your Network Administrator before playing with this icon "just to see what it does."

✔ The Regional Options icon changes the keyboard layout to the one used by people in other countries. This icon doesn't make the Windows 2000 dialog boxes appear in German (although you can order the German version of Windows 2000 from Microsoft). Instead, a foreign keyboard layout makes certain keys produce foreign characters.

✔ The information listed in the System icon turns on network hounds and techno-nerds. Your Network Administrator puzzles over this stuff, not you.

Adding New Hardware

Adding a piece of new hardware to a computer has always been easy. But getting the computer to recognize and work with the new hardware — well, that's another story.

All that has changed for the better with Windows 2000. Nine times out of ten when you add a modem or printer or even a scanner to a Windows 2000 computer, the operating system wakes up and says howdy. In fact, you'll see a notification box on the screen that says something like "Hey, I detect new hardware. Hold on a minute while I set it up." (Or words to that effect.)

Add/Remove
Hardware

If Windows 2000 doesn't see your new hardware, then you have the backup option of running the Add/Remove Hardware Wizard.

Double-click the Add/Remove Hardware icon in the Control Panel to start the wizard. You're asked whether you're looking to add a device or remove one. Make your choice and click Next. Windows 2000 Professional searches and you need to participate only if the device can't be found.

If Windows 2000 Professional is unsuccessful, you see a list of possible devices. Choose the right one and go on. You may be asked for a disk of software that came with the device. Just follow the instructions and you're up and running in no time.

You almost never have to use the Add/Remove Hardware Wizard because Windows 2000 Professional uses the Plug and Play hardware standard, which means that just about every piece of hardware available is known to the operating system.

Part III

Using Windows 2000 Applications

The 5th Wave   By Rich Tennant

I wouldn't bring the server down for too long, Walt. The natives look restless.

In this part . . .

Did you know that

- ✔ Fish have no eyelids?
- ✔ A dime has 118 ridges around it? (Count 'em!)
- ✔ Scientist Percy LeBaron Spencer discovered in 1942 that microwaves could cook food after the waves melted a chocolate bar in his pocket?
- ✔ Windows 2000 comes with a bunch of free programs that aren't even mentioned on the outside of the box?

This part takes a look at all the stuff you're getting for nothing. Well, for the price on the sales receipt, anyway.

Chapter 12

The Windows 2000 Desktop, Start Button, and Taskbar

· ·

In This Chapter

▶ Using the Desktop

▶ Making shortcuts

▶ Deleting files, folders, programs, and icons

▶ Retrieving deleted items from the Recycle Bin

▶ Finding out the Start button's reason for living

▶ Putting programs on the Start button menu

▶ Using the taskbar

· ·

*I*n the old days of computing, pale technoweenies typed disgustingly long strings of code words into computers to make the computers do something. Anything.

Windows 2000 Professional brings computers to the age of modern convenience. To start a program, simply click on a button. A slight complication exists, however: The buttons no longer look like buttons. In fact, some of the buttons are hidden, revealed only by the push of yet another button (if you're lucky enough to stumble upon the right place to push).

This chapter covers the three main Windows 2000 Professional buttonmongers: the Desktop, the taskbar, and that mother of all buttons — the Start button.

Making Piles of Junk on the Windows 2000 Professional Desktop

Normally, nobody would think of mounting a desktop sideways. Keeping the pencils from rolling off a normal desk is hard enough.

But in Windows 2000 Professional, your computer monitor's screen is known as the Windows Desktop, and it's the area where all your work takes place. When working with Windows 2000 Professional, you create files and folders right on your new electronic Desktop and scatter those files and folders across the screen.

For example, let's say you need to make a list of ingredients to buy to make a batch of your killer curry powder. Here's how to put the Desktop's functions to immediate use.

Point at just about any Windows 2000 Professional item and click your right mouse button to see a menu listing the things you're allowed to do with that item.

1. **Click on the Desktop with your right mouse button.**

   A menu pops up, as shown in Figure 12-1.

Figure 12-1:
Clicking on the Desktop with your right mouse button brings up a list of options.

Active Desktop	▶
Arrange Icons	▶
Line Up Icons	
Refresh	
Paste	
Paste Shortcut	
Undo Delete	Ctrl+Z
New	▶
Properties	

Too much clutter to even spot the Desktop? Try this tip: Look on the taskbar (the gray strip along the edge of your screen) for an icon that looks like a desktop blotter.

Click the blotter once and all the windows on the desktop obediently turn themselves into buttons on the taskbar. (***Hint:*** Click on the taskbar's buttons to make the clutter reappear, window by window.)

2. **Point at the word New and click on Text Document from the menu that appears.**

   Because you're creating something new — a new list — you should point at the word New. Windows 2000 Professional lists the new things you can create on the Desktop. The possible entries under New are numerous and depend solely on how your computer has been set up and used. Figure 12-2 shows the differences among three computers more or less chosen at random. But for sure, Text Document is a choice on just about every machine because every Windows computer has Notepad, the text program. Choose Text Document, as shown in Figure 12-3.

Figure 12-2:
The list of New things you can do from this menu will vary according to the computer's software, history, and disposition.

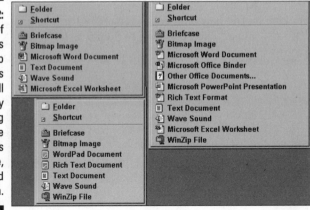

Figure 12-3:
Point at the word New and choose Text Document from the menu.

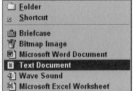

3. **Type a name for the list and press Enter.**

   When the icon for a Text Document appears on the Desktop, Windows 2000 Professional doesn't want you to lose it, so the place for the name is already highlighted. So, the first step is to give the document a name of up to 255 characters. As soon as you start typing, your new title replaces the old name of New Text Document, shown in Figure 12-4.

Figure 12-4:
Start typing to create the icon's new name.

4. Double-click on your new icon and type up your list.

Double-clicking on the new icon calls up Notepad so you can write your little list. Done writing? Then move on to Step 5.

5. Click on Save from Notepad's File menu to save the list (see Figure 12-5).

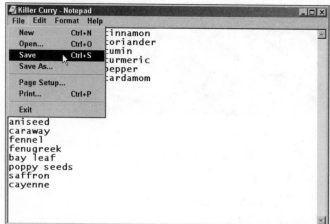

Figure 12-5: Saving your list.

6. Head back to the File menu and choose Print to send the letter to the printer.

7. To store the file, drag the icon to a folder. To delete it, drag the file to the Recycle Bin.

After you finish writing and printing the list, you need to decide what to do with the file. You can simply leave its icon on your Desktop, but that clutters things up. If you want to save the list in a folder, click on the Desktop with your right mouse button and choose Folder from the New menu. Windows 2000 Professional tosses a new folder onto the Desktop, ready for you to drag your list into.

Or, if you want to delete the list, drag the icon into the Desktop's Recycle Bin (described in the next section).

✔ Windows 2000 Professional is designed for you to work right on the Desktop. From the Desktop, you can create new things like files, folders, sounds, and graphics — just about anything. After working with your new file or folder, you can store it or delete it.

✔ You can store your favorite files and folders right on the Desktop. Or, to be more organized, you can drag your files and folders into the folders listed in the My Computer window. (The My Computer program gets a great deal more coverage in Chapter 13.)

✔ Confused about what something is supposed to do? Click on it with your right mouse button. Windows 2000 Professional tosses up a menu listing just about everything you can do with that particular object. This trick works on the Desktop or just about any icon you come across.

✔ Is your Desktop looking rather cluttered? Make Windows 2000 Professional line up the icons in orderly rows: Click on the Desktop with the right mouse button, point at the Arrange Icons option, and choose Auto Arrange from the menu.

Using the Recycle Bin

The Recycle Bin, that little wastebasket with green arrows on the Desktop, is supposed to work like a real Recycle Bin — something you can fish the Sunday paper out of if somebody pitched the comics section before you had a chance to read it.

If you want to get rid of something in Windows 2000 Professional — a file or folder, for example — simply drag it to the Recycle Bin: Point at the file or folder's icon with the mouse and, while holding down the left mouse button, point at the Recycle Bin. Let go of the mouse button, and your detritus disappears. Windows 2000 Professional stuffs it into the Recycle Bin.

But if you want to bypass that cute metaphor, Windows 2000 Professional offers another way to delete stuff: Click on your unwanted file or folder's icon with the right mouse button and choose Delete from the menu that pops up. Windows 2000 Professional asks cautiously whether you're sure that you want to delete the icon. If you click on the Yes button, Whoosh! Windows 2000 Professional dumps the icon into the Recycle Bin, just as if you dragged it there.

So, if you like to drag and drop, feel free to drag your garbage to the Recycle Bin and let go. If you prefer the menus, click with your right mouse button and choose Delete. Or if you like alternative lifestyles, click on the unwanted icon with your left button and push your keyboard's Delete key. All three methods toss the file into the Recycle Bin, where it can be salvaged later or, after it fills up, purged for good.

✔ Want to retrieve something you deleted? Double-click on the Recycle Bin icon, and a window appears, listing deleted items. See the name of your accidentally deleted icon? Drag it to the Desktop. Point at the icon's name and, while holding down the left mouse button, point at the Desktop. Let go of the mouse button, and the Recycle Bin coughs up the deleted item, good as new.

✔ The Recycle Bin's icon changes from an empty wastepaper basket to a full one as soon as it's holding a deleted file.

✔ A full Recycle Bin usually eats up 10 percent of your hard disk space. To free up some space, empty the bin by purging the deleted files for good. Click on the Recycle Bin with your right mouse button and choose Empty Recycle Bin from the menu. Then click on the Yes button after Windows 2000 Professional asks if you're sure that you want to really delete those files and folders that you already deleted once. Cautious program, that Windows 2000 Professional.

✔ You can control how long the Recycle Bin holds on to your deleted files. Click on the Recycle Bin with your right mouse button and choose Properties from its menu. Normally, Recycle Bin waits until your deleted files consume 10 percent of your hard disk before it begins purging your oldest deleted files. If you want the Recycle Bin to hang on to more deleted files, increase the percentage. If you're a sure-fingered clicker who never makes mistakes, decrease the percentage.

Making a shortcut

Some people like to organize their desktop, putting a pencil sharpener on one corner and a box of Kleenex on the other corner. Other people like their tissue box in the top desk drawer. Microsoft knew that one Desktop design could never please everybody, so Windows 2000 Professional enables people to customize their Desktops to suit individual tastes and needs.

For example, you may find yourself frequently copying files to a floppy disk in drive A. Normally, to perform that operation, you open the My Computer icon and drag your files to the drive A icon living in there. But a quicker way exists, and it's called a Windows 2000 Professional shortcut. A shortcut is simply a push button — an *icon* — that stands for something else.

For example, here's how to put a shortcut for drive A on your Desktop; these same steps work when creating any ol' shortcut:

1. **Double-click on the Desktop's My Computer icon.**

   The My Computer folder opens up, showing the icons for your disk drives as well as folders for your Control Panel and Printer. (My Computer gets more coverage in Chapter 13.)

2. **With your right mouse button, drag the 3½ Floppy icon to the Desktop.**

   Point at the 3½ Floppy icon (or any icon you want to create a shortcut to) and, while holding down your right mouse button, point at the Desktop, shown in Figure 12-6. Let go of your mouse button.

3. **Choose Create Shortcut(s) Here from the menu.**

   Windows 2000 Professional puts an icon for drive A on your Desktop, but it looks a little different from the drive A icon you dragged. Because it's only a shortcut — not the original icon — it has a little arrow in its corner, shown in Figure 12-7.

Figure 12-6:
Dragging
the 3½
Floppy icon
to the
Desktop
creates a
shortcut.

Figure 12-7:
The icon on
the left is a
shortcut
that stands
for the icon
on the right.

That's it. Now you don't need to root through the My Computer folders and programs to access drive A. The drive A shortcut on your Desktop works just as well as the real drive A icon found in My Computer and Explorer.

- ✔ Feel free to create Desktop shortcuts for your most commonly accessed programs, files, or disk drives. Shortcuts are a quick way to make Windows 2000 Professional easier to use.

- ✔ If your newly dragged icon doesn't have an arrow in its bottom corner, it's not a shortcut. Instead, you dragged the real program to your Desktop, and other programs may not be able to find it. Drag the icon back to where it was and try again. (You probably mistakenly held down the left mouse button rather than the correct button — the right button.)

- ✔ Windows 2000 Professional's shortcuts are veritable Sherlock Holmeses when it comes to keeping track of moving files. If you create a shortcut to a file or program and then move the file or program to a different spot on your hard disk, the shortcut follows the file or folder to its new location. If your network is running the new Windows 2000 Active Directory, the original can even have a new name and be on a different computer and the shortcut still works.

Uh, what's the difference between a shortcut and an icon?

An icon for a file, folder, or program looks pretty much like a shortcut, except that the shortcut has an arrow wedged in its lower reaches. And double-clicking on a shortcut does pretty much the same thing as double-clicking on an icon: starts a program or loads a file or folder.

But a shortcut is only a servant of sorts. After you double-click on the short-cut, it runs over to the program, file, or folder that the shortcut represents and kickstarts that program, file, or folder into action.

You could do the same thing yourself by rummaging through your computer's folders, finding the program, file, or folder you're after, and personally double-clicking on its icon to bring it to life. But creating a shortcut so that you don't have to rummage so much is often more convenient.

- ✔ If you delete a shortcut — the icon with the little arrow — you're not doing any real harm. You're just firing the servant that fetched things for you, probably creating more work for yourself in the process.

- ✔ If you accidentally delete a shortcut, you can pull it out of the Recycle Bin, just like anything else that's deleted in Windows 2000 Professional.

The Eager-to-Please Start Button

The Start button lives on your taskbar, and it's always ready for action. By using the Start button, you can start programs, adjust the Windows 2000 Professional settings, find help for sticky situations, or, thankfully, shut down Windows 2000 Professional and get away from the computer for a while.

The little Start button is so eager to please, in fact, that it starts shooting out menus full of options as soon as you click on it. Just click on the button once, and the first layer of menus pops out, as shown in Figure 12-8.

Figure 12-8: Click on the taskbar's Start button to see a list of options.

The explosive Table 12-1 shows what the permanent denizens of the Start menu do when you point at them.

Table 12-1	The Start Menu
This Part	**Does This When You Point At It**
Programs ▶	Probably the most used spot. Point here, and a second menu appears, listing available programs and folders containing related programs.
Documents ▶	Point here to see the names of the last 15 files you played with. Spot one you want to open again? Click on its name to reopen it.
Settings ▶	Allows access to the Control Panel and Printer settings, as well as ways to customize the Start button menus and taskbar.
Search ▶	Lost a program or file? Head here to make Windows 2000 Professional search for it.
Help	Clicking here does the same thing as pressing F1 — it brings up the Windows 2000 Professional Help menu.
Run...	Used mostly by old-school, "stick-shift" computer users, it lets you start a program by typing in the program's name and path.
Shut Down...	Click here to shut down or restart Windows.
Start	Clicking on the Start button makes the Start menu shoot out of the button's head.

✔ The Start button's menu changes as you add programs to your computer. That means that the Start button on your friend's computer probably offers slightly different menus than the ones on your own computer.

✔ See the little arrows on the menu next to the words Programs, Documents, Settings, and Search? The arrows mean that when you point at those words, another menu pops up, offering more detailed options.

✔ Need to open a file yet another time? Before you spend time clicking your way through folders, see if it's listed under the Start button's Documents area. You can find the last 15 documents you had open listed there, ready to be opened with a click.

Starting a program from the Start button

This one's easy. To start a program from the Start button, follow these steps:

1. **Click on the Start button.**

2. **After the menu pops out of the button's head, point at the word Programs.**

   Yet another menu pops up, this one listing the names of programs or folders full of programs.

3. **If you see your program listed, click on the name.**

   Wham! Windows 2000 Professional kicks that program to the screen.

4. **If you don't see your program listed, try pointing at the folders listed on the menu.**

   New menus fly out of those folders, listing even more programs.

5. **When you spot your program's name, just click on it.**

   In fact, you don't have to click until you see the program's name: The Start button opens and closes all the menus automatically, depending on where the mouse arrow is pointing at the time.

Still don't see your program listed by name? Head for Chapter 8. You can tell Windows 2000 Professional to find your program for you.

There's another way to load a program that's not listed — if you know where the program is living on your hard disk. Follow these steps:

1. **Choose Run from the Start button menu.**

2. **Type in the program's name.**

3. **Press Enter.**

   If Windows 2000 Professional finds the program, it runs it.

4. **If it can't find the program, though, click on the Browse button.**

   Shazam! Yet another box appears, this time listing programs by name.

5. **Pick your way through the dialog box until you see your program; then double-click on its name.**

6. **Click on the OK button to load it.**

If you don't know how to pick your way through this particular dialog box, head to the section of Chapter 6 on opening a file. (This particular dialog box rears its head every time you load or save a file or open a program.)

Adding a program to the Start button menu

The Windows 2000 Start button works great — but sometimes programs install themselves in the most inconvenient places. For example, let's say you're a big-time user of Quicken. Quicken installs itself a couple of layers down on the Start menu, which is just too tedious. To make it more convenient, you can add Quicken to the menu that pops out of the Start button in just one step.

Click the Start button and drag your mouse along to Programs, then to the Quicken folder, and follow the arrow to still another sub-menu, as shown in Figure 12-9. Right-click the Quicken program and, holding the mouse button down, drag it back to the top of the Start menu. Let go of the mouse button and your menu has a new resident (see Figure 12-10).

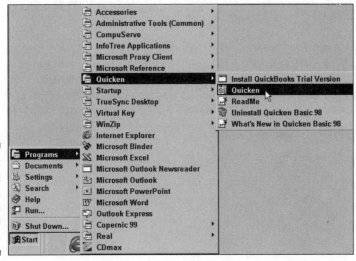

Figure 12-9:
Right-click
the program
file and drag
it to the
Start menu.

Figure 12-10:
A new
shortcut on
the Start
menu.

✔ This drag-and-drop method also works to move something on the menus up or down a step in the hierarchy. Demote something that you'd like to see further down the menu structure just by right-clicking it and dragging it down a level — or vice versa.

✔ Want to get rid of something you've added to the Start menu? Just drag it off onto the desktop. You can leave it there, move it somewhere else, or delete it.

More options for the Start menu

Because the Start button and the Start menu are right there front and center on the Windows 2000 Professional desktop, they're the prime place for personalizing (along with the taskbar). To get to the special settings for the Start menu, right-click on a blank spot on the taskbar and click Properties on the menu that pops up. This opens the box shown in Figure 12-11.

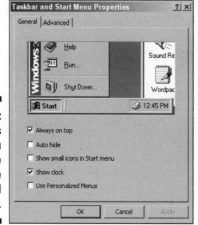

Figure 12-11:
Here's
where you
can fiddle
with the
taskbar and
Start menu.

First, take a look at the General page. This is pretty easy stuff — just click a checkbox and you can see the result in the window at the top of the General page. For example, check Auto Hide and you can see that this option makes the taskbar disappear. (At least most of the time — when Auto Hide is on, just move the pointer to where the taskbar *should* be and the taskbar magically appears again.)

- ✔ Always On Top means the taskbar stays on top of any windows that overlap it.

- ✔ Other check boxes let you decide whether you want the Start menu to be big or small and whether you want the clock displayed on the taskbar.

- ✔ Personalized menus are a weird new development in Windows 2000. If you decide to use personalized menus, your Start menu will keep track of how often you open one program or another. Inevitably, some programs get a lot more attention than others and these favored programs will end up more prominently displayed. Figure 12-12 shows a personalized menu — click on the little double arrows to see the rest of the menu (see Figure 12-13).

Figure 12-12:
Personalized menus mean that the programs you use all the time get a favored position on the menu.

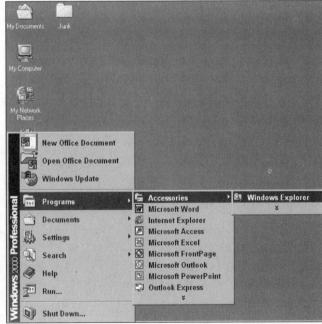

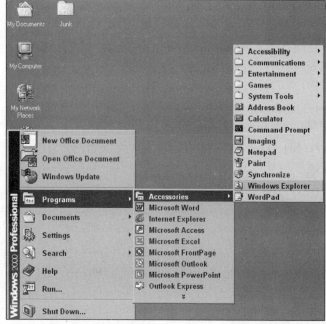

Figure 12-13:
Click the
double
arrows on
the menu to
see all the
entries.

Click the Advanced tab in the Taskbar and Start Menu Properties box (see Figure 12-14) and you see a whole bunch of things you can add to the Start menu, should you feel the impulse to do so.

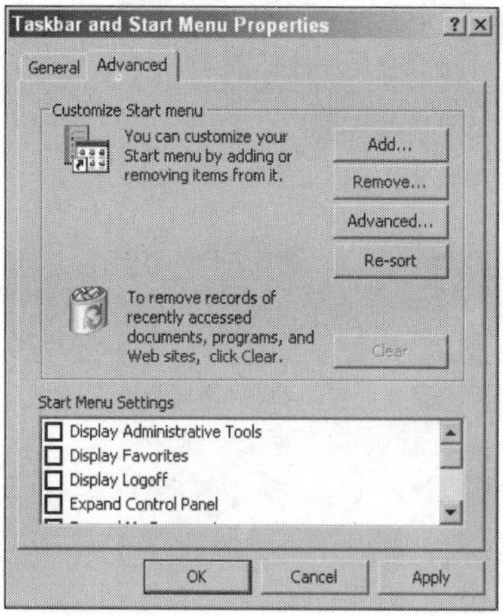

Figure 12-14:
Even more
settings
for the
Start menu.

✔ Click on one or more of the Display check boxes in the box labeled Start Menu Settings and the selected items appear as a basic part of the Start Menu. For example, place a check mark next to Display Favorites to plop your Internet Favorites right on the Start Menu.

✔ Display Logoff puts the logoff option on the Start menu.

✔ The Expand check boxes also put more stuff on the Start menu — but as submenus. For example, click Expand Control Panel and when you go to Start, then Settings, and then Control Panel — wowser! Everything in Control Panel slides off the edge of the menu and you can get at what you want without waiting for a window to open (see Figure 12-15). Whether or not this is worth the additional clutter depends on how often you have to open these windows and how annoying it is for you to take that extra step.

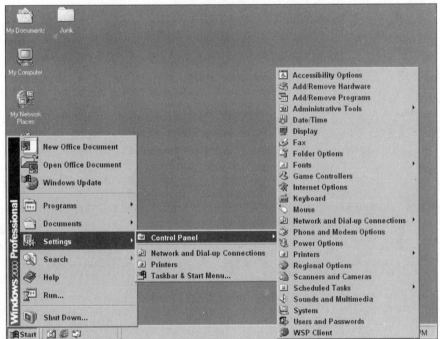

Figure 12-15:
The amazing, expanding Control Panel.

Shutting down Windows 2000 Professional

Although the big argument used to be about whether pasta is fattening, today's generation has found a new source of disagreement: Should a computer be left on all the time or turned off at the end of the day? Both camps have decent arguments, and no real answer exists.

However, if you want to turn off your computer, don't just head for the Off switch. First, you need to tell Windows 2000 Professional about your plans by following these steps:

1. **From the Start menu, choose Shut Down.**

2. **In the box that appears, choose Shut Down from the drop-down list.**

3. **Finally, click OK.**

   That action tells Windows 2000 Professional to put away all your programs and make sure that you saved all your important files.

   You may not even be allowed to shut down the computer you're working on. (Yes, Windows 2000 Professional has rules even for that!)

Just want to log off for lunch? Press Ctrl+Alt+Delete and click the Log Off button. Or use the Start menu Advanced options in the previous section to add the logoff option to your Start menu.

Don't turn off your computer unless you use the Shut Down command from the Start button. Windows 2000 Professional needs to prepare itself for the shutdown, or it may accidentally eat some of your important information.

Organizing the Desktop Mishmash with the Taskbar

Put a second or third window onto the Windows 2000 Professional Desktop, and you'll immediately see the Big Problem: Windows and programs tend to cover each other up, making them difficult to locate.

The solution is the taskbar. Shown in Figure 12-16, the taskbar is that little bar running along the bottom edge of your screen.

Figure 12-16:
The taskbar
lists the
names of all
currently
running
programs
and open
folders.

The taskbar keeps track of all the open folders and currently running programs by listing their names. And, luckily, the taskbar is almost always visible, no matter how cluttered your Desktop becomes.

- ✔ When you want to bring a program, file, or folder to the forefront of the screen, click on its name on the taskbar.

- ✔ If the taskbar does manage to disappear, press Ctrl+Esc; that usually brings it to the surface.

- ✔ If you can only see part of the taskbar — it's hanging off the edge of the screen, for example — point at the edge you can see. When the mouse pointer turns into a two-headed arrow, hold down your mouse button and move the mouse to drag the taskbar back into view.

- ✔ If the taskbar looks too bloated, try the same trick: Point at its edge until the mouse pointer turns into a two-headed arrow and then drag the taskbar's edge inward until it's the right size.

Want to drag and drop a file onto a program or folder that's resting lazily along the screen's taskbar? Here's the secret: Drag the file until it hovers over the program or folder, but don't let go of the mouse button. After a few moments, the taskbar kickstarts the folder or program into action, making it jump into a window on the screen. Then, you can drag and drop your file onto the window to put it inside the program or folder.

Clicking on the taskbar's sensitive areas

Like a crafty card player, the taskbar comes with a few tips and tricks. For one thing, it has the Start button. With a click on the Start button, you can launch programs, change settings, find programs, get help, and order pizza. (Well, you can't order pizza, but you can do all the things mentioned in the Start button section earlier in this chapter.)

But the Start button is only one of the taskbar's tricks; some others are listed in Figure 12-17.

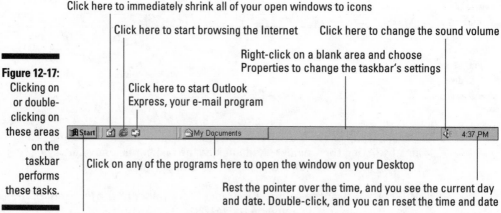

Click here to immediately shrink all of your open windows to icons

Click here to start browsing the Internet   Click here to change the sound volume

Right-click on a blank area and choose
Properties to change the taskbar's settings

Click here to start Outlook
Express, your e-mail program

Figure 12-17:
Clicking on
or double-
clicking on
these areas
on the
taskbar
performs
these tasks.

Click on any of the programs here to open the window on your Desktop

Rest the pointer over the time, and you see the current day
and date. Double-click, and you can reset the time and date

Click here to see the Start menu, which lets you start programs,
load files, change settings, find files, or just get help

Hover the mouse pointer over the clock, and Windows 2000 Professional shows the current day and date. Or if you want to change the time or date, a double-click on the clock summons the Windows 2000 Professional time/date change program.

If you have a sound card installed, a click on the little speaker brings up the volume control. Slide the volume knob up for louder sound; slide it down for peace and quiet. (Or click on the Mute box to turn the sound off completely.)

✔ Other icons often appear next to the clock, depending on what Windows 2000 Professional is up to. If you're printing, for example, you'll see a little printer down there. Laptops sometimes show a battery monitor. As with all the other icons, a double-click on the printer or battery monitor brings up information about the printer or battery's status.

✔ Want to minimize all your Desktop's open windows in a hurry? Simply click on that tiny icon that looks like a pad and paper just to the right of the Start button. Can't find that icon? Then right-click on a blank part of the taskbar and choose the Minimize All Windows option from the pop-up menu. All the programs keep running, but they're now minimized to icons along the taskbar. To bring them back to the screen, just click on their names from the taskbar.

Customizing the taskbar

Although Windows 2000 Professional starts the taskbar along the bottom of the screen, it doesn't have to stay there. If you'd prefer that your taskbar hang from the top of your screen like a bat, just drag it there. Point at a blank spot of the taskbar and, while holding down your mouse button, point at the top of the screen. Let go of the mouse button, and the taskbar dangles from the roof, as shown in Figure 12-18.

Figure 12-18: You can move the taskbar to any side of the screen by dragging it there.

Prefer it along one side? Then drag it there, as shown in Figure 12-19. (The buttons become more difficult to read, however.)

Figure 12-19:
The taskbar's buttons become harder to read when placed along one side.

If the taskbar is starting to look too crowded, you can make it wider by dragging its edges outward, as shown in Figure 12-20.

Figure 12-20:
Dragging the taskbar's edge upward gives the icons more room to display their titles.

To change other taskbar options, right-click on a bare taskbar area and choose Properties from the pop-up menu. From there, you can make the taskbar always stay on top of the current pile of windows, make the taskbar automatically hide itself, hide the clock, and shrink the Start menu's icons — among other things. Whenever you click on an option button, a handy on-screen picture previews the change. If the change looks good, click OK to save it.

Toolbars on the taskbar

You can do even more to set up the taskbar so that it suits you by adding a toolbar or two. *Toolbars* are little collections of your most used icons and commands: By gathering your favorites and placing them along the taskbar at the bottom of your screen, you can reach them over and over again. Ain't repetition grand?

To display a toolbar, right-click on a blank spot in the taskbar along the screen's bottom edge and select Toolbars from the pop-up menu. A list of available toolbar names appears; click on a toolbar name to select it. (Toolbars with checkmarks are already alive and kicking on your taskbar.) To remove a toolbar, click on the name to remove the checkmark.

Already on the scene is the Quick Launch toolbar showing icons for the Desktop, Internet Explorer, and Outlook Express. Just point to an icon to open a helpful little box that describes what the icon does.

 The Desktop icon (shown here) is particularly handy.

If you have a bunch of open windows and need to get at an icon or something on your Desktop, just click the Desktop icon, and everything open is mini-mized to the taskbar — even windows that don't have a minimize button. Windows 2000 Professional forces them to the taskbar — out of the way — until you click on a minimized icon to open it again.

You can add your own favorite programs to Quick Launch. Just find the pro-gram's icon and click it with your mouse. Hold the mouse button down and drag the icon to the Quick Launch pad. Leggo of the mouse.

Figure 12-21 shows the CD Player icon being dragged onto Quick Launch. After the mouse lets go, the CD Player is ready for action. Click on it and the program starts.

Figure 12-21:
Drag an icon
to the Quick
Launch
toolbar and
a shortcut to
the program
is added.

Not interested in something on the Quick Launch toolbar? Just right-click on it and select Delete from the pop-up menu. It's just a shortcut, so you can always replace it if you want. *Except* don't delete the Desktop icon — you won't be able to get it back.

Adding a toolbar to the taskbar

Quick Launch is just one of the toolbars that can be shown on the taskbar. Right-click on a blank spot on the taskbar and select Toolbars. Out springs a list of the possible toolbars that can be shown on the taskbar. (See Figure 12-22.)

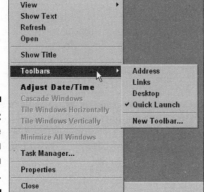

Figure 12-22: Pick the toolbar you want from this menu.

Address toolbar

Select the Address toolbar and the Address field shown in Figure 12-23 pops open on your taskbar.

Figure 12-23: Use the Address toolbar to make those essential Internet connections.

You can type in local intranet addresses or Internet addresses here for a quick connection. You can even enter local addresses to open a folder on your hard drive. Click the arrow to the side of the text box to open a list of past addresses you entered.

Links toolbar

Select the Links toolbar to display the links that are ordinarily shown at the top of your Internet Explorer window. Like the Address toolbar, this is another way to make quick connections — in this case to the sites represented by the links.

Links are properly a part of Internet Explorer, so check out Chapter 16 for information on how to make and use links.

Desktop toolbar

Yes, it's true that you can always get to your Desktop by clicking the Desktop icon in the Quick Launch toolbar, but you can also make a toolbar where every icon on your Desktop is represented.

The Desktop toolbar looks like Figure 12-24.

Figure 12-24:
The Desktop toolbar is sort of ungainly in its natural state.

As you can see, this toolbar isn't very useful because each button is so large. However, if you right-click directly on the Desktop label and then click Show Text (which turns off the text labeling), you get a toolbar that looks like Figure 12-25. Can't remember what an icon controls? Just point the mouse at it and a magical box tells you.

Figure 12-25:
The Desktop toolbar with the text turned off.

Just to make things complicated, Windows 2000 Professional has two different kinds of toolbars. (The more famous ones are the rows of buttons at the top of various windows. Find out more about those guys in Chapter 3.)

Remember this, too: A toolbar and a taskbar are different creatures. The taskbar always contains the Start button. The toolbars are ways to add additional handy items to the taskbar.

Chapter 13

Exploring without Risk

● ●

In This Chapter

▶ Understanding file managers

▶ Looking at folders

▶ Loading a program or file

▶ Deleting and undeleting files

▶ Copying, moving, and renaming files

▶ Using legal filenames

▶ Copying a whole floppy disk

▶ Getting information about files

▶ Finding files that aren't shown

● ●

*E*xploring has always been a perilous business (consider the sorry fates of Magellan, Hudson, and Captain Cook, for example) so it's all-too-appropriate that the program for figuring out everything on your computer is called the Windows Explorer. With this Explorer, it's definitely possible to get lost and wander around for a while, but at least it's not actively dangerous. In this chapter, we take a look at Explorer and its cousin, My Computer (which lives on your Desktop). Though they have a few minor differences, Explorer and My Computer are just two different doors into the same place.

Why Are the Windows Explorer and My Computer Programs So Scary?

Everybody organizes his or her computer differently. (Some people don't organize their computers at all.) And whether you use Explorer or My Computer to poke around your computer's innards depends completely on which one you like the best. To start with Explorer, right-click on the Start button, then choose the word Search from the pop-up menu. The Explorer window that opens may look something like the one in Figure 13-1 — or it may not.

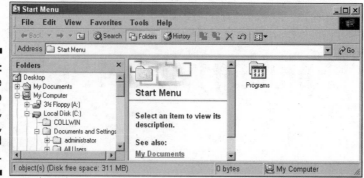

Figure 13-1:
You use
Explorer to
print, copy,
move,
rename, and
delete files.

If you like the way your Explorer looks — you can keep it. But if you'd like another view, well, click once on the word View at the top of the window and slide down to the part of the menu that reads

- ✔ Large Icons
- ✔ Small Icons
- ✔ List
- ✔ Details
- ✔ Thumbnails

and choose one. Each of the View options shows the icons in a different way, displaying different amounts of information. Clicking on those options simply changes the way Windows 2000 Professional displays the icons — it doesn't hurt anything.

The toolbar isn't living on top of your window? Then put it there by selecting Toolbar from the View menu. That little bar of buttons that you see in Figure 13-1 now appears atop your window like a mantel over a fireplace.

Does your Explorer look too messy? Click the Tools menu and select Folder Options. On the General page, look for the Web View section and click the option button for Use Windows Classic Folders and click OK. Then your Explorer looks more like Figure 13-2.

When you create a file or folder, Windows 2000 Professional scrawls a bunch of secret hidden information on the file: its size, the date you created it, and even more trivial stuff. To see what Windows 2000 calls these files and folders behind your back, select View from the menu bar and then select Details from the menu (Figure 13-3).

You can get an Explorer-like view of most folders. Just right-click on the folder and select Explore from the menu that pops up (see Figure 13-4).

Figure 13-2:
Clean up the
Explorer by
getting rid of
the Web
look.

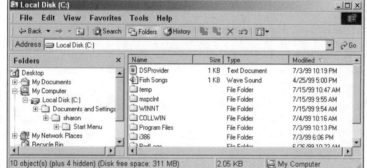

Figure 13-3:
This is the
Details view
when you're
Exploring.

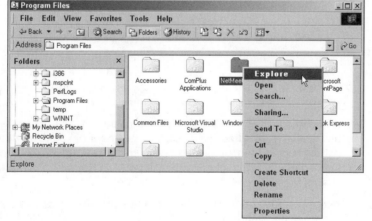

Figure 13-4:
Open a
folder by
right-clicking
it and
selecting
Explore.

Double-click a folder and you get just a single pane in your window. Figure
13-5 shows the same folder — the regular Explorer view on the left and the
single pane view on the right.

Figure 13-5:
On the left is
the Explore
view and on
the right is
the single
pane view.

The My Computer program lets you sling files around, just like Explorer, with one difference. My Computer defaults to the single pane view. Double-click the My Computer icon and it opens to a window with just one pane. Wanna see My Computer in Explore style? Just right-click the My Computer icon and then select Explore.

My Computer has the same View menu as Windows Explorer so you can choose to swap your large icons for small ones or get all the details you'd ever want.

- ✔ In a way, learning how to deal with files is like learning how to play the piano: Neither skill is obvious or intuitive, and you'll probably hit some bad notes with both. Don't be frustrated if you don't seem to be getting the hang of it. Liberace hated file management at first, too.

- ✔ Tired of using a menu to get the Explorer view? Then press the Shift key while double-clicking on any folder you want to explore.

- ✔ If you can't remember what those little tool buttons in Explorer do, rest your mouse pointer over them. Windows 2000 pops up with a helpful box summing up the button's mission, and a further explanation often appears along the bottom of the window.

- ✔ Although some of the additional file information available when using the Details view is handy, it can consume a lot of space on your screen, limiting the number of files you can see in the window. Displaying only the filename is often a better idea. If you want to see more information about a file or folder, try the following tip.

- ✔ Hold down Alt and double-click on a file or folder to see its size, date, and other information.

- ✔ With the Alt and double-clicking trick (described in the preceding paragraph), you can also change a file's attributes.

At first, Windows 2000 displays filenames sorted alphabetically by name in the Explorer and My Computer windows. But by right-clicking on a folder and choosing the different sorting methods in the Arrange Icons menu, you display the files in a different order. Windows 2000 puts the smallest files at the top of the list, for example, when you choose sort by Size. Or you can choose sort by Type to keep files created by the same application next to each other. You can also choose sort by Date to keep the most recent files at the top of the list.

Fiddling Around with Folders

This stuff is really boring, but if you don't read it, you'll be just as lost as your files.

A *folder* is a workplace on a disk. Hard disks are divided into many folders to separate your many projects. You can work with the spreadsheet, for example, without having all the word-processing files get in the way.

Any disk can have folders, but hard disks need them the most because they need a way to organize their thousands of files. By dividing a hard disk into little folder compartments, you can more easily see where everything sits.

The Explorer and My Computer programs enable you to move around to different folders and peek at the files you've stuffed inside each one. It's a pretty good organizational scheme, actually. Socks never fall behind a folder and jam the drawer.

✔ Folders can be inside folders to add a deeper level of organization, like adding drawer partitions to sort your socks by color. Each sock color partition is a smaller, organizing folder of the larger, sock-drawer folder.

✔ Of course, you can ignore folders and keep all your files right on the Windows 2000 Desktop. That's like tossing everything into the back seat of the car and pawing around to find your tissue box a month later. Stuff you've organized, however, is a lot easier to find.

✔ If you're eager to create a folder or two (and it's pretty easy), page ahead to this chapter's "Creating a Folder" section.

✔ Just as manila folders come *from* trees, computer folders use a tree metaphor, as shown in Figure 13-6, as they branch out from one main folder to several smaller folders.

Want all your folders to look the same? Open a folder and use the Tools menu to set it up the way you like: Click the Tools menu and select Folder Options. Click the View tab. At the top of the page is a button that reads Like Current Folder. Click it and then the OK button.

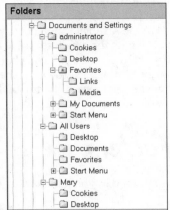

Figure 13-6:
The structure of folders inside your computer is tree-like, with main folders branching out to smaller folders.

Peering into Your Drives, Folders, and Network Storage Tanks

Knowing all the folder stuff described in the previous section can help you blend in with the people behind the counter at the computer store. But what really counts is knowing how to use Windows Explorer and My Computer to flip through the folders and get to a file you want. Never fear. Just read on.

Seeing the files on a disk drive

Like everything else in Windows 2000, disk drives are represented by buttons, or icons, shown in Table 13-1.

Table 13-1 Disk Drives, Networked Drives, and Other Containers

This Icon	Stands for This	Use It Like This
3½ Floppy (A:)	Floppy disk	Double-click here to see the files stored on a floppy disk in a floppy disk drive.
Local Disk (C:)	Hard disk	Double-click here to see the files stored on a hard disk that lives inside your computer or on the network.

This Icon	Stands for This	Use It Like This
	Shared Hard Disk	The little hand shows that you're sharing this hard disk with others on the network
Compact Disc (D:)	CD-ROM drive	Double-click here to see the files stored on a compact disc in a CD-ROM drive connected to your computer or network.
	Folder on your computer	Double-click here to see the files in a folder.
Shared Folder on SRV1 (E:)	Folder or hard disk on your network	Double-click here to see the files in a folder or hard disk that's being shared on your network.
	Unavailable share	Represents a shared drive or folder on the network that's unavailable. Sometimes a double-click will bring it back to life, other times you may have to consult a network personage.

The little icons resemble the types of disk drives they represent — if you sort of squint a little. For example, a floppy disk icon floats above the floppy drive in Table 13-1; a floating compact disc represents your CD-ROM drive. Double-click on either of those icons to see the files and folders stored on those disks and drives.

Hard disks — the little rectangles — don't have anything hovering over them except that nagging suspicion that they'll fail horribly at the worst possible moment.

✔ If you're kinda sketchy on those disk drive things, then you probably haven't read Chapter 2. Trot back there for a refresher course.

✔ Double-click on a drive icon in My Computer, and a window comes up to display the drive's contents. For example, put a disk in drive A and double-click on My Computer's drive A icon. A new window leaps up, showing what files and folders live on the disk in drive A.

✔ Click on a drive icon in Explorer, and you see the drive contents displayed on the right side of the window.

✔ A second window comes in handy when you want to move or copy files from one folder or drive to another, as discussed in the "Copying or Moving a File or Folder" section later in this chapter.

  ✔ If you click on a floppy drive icon when no disk is in the drive, Windows stops you gently, suggesting that you insert a disk before proceeding further.

Seeing what's inside a folder

Because folders are really little storage compartments, Windows 2000 uses a picture of a little folder to stand for each separate place for storing files.

To see what's inside a folder (whether you've viewing the folder icon in My Computer, Explorer, or on the Desktop itself), just double-click on the folder's picture. A new window pops up, showing that folder's contents.

Folder opening looks a little different in Windows Explorer. In Explorer, folders line up along the left side of a window. One folder, the one you're currently exploring, has a little box around its name, as shown in the Scanned Images folder in Figure 13-7

The files living inside that particular folder also appear on the right side of the window. In Figure 13-7, the file view is set to Thumbnails, which works great for pictures but looks dumb for regular files.

Figure 13-7: When you click on a folder on Explorer's left side, that folder's contents appear on the right side of the window.

To peek inside a folder while in Explorer, click on the folder name on the left side of the window. You see two things: That folder's next level of folders (if it has any) appear beneath it on the left side of the window, and that folder's filenames spill out into the right side of the window.

✔ As you keep climbing farther out on a branch and more folders appear, you're moving toward further levels of organization. If you climb back inward, you reach files and folders that have less in common.

✔ Yeah, this stuff is really confusing, but keep one thing in mind: Don't be afraid to double-click, or even single-click, on a folder just to see what happens. Clicking on folders just changes your viewpoint; nothing dreadful happens, and no tax receipts fall onto the floor. You're just opening and closing file cabinet drawers, peeking into folders along the way.

✔ To move back up the branches in Explorer, double-click on a folder closer to the left side of the window. Any folders beneath that folder are now hidden from view.

✔ Sometimes a folder contains too many files to fit in the window. To see more files, click on that window's scroll bars. What's a scroll bar? Time to whip out your field guide, Chapter 6.

Don't bother reading this hidden technical stuff

Sometimes programs store their own special information in a data file. These special programs may need to store information about the way the computer is set up, for example. To keep people from thinking that those files are trash and deleting them, the program hides those files.

You can view the names of these hidden files and folders in My Computer, however, if you want to play voyeur. Select Folder Options from the Tools menu. When the dialog box appears, click on the tab marked View, select the Show hidden files and folders button and then click on the OK button.

The formerly hidden files appear alongside the other filenames. Be sure not to delete them,

however: The programs that created the hidden files will gag, possibly damaging other files.

When you're done peeking, click the Do Not Show Hidden Files And Folders button just above the Show Hidden Files And Folders button, and click the OK button. Doing so stashes the files away, hidden from view.

As you can see, the View page gives you many opportunities for poking around and trying different settings. Fortunately for those of us who tend to forget where we were when we started, there's a Restore Defaults button on the same page. Click that button and all the settings go back to the way they were when Windows 2000 was installed (and you can start fiddling all over again).

While in Explorer, move the mouse pointer over the bar separating a folder on the left from its filenames on the right. When the pointer turns into a mutant two-headed arrow, hold down the mouse button. Then move the bar to the left to give the filenames more room, or to the right to give the folders on the left more room. Let go of the mouse when the split is adjusted correctly and the window reshapes itself to the new dimensions.

Can't find a file or folder? Instead of rummaging through folders, check out the Search command described in Chapter 8.

Loading a Program or File

A file is a collection of information on a disk. Files come in two basic types: program files and data files.

- ✔ *Program files* contain instructions that tell the computer to do something: balance the national budget or ferret out a fax number.

- ✔ *Data files* contain information created with a program, as opposed to computer instructions. If you write a letter to the grocer complaining about his soggy apricots, you're creating a data file.

To open either kind of file in Windows 2000, double-click on the icon next to the filename. A double-click on a program file's icon brings the program to the screen, whether that file's listed in My Computer, Explorer, or even the Find program. When you double-click on a data file, Windows 2000 loads the file and the program that created it. Then Windows 2000 brings both the file and the program to the screen at the same time.

- ✔ Windows 2000 sticks little icons next to filenames so you know whether they're program or data files. In fact, even folders get their own icons so you won't confuse them with files. Chapter 24, at the tail end of the book, provides a handy reference for figuring out what icon is what. (That's because the tail end of this book is much easier to find than this particular chapter.)

- ✔ Because of some bizarre New School of Computing mandate, any data file that Windows recognizes is called a document. A document doesn't have to contain words; it can have pictures of worms or sounds of hungry animals.

If the program or folder you're after is already highlighted, just give the Enter key a satisfying little pound with your index finger. That not only keeps your computer from getting out of line, but it shows you how many different ways Windows 2000 lets you do things (which means that you don't need to worry about remembering them all).

Deleting and Undeleting Files and Folders

Sooner or later, you'll want to delete a file that's not important anymore — yesterday's lottery picks, for example, or something you stumble on that's too embarrassing to save any longer. But suddenly you realize that you made a mistake and deleted the wrong file. Not to worry: The Windows 2000 Recycle Bin can probably resurrect that deleted file — if you're quick enough. The next two sections show how to delete a file and retrieve it quickly.

Getting rid of a file or folder

To permanently remove a file from the hard disk, click on its name. Then press the Delete key. This surprisingly simple trick works for files, programs, and even folders.

The Delete key deletes entire folders, as well as any additional folders lurking inside them. Before you press that Delete key, make sure that you've selected only the file or folder that you want to delete.

   ✔ When you press Delete, Windows tosses a box in your face, asking whether you're sure. If you are, click the Yes button.

   ✔ As soon as you find out how to delete files, you'll want to read the very next section, "How to undelete a file or folder."

Deleting a shortcut from the Desktop, My Computer, or Explorer just deletes a button that loads a program. You can always put the button back on later. Deleting an icon that doesn't have the little shortcut arrow removes that file from the hard disk and puts it into Recycle Bin, where it will eventually disappear. See the following section to find out which file has to walk the plank first.

How to undelete a file or folder

Sooner or later, your finger will push the Delete key at the wrong time, and you'll delete the wrong file. A slip of the finger, the wrong nudge of a mouse, or if you're in California, a small earthquake at the wrong time can make a file disappear. Zap!

Eeek! When the temblors subside, double-click the Recycle Bin, and the Recycle Bin box drops down from the heavens.

To retrieve a file or folder from the Recycle Bin, just right-click on the file or folder and click Restore from the pop-up menu (see Figure 13-8). The file or folder you so rashly trashed is returned to its original place.

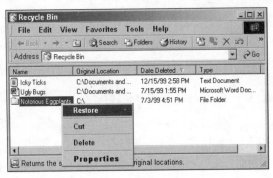

Figure 13-8: Recycle Bin drops down from the heavens to save the day.

 ✔ After the file's transported back to its original place, it's as good as new. Feel free to store it in any other folder for safekeeping.

 ✔ Recycle Bin normally holds about 10 percent of your hard disk's space. For example, if your hard disk is 800MB, the Recycle Bin holds on to 80MB of deleted files. When it reaches that limit, it starts deleting the oldest files to make room for the incoming deleted files. (And the old ones are gone for good, too.)

Copying or Moving a File or Folder

To copy or move files to different folders on your hard disk, use your mouse to drag them there. But first, a warning.

After installing a program to your hard disk, don't move the program or its folders around. An installation program often wedges a program into Windows 2000 pretty securely; if you move the program, it may not work anymore.

Now that the warnings have been issued, here's how to move a file to a different folder on your hard disk:

1. **Move the mouse pointer until it hovers over the file you want to move and then press and hold down the mouse button.**

2. **While holding down the mouse button, point at the folder to which you'd like to move the file.**

   The trick is to hold down your mouse button the whole time. As you move the mouse, its arrow drags the file along with it. For example, Figure 13-9 shows a complaint letter named Gas Prices being moved to the Gripes folder.

Figure 13-9: Drag the complaint about gas prices to the Gripes folder.

3. **Release the mouse button.**

   When the mouse arrow hovers over the place to which you'd like to move the file, take your finger off the mouse button. The file drops into its new home.

Moving a file by dragging its name is pretty easy, actually. The hard part often comes when trying to put the file and its destination on-screen at the same time. You often need to use both Explorer and My Computer to put two windows on-screen. When you can see the file and its destination, start dragging.

However, both Explorer and My Computer do some awfully dumb things that confuse people. For instance, when you drag a file from one folder to another on the same drive, you *move* the file. When you drag a file from one folder to another on a different drive, you *copy* that file.

I swear I didn't make up these rules. And it gets more complicated: You can sometimes click on the file and hold down Ctrl or Shift to reverse the rules. Table 13-2 can help you keep these oafish oddities from getting too far out of control.

Table 13-2	Moving Files Around
To Do This	*Do This*
Copy a file to another location on the same disk drive	Hold down Ctrl and drag it there.
Copy a file to a different disk drive	Drag it there.
Move a file to another location on the same disk drive	Drag it there.
Move a file to a different disk drive	Hold down Shift and drag it there.
Make a shortcut while dragging a file	Hold down Ctrl+Shift and drag it there.
Remember these *obtuse* commands	Refer to the handy Cheat Sheet at the front of this book.

Here's an easy way to remember this stuff when the book's not handy: Always drag icons while holding down the right mouse button. Windows 2000 is then gracious enough to give you a menu of options when you position the icon, and you can choose among moving, copying, or creating a shortcut.

Selecting More than One File or Folder

Windows 2000 lets you grab an armful of files and folders at one swipe; you don't always have to piddle around, dragging one item at a time.

To pluck several files and folders from a list, hold down Ctrl as you click on the names. Each filename stays highlighted as you click on the next one.

To gather several files or folders that appear next to each other, click on the first one. Then hold down the Shift key as you click on the last one. Those two items are highlighted, along with every file and folder between them.

Windows 2000 also lets you lasso files and folders: Point slightly above the first file or folder you want to select. Then, while holding down the mouse button, point at the last file or folder. The mouse creates a lasso to surround your files. Let go of the mouse button, and the lasso disappears, leaving all the surrounded files highlighted.

- ✔ You can drag these armfuls of files in the same way as you drag one file.

- ✔ You can delete these armfuls, too. Just press the Delete key while they're all lassoed.

- ✔ You can't rename an armful of files all at one time. To rename the files, you have to go back to piddling around with them one file at a time.

Renaming a File or Folder

If you're a he-man stuck with a name like Pink Gardenia, you can go to court to change it to something more masculine like Blue Gardenia. Changing a file-name requires even less effort:

1. **Click on the file or folder's name to select it.**

2. **Wait a second, and then click on the file's name — its title — running beneath or next to it.**

   The old filename appears highlighted.

3. **Start typing the new filename in the text box.**

   The original filename disappears when you do this. If something awful happens, read the section about legal filenames coming up next.

4. **Press Enter or click on the Desktop when you're through.**

- ✔ When you rename a file, only its name changes. The contents are still the same, the file remains the same size, and it's still in the same place on your hard disk.

- ✔ You can't rename groups of files this way. The programs spit in your face if you even try.

- ✔ You can rename folders this way, too, although you should only rename folders that you created yourself. In particular, don't rename a folder that a program created for itself upon installation; Windows 2000 often grows accustomed to that folder's name, and doesn't like changes.

Sometimes clicking on filenames to rename them is tricky business. If you're having trouble renaming a file, just click on the file or folder with your right mouse button and choose Rename from the menu that pops up. Handy button, that right mouse button.

Using Legal Folder Names and Filenames

In the Cro-Magnon days of computing, DOS was pretty picky about what you could and couldn't name a file or folder, and Windows 2000 still plays along. If you stick to plain old letters and numbers, you're fine. But don't try to stuff any of the following characters in a filename:

```
: / \ * | < > ? "
```

In fact, if you try to use any of those characters, Windows 2000 bounces an error message to the screen, and you have to try again.

For example, these names are illegal:

```
1/2 of my Homework
JOB:2
ONE>TWO
He's no "Gentleman"
```

These names are legal:

```
Half a Term Paper
JOB2
Two is Bigger than One
A #@$%) Scoundrel
```

✔ Unlike third graders who must face those ghastly multiplication tables, you have no major reason to memorize the characters you can't use. Just type in the filename you want, and Windows 2000 immediately lets you know if you've transgressed, so you can try again.

✔ Just as in earlier versions of Windows, Windows 2000 programs tack three identifying letters onto the end of all the files they create. By looking at that three-letter filename extension, Windows 2000 knows what program created that particular file. Normally, Windows 2000 hides those extensions so they're not confusing. But if you happen to spot filenames like savvy.doc, readme.txt, and nude.bmp on the hard disk, you know that those filename extensions have been added by the Windows 2000 programs WordPad (doc), Notepad (txt), and Paint (bmp). The picture on the file's icon provides the biggest clue to the file's contents.

If you really want to see a filename's extension, click on Folder Options from the folder's Tools menu and then click on the tab marked View. Finally, make sure that no check mark shows up in the little box that says Hide Extensions For Known File Types. Windows 2000 then reveals your file's extensions. (Click on the box again to remove the extensions from your sight.)

If you ever see a filename with a squiggly tilde thing in it, like in wigwam~1.txt, you are witnessing Windows 2000's special way of making file names that older programs can use. Programs that predate Windows 95 expect files to have names no longer than eight characters; Windows 2000 whittles down long filenames so those older programs can use them. (Windows 2000 remembers the long filename for itself.)

Copying a Complete Floppy Disk

To copy files from one disk to another, drag 'em over to their new home, as described a few pages back in the section "Copying or Moving a File or Folder." To copy an entire disk, however, you can use the Copy Disk command.

What's the difference? When you copy individual files, you're dragging specific filenames. But when you copy a disk, the Copy Disk command duplicates the entire floppy disk exactly: This command even copies the empty parts of the source disk! (That's why it takes longer than just dragging the files over.)

✔ The Copy Disk command can copy only floppy disks that are the same size or capacity. Just as you can't pour a full can of beer into a shot glass, you can't copy one disk's information onto another disk unless they hold the same amount of data.

✔ All this capacity and size stuff about disks and drives is slowly digested in Chapter 2.

Here's how to make a complete copy of a floppy disk:

1. **Put your floppy disk in the disk drive.**

2. **Click on the disk drive's icon with your right mouse button and choose Copy Disk from the menu.**

   A window appears, listing Copy From: on the left side and Copy To: on the right side.

3. **Follow the instructions on the screen.**

   In a few moments, your computer creates an exact duplicate of your floppy disk, and then politely asks whether you'd like to create another.

Creating a Folder

To store new information in a normal file cabinet, you grab a manila folder, scrawl a name across the top, and start stuffing it with information.

To store new information in Windows 2000 — for example, a new Exercise Tracking program or a ginseng root diet — you do the same thing: Create a new folder, think up a name for the new folder, and start moving or copying files into it.

New, more organized folders make finding information easier, too. For example, you can clean up a crowded My Documents folder by subdividing it into two folders. Here's how to create new folders in the My Documents folder to sort out all the edibles.

1. **Open My Documents by double-clicking on it.**

2. **Right-click on a blank spot in My Documents and select New and then Folder from the pop-up menus.**

   Figure 13-10 shows the action.

Figure 13-10: Make a new folder inside the My Documents folder.

3. Type the new folder's name and press Enter.

For example, we're naming our new folder Vegetable Matters.

Remember, Windows 2000 can sometimes be picky about the names you give to folders and files. For the rules, check out the "Using Legal Folder Names and Filenames" section earlier in this chapter.

After you type the folder's name and press Enter, the new Vegetable Matters folder is complete and ready to collect the veggie files. For impeccable organization, we're following the same steps and making a folder called Fruit Files. After dragging files into their respective folders, the My Documents folder looks a good deal tidier, as shown in Figure 13-11. (We're still arguing about whether tomatoes are fruit or vegetables.)

Figure 13-11:
After
moving
files into
folders,
the My
Documents
folder
looks much
neater.

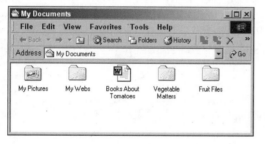

✔ To move files into a new folder, drag them there. Just follow the directions in the "Copying or Moving a File or Folder" section.

✔ When copying or moving lots of files, select them all at the same time before dragging them. You can chew on this stuff in the "Selecting More than One File or Folder" section.

✔ Just as with naming files, you can use only certain characters when naming folders. (Stick with plain old letters and numbers, and you'll be fine.)

Dragging, Dropping, and Running

You can drag files around in Windows 2000 to move them or copy them. But there's more: You can drag a file outside of the Explorer or My Computer window and drop the file into other windows. This action loads the file into other files and programs. For example (as shown in Figure 13-12), you can drag the Egypt file into the Paint window and let go of the mouse button. Paint loads the Egypt file, just as if you'd double-clicked on it in the first place.

This feature brings up all sorts of fun possibilities. If you have a sound card, you can listen to sounds by dropping sound files into the Media Player or Sound Recorder windows. You can drop text files into Notepad to load them quickly. Or you can drop WordPad files into WordPad.

✔ Okay, the first thing everybody wants to know is what happens if you drag a sound file into WordPad? Or a WordPad file into Notepad? Or any other combination of files that don't match? Well, Windows 2000 either embeds one file into the other — a process described in Chapter 10 — or displays a box that says it's getting indigestion. Just click on the OK button, and things return to normal. No harm done, either way.

✔ The second question everybody asks is "why bother?" You can just double-click on a file's name to load it. That's true. But this way is more fun and occasionally faster.

✔ Never dragged and dropped before? Chapter 3 contains complete instructions.

Figure 13-12:
To make things easier when loading files, Windows 2000 lets you drag files from one window into another.

Making Windows Explorer and My Computer List Missing Files

Sometimes Windows 2000 snoozes and doesn't keep track of what's really on the disk. Oh, it does pretty well with the hard disk, and it works pretty well if you are just running Windows 2000 programs. But Windows 2000 can't tell when you've just inserted a new floppy disk. Also, if you create a file from within a DOS program, Windows 2000 may not know that the new file is there.

If you think the Windows 2000 Explorer or My Computer window is holding out on you, tell it to refresh, or take a second look at what's on the floppy disk or hard disk.

You can click on View from the menu bar and choose Refresh from the pull-down menu, but a quicker way is to press the F5 key. (It's a function key along the top or left side of the keyboard.) Either way, the programs take a second look at what they're supposed to be showing and update their lists if necessary.

Press the F5 key whenever you stick in a different floppy disk and want to see what files are stored on the disk. Windows 2000 then updates the screen to show that new floppy's files, not the files from the previous disk.

Chapter 14

Facing the Fax

● ●

In This Chapter

▶ Setting up fax service

▶ Sending a fax

▶ Receiving a fax

▶ Looking at faxes you've sent

▶ Looking at faxes you've received

▶ Creating customized fax cover sheets

▶ Other fun fax stuff

● ●

*E*lectronic communication is definitely the wave of the present, so it's a good thing that Windows 2000 is well equipped to keep you connected to the rest of the world. Thanks to the nifty fax service that Windows 2000 offers, faxing a text document or a graphic image is as easy as clicking Print from an open document in a Windows-based program. The prospect of facing the fax may fill you with fear, but it's actually not that hard to get your fax service up and running — if you know what you're doing, that is.

To use the fax service that's part of Windows 2000, all you need is Windows 2000 and a fax device, usually a fax modem.

Be sure that your modem supports fax capabilities, though it's a rare modem that doesn't.

If your fax modem was installed properly when you installed Windows 2000, chances are excellent that Windows 2000 detected the device and installed fax service and the fax printer. If this is not the case, use the Add/Remove Hardware Wizard in the Control Panel to install the fax components of Windows 2000. See Chapter 11 for instructions on how to use the Add/Remove Hardware Wizard.

This chapter shows you how to set up your fax service, create a fax cover sheet, send a fax, look at faxes you've sent and received, create and manage personal fax cover sheets, and, last but not least, clue you in on some other important fax functions in Windows 2000. By the time we're done, we hope we'll have banished the fear of the fax forever.

Setting Up to Send and Receive Faxes

Before using your fax device, make sure that it's properly configured to send and receive faxes. The Windows 2000 fax service offers some handy-dandy options, but let's start with the basics.

Opening the Fax Service Manager

To open the Fax Service Manager and check out the Windows 2000 fax service, follow these steps:

1. **Click the Start button and then choose Programs, Accessories, Communications, Fax, and Fax Service Management from the menus that pop up.**

   The Fax Service Management page opens (see Figure 14-1).

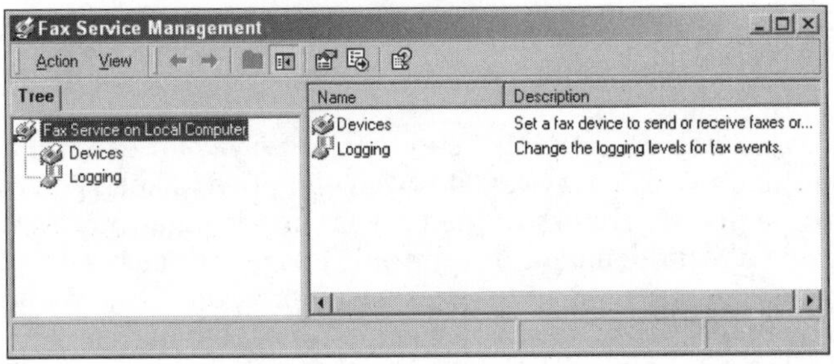

Figure 14-1:
The basic fax configuration window.

2. **In the Fax Service Management window, click on Devices on the left side of the window.**

   This brings up a list on the right-hand side of the window showing the fax device(s) attached to your computer (see Figure 14-2).

   Most likely, you will have just one fax device, but if you happen to have more than one, you should see multiple entries displayed here.

In the right-hand window, you can see how the fax is set up. The most important entries are Send, which tells you whether your fax device is set up to send faxes; Receive, which tells you whether you're set up to receive faxes; and the Device Status, which gives the availability of the device. (You may have to drag the scroll bar at the bottom of the window to see the entries off to the right.)

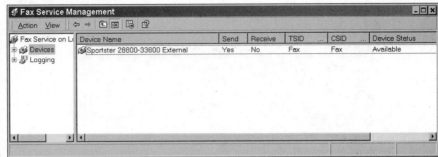

Figure 14-2:
Checking
the setup for
sending and
receiving
faxes.

If the Send and Receive settings are okay with you and the Device Status is
"Available," then you can just close this window (click on the X box in the
upper-right corner) and get on with your life.

Configuring your fax settings

In order to start faxing, you first have to tweak your fax modem to get it properly set up. If you want to establish (or change) a setting for the fax modem,
follow these steps:

1. **Click the Start button and then choose Programs, Accessories,
   Communications, Fax, and Fax Service Management from the menus
   that pop up.**

2. **Click on Devices on the left side of the window.**

   This brings up a list on the right-hand side of the window showing the
   fax device(s) attached to your computer (refer to Figure 14-2).

3. **Right-click the device you want to fix (as shown in Figure 14-3), and
   choose Properties from the menu that pops up.**

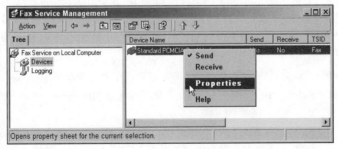

Figure 14-3:
Preparing to
change your
device's
properties.

A typical fax modem's Properties page is pictured in Figure 14-4.

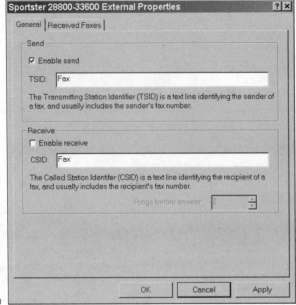

4. **On the General tab of the Properties page, check the Enable Receive box in the Receive section.**

   This prepares your fax device to receive incoming faxes. The Enable Send checkbox is checked by default, so leave it alone.

   Leave the TSID and CSID boxes alone under the Send and Receive sections.

   The only other setting you *might* want to consider changing here is Rings Before Answer, which determines how many times the incoming phone line will ring before the fax device picks up the call. The default is 2, but if you'd like to increase or decrease that number, use the little up and down arrows to put your favorite number in the box, or just type it in.

5. **Click the Received Faxes tab to specify what happens to incoming faxes on your computer.**

   Basically, you can do one (or more) of three things with incoming faxes:

   • **Print:** Check the Print On box and use the drop-down list to specify which printer to use.

   • **Save to a folder on your computer:** Be sure that the Save In Folder box is checked. If you're not satisfied with the default folder that Microsoft Fax offers as the location to which incoming faxes should be saved, click on the little button with three dots on it to the right of the folder name and make your own choice.

- **Send to an e-mail box:** The setting to send incoming faxes to an e-mail box can only be made after an Administrator performs some voodoo rites on your machine and on the network. The option isn't available until that happens.

6. **Click OK to return to the Fax Service Management screen and the hard part is all done.**

7. **Click the close box in the upper-right corner of the Fax Service Management window to make it go away.**

All that remains now is to fill in some information on a cover sheet so that the people you're faxing will know who you are. And this is exactly what the next section tells you, so don't stop reading yet!

Configuring your cover sheets

It's usually a good idea to include a cover sheet with a fax you're sending to somebody so they know who you are, what your fax number is, how many pages the fax is supposed to be, and so forth. To enter the default information to be used on fax cover sheets, follow these steps:

1. **Click the Start button then choose Settings and then Control Panel.**

2. **Double-click the Fax icon in the Control Panel.**

   The Fax Properties page appears (see Figure 14-5), which is where you fill in the default info that appears on every cover page.

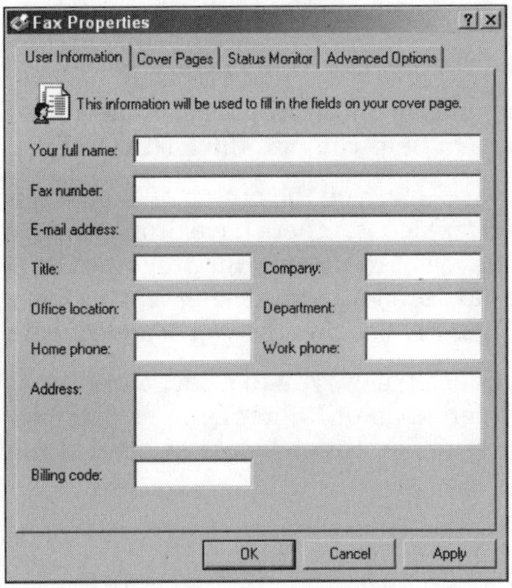

Figure 14-5:
Provide cover sheet information that goes with all your outgoing faxes.

3. **On the User Information tab, fill in the information that you want to print on your fax cover pages.**

If you want, you can type something in every field. At the minimum, include your name and fax number.

Remember, if you change your mind about the way these fields are filled in, you can always come back here and type in new information later.

4. **Click OK when you're all done to close the Fax Properties box.**

If you're all wrought up about creating cover pages for your faxes, see "Creating personal fax cover sheets" later in this chapter.

Sending a Fax

The big moment has come where you send a fax streaming through the phone lines. The procedure to send a fax will vary just a little according to the program you're using. In this section, we show you how to send a fax using WordPad, which gives you the general idea.

1. **Start the program that created the document that you want to send.**

For our example, click the Start button and choose Programs, then Accessories, and then WordPad.

2. **If you want to send an existing document, click File and then Open and double-click the document you want to send. If you want to send a new document, simply type it up.**

3. **Send it by clicking on the File menu and selecting Print.**

4. **In the Print dialog box, choose Fax as the printer.**

5. **Click Print (or OK, depending on the application) and the Fax Wizard pops up out of nowhere to help you out. Click Next to keep going.**

Nearly all Print dialog boxes give you the option of choosing a printer. Some show printer (and fax) icons, others have drop-down list boxes with printer (and fax) choices. Whatever form your program's Print dialog box takes on, choosing the Fax "printer" and clicking Print or OK whisks you off to the Fax Wizard. Figure 14-6 shows the WordPad Print dialog box.

If the Print dialog box doesn't allow you to select a printer, then you can usually choose the Printer Setup or Printer Options entry on the File menu to specify a printer or Fax option before selecting Print.

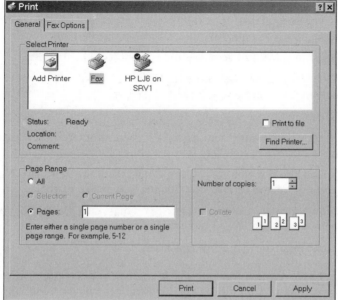

Figure 14-6:
Click the
Fax icon to
send the
document
as a fax.

6. On the Recipient and Dialing Information screen, type in the name and fax number of the person you're trying to send a fax to.

To specify the recipient of your long-awaited fax, type a name into the box labeled To. If this fax involves a local call and you'd like to take a little shortcut, click the Dial Exactly As Typed (No Prefixes) checkbox, which grays out the Location option and the Area Code section of the fax number. But if you're taking the plunge and sending your first fax long distance, you can ignore the Location option (assuming your fax recipient lives in the USA, of course) and type the area code and phone number into the Fax Number boxes.

If you already have an address book in Outlook, you can click Address Book to browse for someone's name and fax number. This is especially handy if you're sending a fax to multiple recipients.

Sending a fax to multiple recipients isn't difficult at all; just type each recipient's name and fax number into the appropriate boxes (or you can retrieve this information from your address book) and click Add to add each person to the recipient list. If you want to drop a recipient, highlight that person's name and click Remove.

When you're done here, click Next to continue.

7. The Preparing the Cover Page screen gives you the opportunity to add a cover page from a template or add a note on the cover page.

To add a cover page from a template, check the box labeled Select A Cover Page Template With The Following Information, and then choose your weapon from the drop-down list. Windows 2000 includes several cover sheet templates, and if you've created a personal fax cover sheet (more about this shortly), it appears on this list, too.

Type the subject of your fax into the Subject Line box.

If you want to include a note to the fax recipient on the cover sheet, type the text of the note into the Note box.

When you're sure that your cover sheet is perfect, click Next to continue.

8. **On the Scheduling Transmission screen, the default setting is to send the fax now. Leave it that way and click Next.**

9. **Review the information on the Completing the Send Fax Wizard screen before sending your fax out to face the world.**

   If you notice anything you'd like to change, click Back until you reach the screen where you can correct your mistake.

10. **Click Finish and your fax zips away.**

So what happens now, you may ask. If you've chosen to send your fax immediately, you see a "printing" dialog box generated by whatever application you're using. Next, you see the Windows 2000 Fax Monitor window, which keeps you up-to-date on the progress your fax is (or isn't) making. If you decide you'd rather hang up before the fax has been transmitted, click End Fax Call. Or, if you really want to find out the gory details of when your fax went through, and so on, click Details. When you're all done sending your fax, click the close button in the upper-right corner of the Fax Monitor window to clear it and you're all set.

Receiving a Fax

Once you turn on the fax receiving capability (see the earlier section "Configuring your fax settings" for all the wonderful details), your computer automatically receives faxes whenever someone sends you one. But if you have a fax modem that shares a voice line, you'll want to set the fax service to receive only when you say to receive.

1. **Double-click the Fax icon in the Control Panel.**

2. **Click the Status Monitor tab and select Enable Manual Answer for the first device.**

3. **Click OK.**

When you hear an incoming call, a box opens on your Desktop asking "Answer Call?" If it's a voice call, click No. If you hear a fax tone, click Yes and the fax begins transmitting.

By default, received faxes are deposited in a Received Faxes folder, which you can get to by clicking your way through Start, Programs, Accessories, Communications, Fax, and My Faxes.

Looking at Faxes You've Sent

Viewing faxes you've sent couldn't be much easier; just follow these steps:

1. **Click the Start button, then choose Programs, Accessories, Communications, Fax, and My Faxes from the pop-up menus.**

   This step may sound complicated, but it's actually a snap once you've gotten the hang of how the Windows 2000 menus work.

2. **Double-click on the Sent Faxes folder to display its contents.**

   A list of the sent faxes appears (see Figure 14-7).

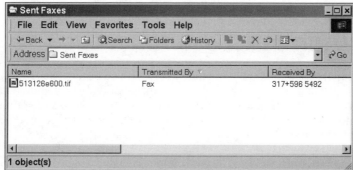

Figure 14-7: The extremely unhelpful listing of faxes sent.

3. **Click on an item to view its description, or double-click on an item to open it for viewing.**

   Since the filenames that Windows 2000 assigns to sent faxes aren't very helpful (to say the least), you may want to skip the description part and proceed directly to opening the item you want to see. Thanks to the nifty fax-viewing feature built into Windows 2000, you can see exactly what you sent.

When you finish looking at the sent faxes, use the close box in the upper-right corner to close the Sent Faxes window. Either way, you return to the My Faxes window.

Looking at Faxes You've Received

This procedure is essentially the same as looking at faxes you've sent, except you need to click on the Received Faxes folder to view its contents.

1. **Click the Start button, then choose Programs, Accessories, Communications, Fax, and My Faxes from the pop-up menus.**

2. **Double-click on the Received Faxes folder to display its contents.**

   A list of received faxes appears.

3. **Click on an item to view its description, or double-click on an item to open it for viewing.**

   The filenames that Windows 2000 assigns to sent faxes are totally useless, so proceed directly to opening the item you want to see.

When you're all done, use the close box in the upper-right corner to close the Received Faxes window, which lands you back in the My Faxes window.

Customizing Fax Cover Sheets

Personal fax cover sheets are nice to have if you don't always want to stick to the party line. They can let you show a little individuality and creativity, and they can convey a less formal tone than your "official" fax cover sheets. This section shows you how to create and manage personal fax cover sheets on your computer.

Sometimes, however, your organization may have a wet blanket (possibly your boss) who wants things done a certain way each and every time. If this person has control over your computer and has disabled Windows 2000's personal fax cover sheet capabilities, read no further. Until you can convince him or her to change his mind, the instructions here do you no good since the options they describe are unavailable.

Creating personal fax cover sheets

To create a new personal fax cover sheet on your computer, follow these steps:

1. **Double-click the Fax icon in the Control Panel.**

   This opens the Fax Properties page.

2. **Click the Cover Pages tab.**

   Any personal fax cover pages that already exist on your system appear in the list on this screen.

3. Click New to create your personal fax cover page.

What you see now is the Windows 2000 Fax Cover Page Editor. Using this program, you can design your very own fax cover page; you can add text, lines, or shapes to your cover page, change the spacing and alignment of items on it, and much more.

You can also insert predefined fields using the Insert menu. What this means is that Windows 2000 takes the information that you filled in on the User Information tab of the Fax Properties page (your name, fax number, company name, and so on) and places it wherever you want on the fax cover page you're creating (see Figure 14-8). Or, add a message field that can include a note, subject line, indication of the date and time your fax is sent, or the number of pages to be faxed.

Figure 14-8:
Great fun making your own fax cover pages.

Click the Help menu and select Help Topics for specifics on creating different elements. When your personal fax cover page is perfect, click File and then Save to save it (be sure to give it a memorable name) and close the Fax Cover Page Editor using the close box in the upper-right corner of the screen.

Viewing personal fax cover sheets

If you've created a new personal fax cover page or if you're just plain nosy and want to see what a personal fax cover page stored on your computer looks like, do the following:

1. Double-click the Fax icon in the Control Panel, and click the Cover Pages tab.

2. **Select the personal fax cover page you'd like to see by clicking on its name.**

3. **Click Open to view it.**

   This opens the Fax Cover Page Editor and displays the personal fax cover page you've selected for viewing and editing. When you're done admiring it, close the Fax Cover Page Editor using the close box in the upper-right corner of the screen.

Other Fax Stuff You May Want to Know About

Lest we leave you with an incomplete picture of Windows 2000's fax capabilities, we thought we'd fill you in on what some of the other fax options do. Here, in the order they appear on the pop-up menus, is a brief guide to the remaining Windows 2000 fax functions.

Using the fax queue

Whenever you send a fax, it's automatically added to the fax queue, which is just a fancy British way of saying that you're making the fax stand in line and wait its turn. Actually, if you tend to send your faxes out immediately, you may never have to concern yourself with the fax queue at all; it's intended primarily for those of us who line our faxes up like airplanes on a runway and send them on their way serially, sometimes hours after we've prepared them.

Viewing the fax queue is useful if you're unsure whether a particular fax has already been sent, or if you suddenly decide that you don't want to send one (or more) of the faxes in the queue at all. The queue is also the place to go if you need to pause or resume faxing, set the fax as the default printer, and more.

To get at the Windows 2000 fax queue, click the Start button, and then select Programs, Accessories, Communications, Fax, and Fax Queue from the pop-up menus.

My Faxes: Common Coverpages folder

Earlier sections in this chapter outline the uses of the My Faxes window. The first two items in My Faxes are the Sent Faxes and Received Faxes folders; the third (and last) is the Common Coverpages folder.

The Common Coverpages folder is where the common — that is, non-personal (or "official") — fax cover pages are stored on your computer. Periodically, you may want to check what's in here to see whether any cover sheets need to be updated, or you may want to remove cover sheets you no longer use. Here are the steps you need to follow to manage common cover sheets:

1. **To access the Common Coverpages folder, click the Start button and choose Programs, Accessories, Communications, Fax, and My Faxes from the pop-up menus**.

   This opens the My Faxes window, where you see three items: Common Coverpages, Received Faxes, and Sent Faxes.

2. **Double-click the Common Coverpages folder to open it.**

   You now see a list of the common cover sheets stored in this folder.

3. **Double-click on a cover sheet to view and/or edit it.**

   This opens the Fax Cover Page Editor, which enables you to look at and/or make changes to the cover sheet file you selected.

When you're done with the Fax Cover Page Editor, close it using the close box in the upper-right corner of the screen. That's all there is to it.

Sending a quickie fax

This last Windows 2000 fax option is to send a minimalist fax, consisting of no more than a cover sheet. The Send Cover Page Fax command is the fastest way to accomplish this since it gives you direct access to the Send Fax Wizard. Here's what you need to do:

1. **Click the Start button and choose Programs, Accessories, Communications, Fax, and Send Cover Page Fax from the pop-up menus.**

   This fires up the Send Fax Wizard, so you see its friendly welcome screen.

2. **Follow the steps of the Send Fax Wizard to finish sending your cover page-only fax.**

   See the section "Sending a Fax" in this chapter for more-specific scoop on the Send Fax Wizard.

   Before you know it, your "quickie" fax makes its way out into the world.

Chapter 15

Little Accessories that Clog the Start Button's Programs Menu

. . . .

In This Chapter

▶ Getting to know Windows 2000 Professional accessories

▶ Figuring out differences between NT 4 and Windows 2000

. . . .

*W*indows 2000 Professional comes with a lot of free programs, but not all of them will appear on your particular computer. Depending on the generosity of your Network Administrator, the programs described in this chapter may differ from the number of programs installed on your particular computer.

Don't expect these little programs to work wonders. Microsoft programmers squirm a little in their chairs if you even call them programs. No, Microsoft calls these things *applets* — mini-programs designed to demonstrate what a real Windows 2000 Professional program could do if you would just head back to the software store and buy one. However, if your needs are simple, these simple programs may just fill those needs. But when your needs start growing, your software budget will probably have to grow, too.

Either way, this chapter explains what comes free in the Windows 2000 Professional box. And if you don't find a confusing little freebie program covered here, check out Chapter 16, where you find more of the network-related goodies explained in fuller detail.

 If the menus leading off the Start button look a little stunted, it's because they are. By default, Windows 2000 only displays the items you've used most recently. To re-expand the menus and see all the items they contain, just click the double arrows at the bottom of each menu.

Briefcase

What it does: Want to move files between your laptop and desktop computers — and not get the different versions of the files mixed up? The Windows 2000 Briefcase lets you connect two computers with a serial or parallel cable and shoot files between them. Or, you can simply copy files back and forth with a floppy disk. Best yet, Briefcase can tell which file is most up-to-date, so you always keep the current copy.

Where it lives: To open Briefcase, right-click anywhere on the Desktop, click New, then click Briefcase.

How to use it: Briefcase works as a specialized folder that keeps track of the dates and times on your files. Start by dragging the desired files directly onto the Briefcase icon on the Desktop.

Working with floppies? Just drag the Briefcase icon onto a floppy's disk drive icon, and take that floppy to your other computer. Then open the floppy on the other computer, open the Briefcase icon, and work on the files from within the Briefcase icon. When you're done, reinsert the floppy into your main computer and drag the Briefcase icon back onto that computer. Briefcase looks at the files and constantly makes sure that you're replacing older files with newer ones.

If you're working with cables or networks, drag the Briefcase icon onto the other computer's icon on the Desktop, and work from there. Either way, by always working on the files inside the Briefcase icon, you can keep from accidentally overwriting your new files with old ones — a common occurrence when moving files from computer to computer.

If you're upgrading from Windows NT, you'll notice that what was My Briefcase has been renamed Briefcase and it's no longer on the Desktop by default. Follow the instructions in this section to put it there and you're all set.

Briefcase depends on both computers to display the correct time and date. If you're counting on using Briefcase, make sure that the clocks on both computers are accurate.

Calculator

What it does: Calculator is, well, a calculator — as shown in Figure 15-1. It looks simple enough, and it really is — unless you've mistakenly set the view to Scientific mode and see some nightmarish logarithmic stuff. To bring the calculator back to normal, choose View and select Standard.

Figure 15-1:
Calculator
works like
those simple
calculators
given away
free at trade
shows.

Where it lives: Open the Start menu, choose Programs, choose Accessories, and click on the Calculator icon.

How to use it: To punch in numbers and equations, click on the little number buttons, just as if it were a normal calculator. When you click on the equal sign (=), the answer appears at the top in the display window. For an extra measure of handiness, you can copy the answers to the Clipboard by pressing Ctrl+C (holding down the Ctrl key and then pressing C). Then click in the window where you want the answer to appear and paste the answer by pressing Ctrl+V. This method is easier than retyping a number like 3.14159265.

✔ Unlike in other Windows programs, you can't copy Calculator's answer by running the mouse pointer over the numbers. You have to press Ctrl+C or click on the Edit menu item and choose Copy.

✔ If the mouse action is too slow, press the Num Lock key and punch in numbers with the numeric keypad.

✔ The asterisk is the multiply sign, and the forward slash (located under the question mark key) means division.

CD Player

What it does: Adding a CD-ROM drive to a computer doesn't always add multimedia capabilities as much as it adds a little Bachman Turner Overdrive to your lunch hour. Most multimedia computer owners tend to pop a music CD into their computer's CD-ROM drive now and then. CD Player, shown in Figure 15-2, lets you keep track of which songs are playing, arranges the song order, fast-forwards past the bad stuff, and performs other basic CD player tasks.

Figure 15-2:
CD Player
lets you play
CDs and
hear music
using your
computer's
CD-ROM
drive.

Where it lives: Open the Start menu, choose Programs, choose Accessories, choose Entertainment, and then click on the CD Player option.

How to use it: When you put a CD in the drive, the CD Player offers to download artist, title, and track information for this CD from the Internet. If you click OK on the New Album Found box, Windows 2000 activates your Internet connection and provides you with an astonishing array of information about the disc you've casually popped into your drive. You can also choose among various play modes (Standard, Random, Preview, and so on), skip one or more track(s), scan the CD for the track you want, and much more. These days, using CD Player is like having a regular programmable CD player on your desk — except most computer speakers aren't quite as good as the ones you have at home.

✔ Music too loud? Click on the little speaker in the corner of the taskbar. An easy-to-use sliding bar lets you raise or lower the volume — no more frantic searching to save your ears.

Don't forget — most CD-ROM drives come with a headphone jack along the front of the computer so your Beethoven symphonies don't disturb your coworkers.

✔ Don't remember what some of those buttons do? Just rest your mouse pointer over the button, and Windows 2000 Professional sends a message to the screen to help you out.

✔ Looking for a certain song, but can't remember which one it is? Click the Mode button and select Preview. CD Player automatically plays the first few seconds of each song on the CD until you recognize the one you're after.

✔ As soon as you insert an audio CD, Windows 2000 Professional automatically begins playing it — as long as your CD-ROM drive supports that feature. To stop Windows 2000 Professional from immediately playing the CD, hold down the Shift key while inserting the CD into the CD-ROM drive.

Character Map (Adding the à in Voilà)

 What it does: Adds weird foreign characters, such as à, É, or even £, Figure 15-3 shows the Character Map box, which lists every available character and symbol.

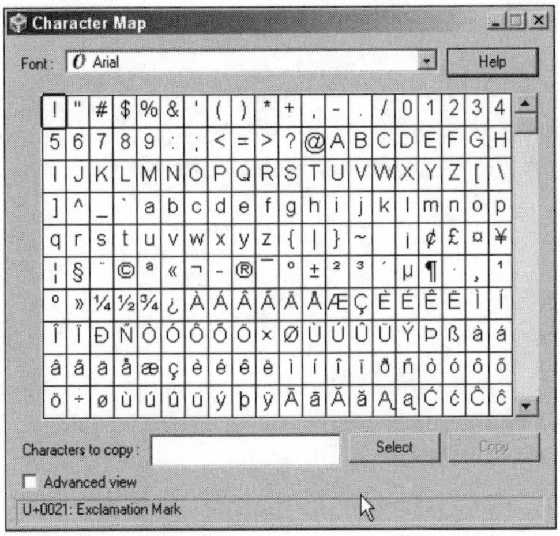

Figure 15-3: Character Map makes it easier to find and use foreign symbols.

Where it lives: Open the Start menu on the taskbar, choose Programs, choose Accessories, choose System Tools, and click on Character Map.

How to use it: Follow these steps to put a foreign character in your work:

1. **Make sure that the current font — the name for the style of the characters on the page — shows in the Character Map's Font box.**

   Not showing? Then click on the down arrow and select the font when it appears in the drop-down list.

2. **Scan the Character Map box until you see the symbol you're after; then pounce on that character with a double-click.**

   The symbol you select appears in the Characters to Copy box.

3. **Click on Copy to send that character to the Clipboard.**

4. **Click on the X in the upper-right corner to close the Character Map box.**

5. **Click in the document where you want the new symbol or character to appear.**

6. **Press Ctrl+V, and the new character pops right in there.**

   (Give it a second. Sometimes it's slow.)

The symbols in the Character Map box are easier to see if you hold down the mouse button and move the pointer over them.

✔ When working with foreign words, keep the Character Map handy as an icon, ready for consultation.

✔ For some fun symbols like ✌, ⌂, &, ☎, ❛, ☠, and check box symbols, switch to the Wingdings font. It's full of little doodads to spice up your work.

✔ You can grab several characters at a time by double-clicking on each of them and then copying them into your work as a chunk. You don't have to keep returning to the Character Map for each one.

ClipBook Viewer

What it does: ClipBook Viewer (see Figure 15-4) lets you see the things that you've cut or copied and are preparing to paste. It's also a way of posting documents for others on your network to view.

Figure 15-4:
ClipBook Viewer lets you see items that have been cut or copied and are ready to be pasted.

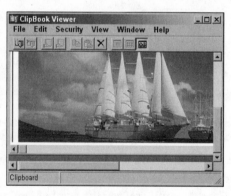

Where it lives: Open the Start menu on the taskbar, choose Run, then type **clipbrd**.

How to use it: Flip to Chapter 10 for all the details on using the ClipBook Viewer.

Games

What it does: The four games that come with Windows 2000 (Freecell, Minesweeper, Pinball, and Solitaire) are one of the more frivolous — and fun — aspects of the operating system. All four of these games may be familiar to you if you've used Windows 95/98 before. Freecell and Solitaire are one-person card games; in Minesweeper the goal is to find all the mines without getting blown up; and Pinball is a virtual version of exactly what its name implies.

Where it lives: Open the Start menu on the taskbar, choose Programs, choose Accessories, choose Games, then click on the game you'd like to play.

How to use it: When to use it (when your boss isn't looking) might be a better question. If you open a game and look at its Help file, each provides you with the specific rules of the game and more. Have fun!

If you don't see the games, it's possible that the Network Administrator has made them unavailable. Some particularly cranky Network Administrators do this because they have the strange idea that some people might play Solitaire rather than work. Hmmph.

Imaging

What it does: Imaging lets you peek inside a file containing graphics and see the file's contents. Imaging is the program that Internet Explorer often uses to look at pictures while you're browsing the Internet's World Wide Web.

Where it lives: Open the Start menu on the taskbar, choose Programs, choose Accessories, and click on Imaging.

How to use it: Internet Explorer automatically brings up Imaging when it needs it. But if you want to peek inside a picture, double-click on the picture's icon from within My Computer or Explorer. If it's capable, the Imaging program usually loads the picture and brings it into view.

- Imaging can peer inside files saved in various graphics formats: TIF, BMP, JPG, and PCX. However, it can save files in only three formats: BMP, TIF, and JPG.

- Sharon likes Imaging's Annotation feature, as shown in Figure 15-5. With this feature, she can make a "rubber stamp" that says "THIS PROJECT IS DOOMED," including the date on which the doom is predicted and stamp it all over her favorite images.

- If you find yourself using Paint a lot, give Imaging a try.

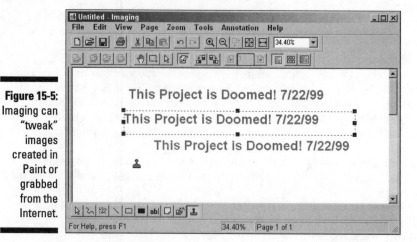

Figure 15-5:
Imaging can
"tweak"
images
created in
Paint or
grabbed
from the
Internet.

Media Player

What it does: Media Player can play sounds from a sound card, connect to MIDI keyboards, and can access CD-ROM drives for both sound and data. Media Player can even play video stored in files or on video discs.

Where it lives: Open the Start menu on the taskbar, choose Programs, then Accessories, then Entertainment, and click on Windows Media Player.

How to use it: From within Explorer or My Computer, double-click on the media file you want to play; Media Player rises to the task. (You can find pictures of icons containing videos, sounds, and music in Chapter 24.)

> ✔ Windows 2000 Professional comes ready to run with some of the most popular sound cards. Other sound cards or CD-ROM drives come with special drivers on a floppy disk that is boxed with the package.
>
> ✔ Sound cards and CD-ROM drives are covered in Chapter 2.

Notepad

What it does: Windows comes with two word processors, WordPad and Notepad. WordPad is for the letters you're sprucing up for other people to see. Notepad is for quick notes you're going to keep for yourself.

Where it lives: Open the Start menu on the taskbar, choose Programs, choose Accessories, and click on Notepad.

How to use it: Notepad loads more quickly than WordPad. Double-click on the Notepad icon, and it leaps to the screen more quickly than you could have reached for a notepad in your back pocket. You can type in some quick words and save them on the fly.

Notepad's speed comes at a price, however — it stores only words and numbers. Notepad doesn't store any special formatting, such as italicized letters, and you can't paste any pictures into it, as you can with WordPad. It's a quick, thrown-together program for your quick, thrown-together thoughts.

✔ Notepad tosses you into instant confusion: All the sentences head right off the edge of the screen. To turn one-line, runaway sentences into normal paragraphs, turn on the Word Wrap feature by choosing the Format menu and clicking on Word Wrap.

✔ Notepad prints kind of funny, too: It prints the file's name at the top of every page. To combat this nonsense, choose File and then click on Page Setup. A dialog box appears, with a funny code word in the Header box. Delete the word and click on the OK button. If you want to get rid of the automatic page numbering, clear out the Footer box as well.

✔ Here's another printing problem: Notepad doesn't print exactly what you see on-screen. Instead, it prints according to the margins you entered in Page Setup under the File menu. This quirk can lead to unpredictable results.

✔ Although Notepad leans toward simplicity, it has one fancy feature that not even WordPad can match. Notepad can automatically stamp the current time and date at the bottom of your page whenever you open it. Just type **.LOG** in the very top, left-hand corner of a file and then save the file. Then whenever you open it again, Notepad stamps the bottom of the file with the current time and date, and you can jot down some current notes.

✔ Don't try the .LOG trick by using lowercase letters and don't omit the period. It doesn't work.

✔ To stick in the date and time manually, press F5. The time and date appear, just as they do in the .LOG trick.

Paint

What it does: Love the smell of paint and a fresh canvas? Then you'll hate Paint. After working with real fibers and pigments, you'll find the Windows 2000 Professional computerized graphics program, Paint, to be a little sterile. But at least you don't have any mess. Paint creates pictures and graphics to stick into other programs.

Where it lives: Open the Start menu, choose Programs, choose Accessories, and click on the Paint icon.

How to use it: Paint offers more than just a paintbrush. It has a can of spray paint for that airbrushed look, several pencils of different widths, a paint roller for gobbing on a bunch of paint, and an eraser for when things get out of hand.

In addition to capturing your artistic flair, Paint can team up with a digital camera or scanner to touch up pictures in your PC, as shown in Figure 15-6. You can create a flashy letterhead to stick into the letters you create in WordPad. You can even create maps to paste into your party fliers.

Figure 15-6:
With Paint,
you can
create
pictures
(like this
one) and
touch up
scanned-in
photos and
taxes.

✔ You can copy drawings and pictures from Paint and paste them into just about any other Windows 2000 Professional program.

✔ You can cut out or copy chunks of art from the Paint screen using the select or free-form select tools described later in this section. The art goes onto the Windows 2000 Professional Clipboard, where you can grab it and paste it into any other Windows program. (Paint doesn't support "Scraps," which we cover in Chapter 10.)

✔ Paint enables you to add text and numbers to graphics, so you can add street names to maps, put labels inside drawings, or add the vintage year to your wine labels.

Anything you create in Paint you can turn into wallpaper and use as a backdrop for your Desktop. Just save your fun new file, open the File menu and then select the Set as Wallpaper (Tiled) or Set as Wallpaper (Centered) options. More detailed information about wallpaper installation lurks in Chapter 11.

Phone Dialer

What it does: From its name, you might expect that this accessory exists only to dial phone numbers for you. Not true. Using Phone Dialer, you can make regular and Internet voice phone calls, video calls, or participate in a video conference call — right from your PC.

Where it lives: Open the Start menu, choose Programs, choose Accessories, choose Communications, and then click on Phone Dialer.

How to use it: To use Phone Dialer to dial a plain old phone call and to add a number to your speed dial list, follow these steps:

1. **Open Phone Dialer as described in "Where it lives" above.**

2. **Click on Dial.**

3. **Click on the circle next to Phone call and type in the phone number you'd like to call.**

4. **Click on Place Call.**

5. **If you wish to add the phone number you're calling to your speed dial list, check the Add Number to Speed Dial List box.**

   Doing this enables you to dial this person's number by double-clicking on their name on the speed dial list.

In addition to Phone Dialer, you may need some equipment to make your telephonic dreams come true. A sound card is pretty much the minimum ante for telephonic operations; if you don't have one, forget about those Internet voice calls. If you wish to speak your piece during an Internet voice call or in a conference situation, you'll need a microphone. And if you wish to see and be seen during a video conference, you'll need a camera too, so tell your boss to start saving that supply budget.

Configuring Phone Dialer for anything except the basic phone call described above is not for the squeamish. This is definitely Network Administrator territory.

Sound Recorder

What it does: Records and plays back sounds.

Where it lives: Open the Start menu from the taskbar, choose Programs, choose Accessories, choose Entertainment, and then click on Sound Recorder.

How to use it: If you have a microphone or a CD-ROM drive, you can make your own sound files that you can associate with a Windows event or even send with e-mail. Here's how you do it:

1. **Open Sound Recorder then select New from the File menu. To begin recording, click the button with the big red dot.**
2. **Start the CD or start speaking into the microphone.**
3. **Click on the button with the black square to stop recording.**

    Figure 15-7 shows the Sound Recorder recording from the CD-ROM drive.

Figure 15-7:
Sound
Recorder
records
what the CD
is playing.

4. **Choose Save from the File menu, give your new file a name, and then click on the Save button.**

   ✔ To record from a microphone, you'll need a sound card because that's what the microphone plugs into.

   ✔ You don't need a sound card to *record* from a CD-ROM drive — but a sound card and speakers are required if you want to *hear* a playback of what you've recorded.

Synchronize

What it does: Synchronizes (updates) online and offline data, including shared folders on another computer and offline Web pages.

Where it lives: Open the Start menu, choose Programs, choose Accessories, then click on Synchronize.

How to use it: Click on Setup to designate what is to be synchronized. Select the checkbox(es) for the item(s) to synchronize. When you're finished selecting items, click on Synchronize, and you're in business.

On most networks, you're connected to the files you're using all the time, in which case Synchronize isn't used. But if you're not connected all the time — you dial in from the field or you connect to certain files over a WAN (wide-area network) — you will use Synchronize to match up the files you've been working on to the files at the other location.

WordPad

 What it does: WordPad isn't quite as fancy as some of the more expensive word processors on the market. For example, you can't create multiple columns like the ones in newspapers or newsletters, nor can you double-space your reports. But WordPad works fine for letters, simple reports, and other basic documents.

Where it lives: Open the Start menu, choose Programs, choose Accessories, and click on WordPad.

How to use it: Double-click on the WordPad icon, and you're ready to start typing in a new document. Select the word File at the top of the program's window, and a menu tumbles down. Choose Open or Save, depending on your whim.

A dialog box pops up, listing the files in the current folder. Select the name of the file you want to open (click on it) or type the name of a new file. Then select OK. That's it.

✔ If you want to open a file that you spot listed in Windows Explorer or the My Computer window, double-click on the file's name. Windows 2000 Professional yanks the file into the right program and brings both the program and the file to the screen.

✔ You can find more explicit instructions on opening a file in Chapter 6. Folders and equally mind-numbing concepts are browbeaten in Chapter 12.

✔ When you save a file for the first time, you have to choose a name for the file, as well as a folder to put it in. WordPad subsequently remembers the file's name and folder, so you don't have to keep typing the filename each time you save the current version of the file.

✔ WordPad can save files in four different formats: A plain text file known as ASCII, a Word 6 file, a Rich Text Format, or a Unicode Text Document.

✔ Sometimes you'll want to open a file, change parts of it, and save the file with a different name or in a different folder. Choose Save As, not Save, and WordPad then treats your work as if you were saving it for the first time. It asks you to enter a new filename and a new location.

✔ Although you can make up filenames on the fly in WordPad, you can't use WordPad to create new folders. That duty falls to the Windows 2000 Professional Explorer or My Computer programs, which we discuss in Chapter 13.

✔ If you're ditching your typewriter for Windows, remember this: On an electric typewriter, you have to press the Return key at the end of each line or else you start typing off the edge of the paper. Computers, in contrast, are smart enough to sense when words are about to run off the end of the screen. They automatically drop down a line and continue the sentence. (Hip computer nerds call this phenomenon *word wrap.*)

Press Enter only when you finish typing a paragraph and want to start a new one. Press Enter twice to leave a blank line between paragraphs.

✔ WordPad works well for most word processing needs: writing letters, reports, or term papers on somber philosophers with weird last names. Unless you're a lousy speller, you'll find WordPad easy to use, and you'll like its excellent price.

System Tools for the Suspicious

Windows 2000 Professional comes with several technical programs designed to make the nerd feel right at home. Like vitamins and exercise for people, these tools are very useful for keeping your computer healthy and happy. Fortunately, they're all at least as easy to use as the treadmill at the gym.

Backup

What it does: Copies all of your computer's files to another area for safekeeping.

Where it lives: Open the Start menu, choose Accessories, choose System Tools, and click on Backup.

How to use it: Everybody knows they're supposed to make backup copies of their computer's information. The problem is finding the time to do it.

The Windows 2000 Professional Backup program isn't anything really special except in one key area: It can handle long filenames. Because the old-school, DOS-based backup programs can only handle eight-character filenames, they can't make reliable Windows 2000 Professional backups.

Of course, the Backup program comes with one of those ubiquitous wizards, which gently leads you through the process of creating a backup or restoring a previously made backup.

Unless you're just going to back up a few records for your gerbil farm, backing up to floppy disks is not a good idea. Floppy disks hold just under a million and a half pieces of information. Backing up a typical hard drive today would require at least a thousand floppies. No one is *that* worried about their data.

Good backup rules are:

- ✔ For a few files (letters, a spreadsheet or two) use a floppy disk.

- ✔ For a lot of files and documents but not everything on the hard drive, get a Zip drive. Zip disks can hold 100 or 250 Mb of information — enough for every data file you're likely to possess.

- ✔ For an entire computer — backing up all files, programs, everything — get a tape drive. Tape drives can back up many, many gigabytes of information very quickly. You can even use the Windows 2000 Backup program to schedule the backup to run while you're away from the computer, milking the gerbils.

On most company networks, backups are scheduled at regular times and performed over the network by the Administrator. In that case, you won't have a backup device on your computer — except perhaps a floppy drive, which you can use for your most treasured files.

Disk Cleanup

What it does: Windows 2000 accumulates lots of junk — files temporarily grabbed from the Internet to make things run faster, other temporary files created by programs that absentmindedly forgot to remove them later, and other pieces of computer litter. Disk Cleanup sweeps all the junky pieces together so you can get rid of them.

Where it lives: Click on the Start button, choose Programs, choose Accessories, then System Tools, and finally, click on Disk Cleanup.

How to use it: When Disk Cleanup opens, select the hard drive you want to tidy up. Disk Cleanup goes to work looking for those deadbeat files that are just taking up room. After it scans your drive, it reports back with a list of things you can get rid of (see Figure 15-8).

Click on the View Files button if you want to see just what Disk Cleanup is proposing to throw out. Click on the checkbox to remove the check mark for anything you don't want discarded. Click on OK when you want to go ahead with the cleaning.

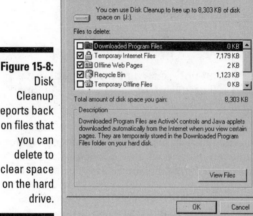

Figure 15-8:
Disk
Cleanup
reports back
on files that
you can
delete to
clear space
on the hard
drive.

✔ Run Disk Cleanup when you need a little more room on your hard drive. You'll know that you need more room when you go to install a new program and the system reports that it needs more space than you have available.

✔ On the More Options page of Disk Cleanup you can have Disk Cleanup look for programs you don't use often (or maybe never), which it will then get rid of (with your approval). This tool is very handy if you inherit a machine from someone. Disk Cleanup can search out the stuff that you'll never use.

Disk Defragmenter

What it does: When a computer reads and writes files on a hard disk, it's as careless as a shoe shopper during the yearly sale at the mall. Files get put into the first place that's handy — files are broken into chunks and scattered every which way. The computer still knows where the files are but picking them up and putting them back in order when you want to use them can be a slow process. Disk Defragmenter reorganizes the hard drive, putting all the files together and organizing them by program and size.

Where it lives: Click on the Start button and choose Programs, then Accessories, then System Tools, and then click on Disk Defragmenter.

How to use it: Open Disk Defragmenter and click on the drive you want to defragment. The program looks at the drive and tells you whether it needs any work. Take the program's advice. (You probably won't have to use the program more than every few months — depending on how much file activity goes on.)

Chapter 16

Talking to Computers Everywhere

- -

In This Chapter

▶ Setting up Outlook Express

▶ Doing the e-mail thing with Outlook Express

▶ Working with newsgroups

▶ Switching identities

▶ Managing a contact list

▶ Setting up Internet Explorer

▶ Exploring the Internet (and intranet)

- -

*W*hen it comes right down to it, work is rarely very exciting in an office cubicle because you're seeing the same ol' things, over and over. Excluding those lunches out, the new blond sales manager, and the latest Dilbert cartoon — things can get downright dull.

However, Windows 2000 comes to the rescue with features that not only help you get your job done but can also perk up your day. Outlook Express, the Windows 2000 mail and news reading program, lets you plan exciting lunches and discuss Dilbert's most recent sociopolitical statement; plus, a mountain of trendy stuff is available for you to explore on the Internet.

This chapter shows you how to open some of the doors in Windows 2000 and start talking to the people on the other side. But be forewarned: This stuff can be downright complicated. Until you learn how to open and close the right computerized doors at the right time, don't be surprised if you find yourself with a few bumps and bruises.

Installing Internet mail is really easy, but you have to follow tons of steps. So if the sight of oodles of installation steps makes you feel a little queasy, politely ask the Network Administrator for help. That's what he's paid for.

Setting Up E-Mail

This section is for those unable to con the Network Administrator into setting up your e-mail. When asked, he just shoved a ratty piece of paper at you and said (with or without an evil glint), "Here's all you need. You're on your own, kid."

Well, you can show *him*. Just hold onto that piece of paper and follow these steps:

1. **Double-click the Outlook Express icon on the Quick Launch section of the taskbar.**

2. **The first window (see Figure 16-1) asks for your name. Type it in and click Next.**

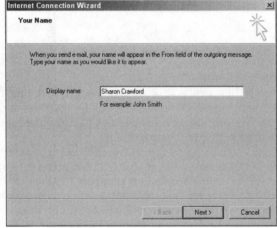

Figure 16-1:
Enter your
name,
which
appears on
your
outgoing
messages,
in this box.

This is the name that displays as the sender of your messages.

3. **In the next window, type in your e-mail address and click Next.**

Your Network Administrator provides you with this information. Most likely, it'll be the same as your Windows 2000 Professional logon name with an @ sign and then the company name and an Internet extension like com or net or org. If you want to set up a new mail account, see the next section "Getting a New (Free) Account."

4. **This next window (see Figure 16-2) is all the stuff that your network administrator provides. Fill in the information and click Next.**

The type and names of the mail servers is not something you can find out except from another person — the Network Administrator, the Internet service provider, or some other user on the network (one with a geeky bent).

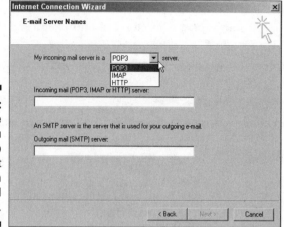

Figure 16-2:
Some of the
stuff you
need to
know to set
up your own
e-mail
account.

5. **Enter your logon name and password for this e-mail account. Click Next.**

   On a well-run network, your e-mail logon name and password should be the same as your network logon name and password. If they are not, please don't quote our book to the network administrator — just enter the e-mail name and password you've been assigned. If you're not on a network, you chose the e-mail logon name and password when you signed up with the Internet service provider.

   Outlook Express can now connect to your Internet mail account to send and receive mail. If you need to change (or just check) any of the information you entered, choose Tools and then Accounts from the Outlook Express menu to open the Internet Accounts dialog box, highlight the account name, and click the Properties button.

Getting a New (Free) Account

Hotmail is a company that pioneered free Internet e-mail accounts. Microsoft bought them up in 1999, which is why you get the option right in the operating system of setting up a Hotmail e-mail account.

If you already have an e-mail account, you can still have a separate Hotmail (or other account) because Outlook Express supports multiple identities — which simply means that you can collect mail from more than one place.

To set up Hotmail with Outlook Express, follow these steps:

1. **Double-click the Outlook Express icon on the Quick Launch portion of the taskbar.**

2. **Click the Tools menu and choose Accounts.**

3. **In the Internet Accounts box, click the Add button and select Mail from the popup menu.**

   The next window that appears — the Internet Connection Wizard — is the same as the one shown in Figure 16-1.

4. **Type in your name and click Next.**

5. **If you already have a Hotmail account, fill in your e-mail address. Otherwise click on the button for setting up a new account.**

6. **Follow the rest of the steps using the Setup Hotmail Account wizard (see Figure 16-3).**

   When you finish, you see that Hotmail has been added to your Outlook Express In Box. Clicking on it shows you your Hotmail folders.

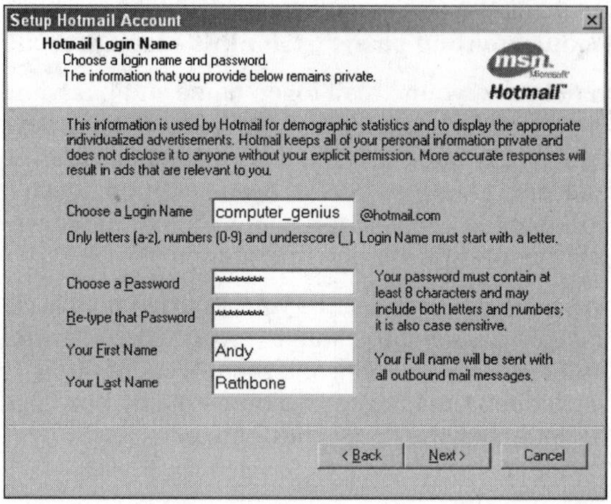

Figure 16-3: Getting a free e-mail account is easy through Outlook Express.

The advantage of an Internet mail account is that you can check your mail from any place where you can get Internet access. Lots of airport kiosks and other places where business travelers congregate have Internet connections and, if you have a Hotmail account, you just go to www.hotmail.com and sign in using your account name and password.

✔ Identities and their uses are covered in the section "No Identity Crisis Here," later in the chapter.

✔ Using Internet Explorer to poke around the Internet is in the "Internet Explorer" section, even later in the chapter.

✔ Hotmail isn't the only free e-mail fish in the sea. Other companies offering free e-mail accounts are sprouting up all over Internet. Some can be used with Outlook Express (though they can be complicated to set up) and others only with a Web browser.

Getting on the Outlook Express

When you're working with Outlook Express, you have a choice: You can work online (remain connected to the Internet at all times), or offline. Working online is probably the better choice if you have a direct connection to the Internet or if you're not worried about tying up a phone line (the one the modem uses to connect to your Internet service provider).

If you work online, your mail is dispatched the second you send it and you have instant access to newsgroups. On the other hand, if you're using your laptop away from work, you're probably better off doing your reading and writing offline and then connecting to send all your messages at once. Working offline saves money on your phone bill.

Doing the Outlook Express Mail Thing

E-mail is the life-blood of many, many companies. It's essential for communication with clients, customers, suppliers and co-workers. Plus, it's excellent for keeping in touch with your fantasy baseball league, not to mention cousins in Pittsburgh or Potsdam.

Filling up your Address Book

When you want to send a postal letter to your Uncle Swifty, you need an address that might include the cellblock number and definitely a zip code. Sending e-mail requires an address, too — just as strange looking, though you don't need a zip code.

The easiest way to address an e-mail is by using the handy Address Book. The Address Book stores all your favorite e-mail addresses — friends, family, business associates, and incarcerated uncles — and protects you from having to remember and retype long e-mail addresses.

To add an address to your Address Book, follow these steps:

1. **Double-click the Outlook Express icon on the Quick Launch portion of the taskbar.**

2. **Click the Addresses button to open the Address Book.**

3. **Click the New button and select New Contact.**

   The Properties box opens as shown in Figure 16-4.

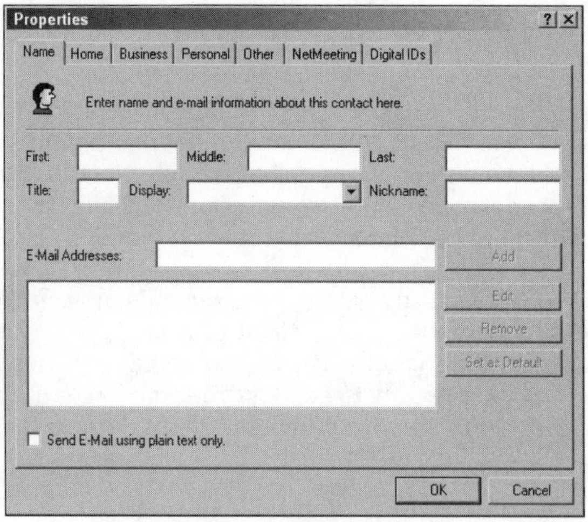

Figure 16-4:
Adding a
name and
address to
the Outlook
Express
Address
Book.

4. **Click the Name tab if it's not already showing and fill in the name and e-mail address. Click on OK.**

   You can also click any of the other tabs and fill in additional information, such as this person's home and business contact information, personal preferences, birthday, anniversary, conferencing information — Outlook Express now lets you keep closer track of your contacts than you'll probably ever want to.

Add other names and addresses to the Address Book by repeating Steps 3 and 4. When you're done, close the Address Book by clicking the button with the X in the upper-right-hand corner of the window.

Sending messages

To send a message in Outlook Express, do the following:

1. **Double-click on the Outlook Express button on the taskbar.**

2. **Click the New Mail button.**

   You now see a blank New Message screen. In the To window, you can type in an e-mail address or click the little Address Book icon to the left to pick a name from your Address Book.

3. **Type in a subject and then a message in the main window, as shown in Figure 16-5.**

Figure 16-5:
When typing
a message,
whatever
is in the
subject line
becomes
the title
of the
message.

4. **Click the Send button.**

   If you're working online, your message spends a brief moment in the Outbox folder, then goes on its merry way. If you're working offline, you may see a dialog box telling you that the message you just typed will be placed in your Outbox folder so it will be ready to send the next time you choose the Send and Receive command.

Receiving messages

When you open Outlook Express, the way Internet mail is delivered to you depends on whether your Internet connection is a dial-up connection or a direct connection. Either way, you can go get your mail when you want it, or you can have it done automatically.

With an automatic connection, when you open your mail program it queries your Internet mail server at once and then as often as you specify thereafter. An automatic connection through the network is done almost instantaneously, and nothing appears to be happening until the mail pops up in your Inbox. If you use a dial-up connection to connect automatically, your mail program opens the phone line, dials your Internet service provider, connects to your mailbox at the Internet service provider, and then puts any messages in your Inbox.

Getting your incoming mail with Outlook Express really couldn't be easier. If you're already online, click the Outlook Express button on the Taskbar and then click Send/Recv. Outlook Express then checks the mail server to see if you have any new messages.

Reading messages

To read a message in your Inbox, just double-click on the message from the list, and the message opens in a window.

If you want to know what any of the buttons mean, just position your pointer over one, and a descriptive box pops open.

If you're used to getting Internet e-mail using other software, you'll notice that Outlook Express shows only the name of the person sending you the mail with no clue as to where it came from. If you want to see all the gruesome details for a message you have open — also known as the Internet header — click the File menu, choose Properties, and then click on the Details tab.

Replying to messages

Sometimes you receive a message that you'd like to answer without having to retype the recipient's messy e-mail address. This is exactly what the Reply button is for. Select the message you'd like to reply to in the Inbox, and then click Reply. You should see something that looks like Figure 16-6.

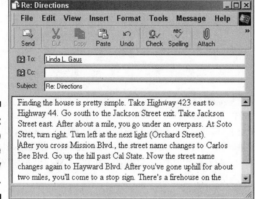

Figure 16-6:
Replying to a message is as easy as can be.

If the original message was sent to more than one person (you can tell by looking at the original message's To: and Cc: line) and you want to reply to everyone, use the Reply All button.

Forwarding messages

Other times, you receive a message that you want to share with someone else. You can forward the message (well, really a copy of the message since the original stays with you) by clicking the Forward button.

This action opens a window that displays the original message and gives you the opportunity to add your own comments, as shown in Figure 16-7.

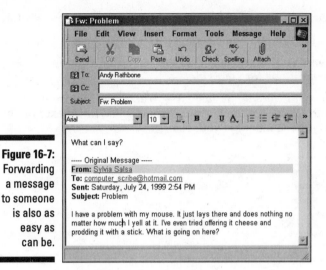

Figure 16-7:
Forwarding
a message
to someone
is also as
easy as
can be.

From this screen, you can send your forwarded message directly on its way
by specifying the recipient in the To: box and then clicking the Send button
or choosing Send from the File menu. Alternatively, you can specify the recipient and then add your own text to the message by clicking in the text
window and typing whatever you have to say. When you're done, send the
message as you usually would.

Printing messages

Some messages are just too important to entrust entirely to your computer,
so sometimes you may want to print out an e-mail message you've received
(or even one you've sent). To print an e-mail message in Outlook Express,
click on the message you'd like to print, then click the Print button. Set the
print options on the Print page if necessary, and click Print.

Setting rules for your messages

These days you can get so much electronic mail that important messages can
get lost in the crowd. Outlook Express can sort messages into folders, add
color highlighting to messages from particular people, automatically reply to
or forward messages, and more. Let's say you want to be sure not to overlook
any new messages from your pal Alan at the Federal Reserve Bank. You can
configure Outlook Express to display his messages in a prominent fashion:

1. **Double-click the Outlook Express icon on the taskbar.**

2. **Click the Tools menu, choose Message Rules, and then choose Mail.**

   This summons the New Mail Rule screen.

3. **In the Conditions section (section 1) at the top of the window, select one or more conditions for your rule.**

   Figure 16-8 shows the first item selected — Where The From Line Contains People. Check out the bottom section called Rule Description to see a spelled-out summary of your rule.

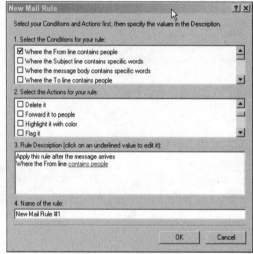

4. **In the second section (Actions), select one or more actions for what you want the rule to do.**

   The action(s) you specify here determine how Outlook Express handles messages that meet the condition(s). In this case, check the box next to Highlight It With Color.

5. **Next click on the highlighted Contains People field in the Rule Description section (section 3) to provide the specifics for the rule.**

   Thus far you've just given the program general information — now you have to tell it whose messages you want handled. When you click Contains People, the Select People dialog box opens.

6. **Type in the e-mail address (or addresses) — or get them from the Address Book — for the people you want covered by the rule and click Add. When you finish entering e-mail addresses (see Figure 16-9), click OK.**

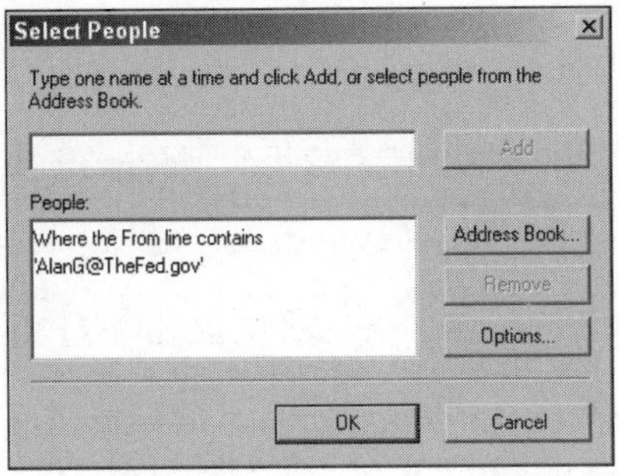

Figure 16-9:
Adding the
names of
people
whose
messages
will be
covered by
your rule.

7. **Back in the New Mail Rule dialog box, click any other highlighted items in the Rule Description section and provide the specifics in the box that appears.**

   For our example, click the highlighted field labeled Color. This opens a dialog box where you can choose what color you want your pal's messages to display in. Click a choice and then OK.

8. **Type in a name for your rule in the Name Of The Rule section and click OK.**

   Your new rule is now listed in the Message Rules box (see Figure 16-10). This is where you go to create, delete or modify rules. You can make rules to apply to mail or to newsgroups or both.

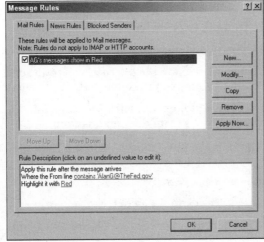

Figure 16-10:
Change or
add rules
to sort
your mail.

Newsgroups

Newsgroups are kind of like giant bulletin boards in cyberspace; they are collections of messages, grouped by subject, that are posted by individuals to a common computer, called a news server. Newsgroups exist for every conceivable topic (and many inconceivable ones!). Once you look, you'll be amazed what you find, whether your interests tend toward the exotic or the mundane.

Outlook Express is your gateway to the wide world of newsgroups. As long as you have Outlook Express and a link to one or more news servers (ask your Network Administrator if you're not sure about the news server part), you're in business.

In the following sections, you find out how to find newsgroups, subscribe to them, and download, read, manage, reply to, and post newsgroup messages. These operations sound as if they should involve a lot of steps, but actually Outlook Express makes working with newsgroups easy, so don't despair.

How to add a news server

Before you can start exploring newsgroups, you need to make sure that Outlook Express can communicate with a news server. News servers almost always have the word *news* in their name and your Network Administrator or Internet service provider can provide you with the information you need. To make the connection to the news server, follow these steps:

1. **Double-click the Outlook Express icon on the Taskbar.**

2. **Click the Tools menu and choose Accounts.**

   If you have a direct connection to the Internet, you're all set. If you use a dial-up connection, make sure you're connected to your service provider.

3. **In the Internet Accounts dialog box, click the News tab. Then click the Add button and select News from the pop-up menu.**

   This opens a window — the Internet Connection Wizard — that looks just like the one back in Figure 16-1!

4. **Fill in your name and click Next.**

5. **Fill in your e-mail address and then click Next again.**

6. **Fill in the name of your news server (see Figure 16-11) and click Next one more time.**

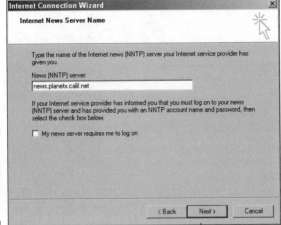

Figure 16-11:
Filling in the
name of
your news
server.

Again, your Network Administrator or Internet service provider can provide you with this information.

After you click the Close button, you see a dialog box asking whether you'd like to download the list of newsgroups available on your news server. If you would (and you have to do this at some point before you begin working with newsgroups), click Yes. This downloading can take quite a while, especially if your news server carries a lot of newsgroups, so sit back and relax until it's done. The good news is that you won't have to do this again. If you'd rather not download the list of newsgroups from the news server now, click No and you can do it later on.

Finding newsgroups

Given the astronomical number of newsgroups out there, how can you find anything in the mess? Outlook Express has a handy-dandy search function that lets you look for specific words in newsgroup names. Here's what you need to do to find the perfect newsgroup(s):

1. **Double-click the Outlook Express icon on the taskbar.**

2. **Click on the entry for the news server in your folders list, and then click the button labeled Newsgroups.**

   This opens the Newsgroup Subscriptions screen shown in Figure 16-12.

3. **In the Display Newsgroups Which Contain box, type the word(s) you want to search for.**

   For example, if you're interested in food (and who isn't) type **food** in the box and a long list appears of newsgroups with food in the title.

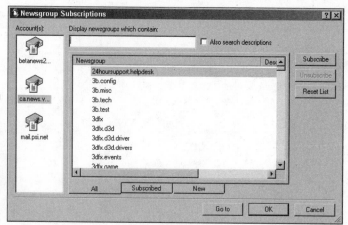

Figure 16-12:
All the possible newsgroups are listed on the All page.

If you can't find a specific newsgroup that you heard about somewhere, it's possible that your news server doesn't carry it. Once again, consult your all-knowing Network Administrator, who may refer your question to your Internet service provider.

Subscribing to a newsgroup

Subscribing to a newsgroup that suits your interests may seem like a big step, but it's actually not a big deal; it doesn't cost anything and you can unsubscribe at any time. To subscribe to a newsgroup, follow Steps 1 through 3 in the "Finding newsgroups" section and then select the entry for the news-group you'd like to subscribe to and click Subscribe. Click OK to clear the Newsgroup Subscriptions screen and you're all set.

Subscribing just means that the newsgroup will be listed in your list of fold-ers in Outlook Express, so you don't have to go looking for it in the full list of newsgroups every time.

Downloading newsgroup messages

Now it's time to download some newsgroup messages so that you can read and reply to them. Here are the steps you need to follow:

1. **Double-click the Outlook Express icon on the Taskbar**

2. **Click on the entry for the news server.**

   You see the name of any newsgroup(s) you've subscribed to just under-neath the entry for your news server.

3. **Click the Settings button and indicate what (if anything) you'd like Outlook Express to download to your computer.**

   - **Don't Synchronize:** Specifies that no newsgroup messages or headers should be downloaded.

   - **All Messages:** Downloads every message that has ever been posted to the newsgroup you've subscribed to. Use this command with caution. Especially if you've chosen a high-traffic newsgroup, you may find yourself overwhelmed with messages. Most people choose All Messages only once; thereafter they use New Messages Only to keep current.

   - **New Messages Only:** Downloads all messages that have been posted to the newsgroup(s) you've subscribed to since the last time you checked. Use this option to keep abreast of what's going on in your favorite newsgroup(s).

   - **Headers Only:** Downloads just the message headers for the news-groups you've subscribed to. The advantage of this option is that it enables you to quickly scan for the postings that really interest you.

4. **Click the Synchronize Account button.**

   Now Outlook Express goes ahead and downloads messages (or parts of messages, if you selected Headers Only in Step 2) to your computer.

Reading newsgroup messages

Reading newsgroup messages really couldn't be simpler; once you've down-loaded messages or message headers from one or more newsgroup(s), click on the entry for a newsgroup in the Folders list, then double-click on a particular message (the messages are listed on the right side of the screen) to open it.

Replying to newsgroup messages

If you're reading a message and you'd like to put in your own two cents, you can click the Reply Group button to post a message to the newsgroup.

Or you can use just the Reply button and your message goes to the person who posted the message you're reading as e-mail.

✔ Note that Outlook Express quotes the message you're replying to by default. If you wish, you can delete part or all of the original text, but make sure you leave enough of it that other people reading the news-group messages will know exactly what you're responding to.

✔ In any newsgroup, make sure you read the group postings for a while before you send a message to the group. Newsgroups are ongoing institutions, each with its own style and traditions. If you simply jump in and ask questions, veteran members will treat you like a loud child in a fancy restaurant — someone to be either ignored or reprimanded.

✔ Many newsgroups have a document called a *FAQ* (Frequently Asked Questions). If you read the group for a while, you'll find out where this document is available. If you read the FAQ before posting, you'll learn what this particular newsgroup's traditions and rules are.

Getting rid of messages you've read

At some point, perhaps sooner rather than later, you may find that your newsgroup habit is taking up too much space on your computer. That means it's time to get rid of newsgroup messages you've already read. Do these things to clean up your act:

1. **Double-click the Outlook Express icon on the taskbar.**

2. **Click the Tools menu and choose Options.**

   The Options box appears, complete with its many tabs.

3. **Click the Maintenance tab and then the Clean Up Now button.**

   This opens the Local File Clean Up window, where you can specify exactly what needs cleaning.

4. **Click the Browse button, make a selection, and click OK.**

   On the Outlook Express screen, select an entry for a news server (if you want to clean up messages from all newsgroups you subscribe to on that server) or an entry for a particular newsgroup (if you only want to clean up messages from this newsgroup).

5. **Choose an option on the Local File Clean Up screen and click the appropriate button. Click Yes to confirm your selection.**

   • **Remove Messages:** Use this option if you'd like to delete the bodies of newsgroup messages only; it leaves the message headers on your computer so you can always go back and find a message that interests you.

   • **Delete:** This option is the more drastic of the two; it removes message bodies and headers too, so if you're sure you're done with the messages in question, try it.

6. **Click Close and then OK to clear the Options box.**

No Identity Crisis Here

Although they may sound like something you'd hear about on "America's Most Wanted," identities are actually no more than a convenient way for several people to share a single computer. Identities may suit you well if you're forced to share your computer at the office, or even if you share your home computer with the kids, because identities allow each person to use Outlook Express to check their own e-mail and maintain an individual contact list.

Adding a new identity

To add a new identity in Outlook Express, follow these steps:

1. **Double-click the Outlook Express icon on the taskbar.**
2. **Click the File menu and choose Identities and then New Identity.**

   This opens the New Identity screen shown in Figure 16-13.

Figure 16-13:
Create a
new identity
if you're
sharing a
computer
with some-
one else.

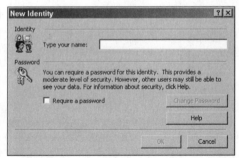

3. **Type your name in the box, and check the Require A Password box if you want to keep your new identity secure.**

   If you've checked the Require A Password box, you need to type your password twice on the Enter Password box, and then click OK.

4. **Click OK to create your new identity.**

   At this point, Outlook Express asks you whether you'd like to switch to your new identity. If you do, click Yes; otherwise, click No. Because you haven't connected to the Internet using this identity before, you'll see the Internet Connection Wizard. Feed it the information it requires, and then you're all set.

If you're working with an alternate (not your Main) identity, the Outlook Express title bar indicates which identity you're currently working with.

Managing identities

If you've created multiple identities, there may come a time when you need to change, add, or remove an identity. Here's what you need to do:

1. **Click the Outlook Express button on the taskbar.**

2. **Click the File menu and then choose Identities and then Manage Identities.**

   This opens the Manage Identities screen (see Figure 16-14), which is command central for adding, changing, and removing identities on your computer.

Figure 16-14:
Manage
your various
identities
here.

3. **To change an identity's properties, select the identity in question and click Properties. Make your changes to the identity and click OK.**

   If this identity requires a password, you must type the password in here before you're allowed to make any changes. In the Properties box, you can change how your name is displayed and the password, if one is required.

4. **To remove an identity, select the identity in question and click Remove. Click Yes to confirm the deletion, or click No to change your mind.**

5. **To add a new identity, click New.**

Outlook Express is pretty good at keeping the various identities separate. Each identity sets his or her own mail and newsgroup options.

Use the Manage Identities dialog box to establish a default identity — the identity used each time you open Outlook Express — by simply placing a check in the box labeled Use This Identity When Starting A Program. Then choose your default identity from the drop-down list. If you don't set a default identity, you'll be asked what identity to use each time you open Outlook Express.

What If My Outlook Isn't Expressed?

You can send and receive mail a lot of different ways. If your network is using a program other than Outlook Express, then the mail instructions in this chapter won't do you a lot of good. The Network Administrator (or more likely, one of your co-workers) will have to brief you on how your particular system works.

Getting Started with Internet Explorer

The Internet Explorer icon is the little doohickey on the Desktop that looks like a big "e" with a ring around it. Internet Explorer is the Microsoft browser, which you can use to navigate the World Wide Web on the Internet and on what's known as an intranet — Web pages that are published on your own network.

Internet, intranet, what's the deal?

The Internet is a worldwide network of networks, connected by different kinds of high-speed data transmission lines. Your company's network may be connected to the Internet by means of modems or by being one of the networks that make up the Internet. Or, if you're not part of the techno-elite, you may not be connected to the Internet at all.

An *intranet*, by contrast, is a network that uses Internet technology (specifically Web technology) to share information. Usually when people say intranet, they mean that the "inside" network uses Web pages.

If you have an intranet, you can use Internet Explorer to visit the Web pages on your network. Internet Explorer can also view Web pages on the Internet. If all of this sounds potentially confusing — it is. The difference between internal information and external information can become very, very cloudy.

This, fortunately, is the problem of the Network Administrator and not yours. However, the administrator's solution may affect how Internet Explorer works for you and how it looks.

Connecting to the Internet

You can connect to the Internet in two ways these days: you can use a so-called direct connection, which means that the entire network your computer is on is connected to the Internet, or you can use a modem to dial up an Internet service provider. Check with your trusty Network Administrator to find out which scenario applies to you. Actually, once you're connected, it hardly matters which way you do things; Internet Explorer walks and talks the same regardless of which kind of connection you're using.

Using Internet Explorer

If you've been living in a cave for years and haven't heard of "the Web," you're probably better off. That way you don't have to unlearn all the harder ways of using browsers and can just enjoy using Internet Explorer. So, brush off those cobwebs and step a little closer.

Firing it up

To run Internet Explorer, double-click on the Internet Explorer button on the taskbar. Figure 16-15 shows the default opening screen — this is the screen that Internet Explorer goes to unless someone has changed the settings. Don't be alarmed if it doesn't look just this way on your computer. Even if the address is the same, Web pages are changed more often than a new baby.

The basic method for using Internet Explorer is to point and click; that is, you point it at a site you'd like to visit, and you're off. To point Internet Explorer at a particular site, click in the Address box and type the Internet address (Uniform Resource Locator or *URL*) of the site you want to visit and press Enter. For example, you can type www.dummies.com in the Address box and you end up at the World Wide Web home page for Dummies Press.

If you connect to Web pages on your local network, you need only type in the name of a local Web server.

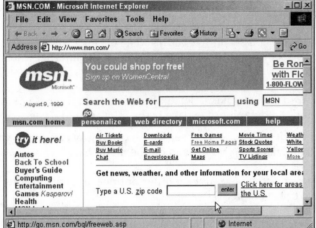

Figure 16-15:
The opening
screen for
a newly
installed,
networked
Internet
Explorer.

Internet Explorer bars and buttons

At the top of the Internet Explorer window, you see the usual bars and buttons. Turning them on and off is pretty easy. Right-click on the menu bar to see a little pop-up menu for the various bars.

The Standard buttons are on the toolbar directly under the menu bar. If you want to see which ones they are, right-click on a blank spot on the menu bar and select Standard buttons. Whoops! They're gone. Right-click on the menu bar and click Standard buttons again. Voila! They're back.

The lesson here is that a check mark before an item on a menu means that item is ON. Click the item and the check mark goes away and the item is OFF.

✔ The Address Bar is the next bar down — below the Standard buttons.

✔ Links are connections to Internet sites. If you display the Links bar, choose Customize Links to add the Web sites you want.

✔ Using the Radio bar to listen to radio stations from all over the world is covered in Chapter 18.

Right-click any button bar that's showing and select Customize. In the dialog box that opens, you can choose what buttons to include on the button bar.

Setting up a home

Just as your television set always shows some channel when you turn it on, your Web browser always shows some portion of the Internet when you start it. The part that shows when you start Internet Explorer is called your home page.

> ✔ Every Web browser has a default home page. In the case of Internet Explorer, the default home page is the Microsoft MSN network.
>
> ✔ When you feel lost and homesick, you can always return to your home page by clicking the Home icon on the menu bar.

To specify your home page and set other options such as browser colors and fonts, follow these steps:

1. **Open Internet Explorer by double-clicking on the Internet Explorer icon on the taskbar.**

2. **Click the Tools menu and choose Internet Options.**

   This opens the Internet Options box (see Figure 16-16), where you can tell Internet Explorer where "home" is, fiddle with colors, and change other settings.

Figure 16-16:
Internet Explorer's Internet Options page lets you "furnish" your home as you please.

3. **Type the address of the page you'd like to use as your home page into the Address box in the Home Page area of the General tab. Alternatively, you can click one of the buttons in the Home Page area to set your home page.**

Here's the lowdown on what the buttons do:

- **Use Current:** To use this option, you need to point Internet Explorer to the page you'd like to make your home, and then click the button.

- **Use Default:** This option automatically makes the Microsoft Network home page (`www.msn.com`) your home page.

- **Use Blank:** This option makes your home like an apartment you've just moved into; your home page is a blank screen, as the button's name implies.

4. **If you want to tinker with your browser's colors, fonts, or languages, use the buttons at the bottom of the General tab.**

If you're bound and determined to decorate your home in your own style, here's what the buttons do:

- **Color:** Click this button to change the colors used to display the text and background of Web pages and the colors used to designate visited and unvisited links. The default color schemes work quite well for most of us; if you get really carried away here you may end up with something you can't read, so be a little careful.

- **Fonts:** Click this button if you're not satisfied with the default font for Web pages and documents where a text font isn't specified. Again, you may have regrets if you choose something really weird, so we advise sticking to trusty ol' TimesNewRoman, an eminently readable text font.

- **Languages:** If you're a multilingual user of Internet Explorer, this option may make your life a little nicer. It enables you to see Web pages that offer content in something other than U.S. English in the language(s) you specify; you can even indicate the order of priority in which the languages should be treated.

- **Accessibility:** Danger! Leave the default settings on this screen alone (everything should be unchecked), otherwise strange things may occur.

5. **When you're done decorating your home, click OK to clear the Internet Options screen.**

Leave the Temporary Internet files area of the General tab alone; messing with these options can only complicate your life. While we're at it, we advise you to leave the History area of the General tab alone too; we get to what it does shortly, so for now, don't touch.

Playing favorites

Internet Explorer's Favorites list can save you a lot of work since it lets you "remember" the location of Web pages you've seen and liked. In this section, you find out how to add a page to your Favorites list and how to keep your Favorites list organized.

To add a page to your Favorites list, do these things:

1. **Open Internet Explorer by double-clicking on the Internet Explorer icon on the taskbar.**

2. **Point Internet Explorer to the page you want to add.**

3. **Click the Favorites button and then the Add button.**

   If you just want to add an entry for this page to your Favorites list and be done with it, click OK. If, however, you think you might like to see this page even when you're not logged onto the Internet, check the box labeled Make Available Offline, and then click OK.

To organize your Favorites list, follow these steps:

1. **Open Internet Explorer by double-clicking on the Internet Explorer icon on the taskbar.**

2. **Click the Favorites button and then the Organize button.**

   This opens the Organize Favorites screen shown in Figure 16-17. Use the four buttons here to sort your Favorites into categories; you can create folders and move Favorites into them, rename Favorites, and delete Favorites.

   Note that if you highlight the entry for a particular Favorite, you can choose to make it available offline (or not) by checking or unchecking the Make Available Offline box.

If you pull down the Favorites menu and look down below the Add Favorites and Organize Favorites options, you notice a whole slew of pre-programmed Favorites. Feel free to organize these Favorites as you wish; if you find them annoying, you can delete the ones you don't want hanging around.

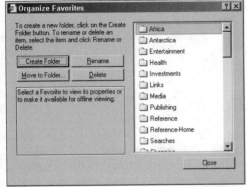

Figure 16-17:
Here's
where you
can keep
your
Favorites
organized.

History repeating itself

Although it sounds like something grander, Internet Explorer's History list is nothing more than a list of Web sites you've visited recently. Like the Favorites list, however, the History list may serve you in good stead; if there's a site you visited recently but forgot to add to your Favorites list, you can probably find it on the History list.

To make History repeat itself, follow these steps:

1. **Open Internet Explorer by double-clicking on the Internet Explorer icon on the taskbar.**

2. **Click the History button.**

   Here you see a list of folders named for dates (today, yesterday, and so on), each of which contains a list of the site(s) you visited on that day.

3. **Search through all these folders and click the site you're looking for.**

   You can also make your life easy and use the Search function. Click the Search button in the History box, type whatever you're looking for into the Search For box, and click Search Now. Voilà — if you see the site you're looking for, simply click it to go there.

4. **If you want to see History from a different perspective, click the View button on the History box and choose how you'd like to see the list displayed.**

   You can choose from four options: By Date, By Site, By Most Visited, or By Order Visited Today.

5. **When you'd like to make History history, click the X box in the upper-right corner of the History window to close it.**

By default, Internet Explorer keeps items on the History list for 20 days. If you'd like to keep items there for a longer or shorter time, click the Tools menu and choose Internet Options. Change the number in the History area of the General tab to suit your taste, or click Clear History to wipe the slate clean.

Searching, searching

The bad news about having access to so much information out there in cyberspace is that sometimes it seems like you'll never be able to find what you want. The good news is that Internet Explorer comes with a powerful set of search functions that can help you find nearly anyone or anything. In this section, we show you how to go looking for that Web page, person, business, or map that's been eluding you.

To search for something on the Internet, do these things:

1. **Open Internet Explorer by double-clicking on the Internet Explorer icon on the taskbar.**

2. **Click the Search button.**

   This opens the Search screen (see Figure 16-18). At this point, you have a choice of searching four different ways or repeating a search you've already done. Here's a brief guide to the options on the Search screen:

   - **Find Web Page:** This option can help you find Web page(s) that contain whatever term you type into the Find A Web Page Containing box.

   - **Find a person's address:** If you're looking for a long-lost friend, this is the option for you. You can search for someone's mailing address or e-mail address by selecting the appropriate item from the Search For drop-down list, then typing in as much information about the person as you have (First Name, Last Name, City, State/Province).

   - **Find a business:** Use this option to search by business name or category (choose which from the Search For drop-down list), then type in as much information about the business as you have (Business name, City, State/Province).

   - **Previous searches:** You can save yourself some work by using this option if you've already run a search that you'd like to re-run. To re-run a particular search, just click on its link.

   - **Find a map:** With this option, you can locate a map of almost anywhere. Search for an Address or Place or Landmark by choosing the appropriate item from the Search For drop-down list, then type in as much relevant information as you have (City, State/Province, Zip/Postal Code).

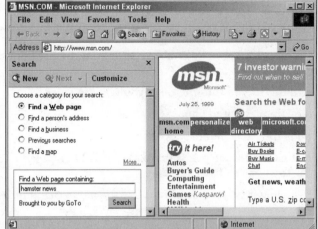

Figure 16-18:
Search can help you find whatever (or whoever) you're looking for.

When you're through searching, click the X in the upper-right corner of the Search screen to close it.

Web browsing offline

If you're a laptop user who's far from home or if you have another reason to be concerned about tying up the phone line you use to connect to the Internet, Web browsing offline is tailor-made for you. This section shows you the basics of using Internet Explorer to look at Web content offline.

Accessing items on your Favorites list

To make an item on your Favorites list available offline, do these things:

1. **Open Internet Explorer by double-clicking on the Internet Explorer icon on the taskbar.**

2. **Click the Favorites button and select Organize.**

   This opens the Organize Favorites window shown back in Figure 16-17.

3. **Click the entry for the page you want to view offline and click on the Make Available Offline checkbox.**

   If you really want to get fancy, click Properties and you can specify the schedule for updating this page and indicate how much content to download (text only, text and pictures, and so on).

Saving Web pages for offline viewing

To save a Web page to your computer for later viewing, follow these steps:

1. **Open Internet Explorer by double-clicking on the Internet Explorer icon on the taskbar.**

2. **Click around 'til you find the page you want to save.**

3. **Click the File menu and choose Save As.**

   This opens the Save Web Page As box.

4. **Double-click the folder you want to save this Web page in. Type a name for the page in the File name box.**

   If you're feeling lazy, you can always use the name that Internet Explorer suggests.

5. **Select a type for the file in the Save As Type box.**

   There are three options here that you should consider: Web page, complete; Web Page, HTML only; and Text Only.

   - **Web Page, complete:** This option saves all of the Web page, from text to pictures.

   - **Web Page, HTML only:** If you choose this option, you save the information on the page, but not the graphics, sound, or other files.

   - **Text Only:** This option does exactly what its name implies; it saves just the text of the page in question.

6. **Click OK.**

Viewing Web pages offline

To view Web pages offline, do this:

1. **Before you disconnect from the Internet, click the Tools menu, and choose Synchronize.**

   This updates the information on the Web page(s) in question before it's too late.

2. **Click the File menu and choose Work Offline.**

   This disconnects you from the Internet.

3. **Open up your Favorites list and click the item you want to view.**

   You see the Web page in all its glory so you can study its content without worrying about your phone bill or whether you might miss an important incoming call.

Part IV

Been There, Done That: Quick References for Moving to Windows 2000 Professional

The 5th Wave   By Rich Tennant

"BETTER CALL MIS AND TELL THEM ONE OF OUR NETWORKS HAS GONE BAD."

In this part . . .

*C*hanging from one operating system to another is like moving into a new house and trying to find the bathroom in the dark. Until you get used to the floor plan, you'll be stubbing your toe now and again. After you figure out where things are, that sense of bafflement disappears, and you can relax. This part of the book is for folks who may have spent some time in the house of Windows NT or even Windows 95 or Windows 98. The floor plan is very similar in Windows 2000 — we just tip you off to where the light switches are.

Chapter 17

Getting My Pro to Look Like My Old Windows

. . . .

In This Chapter

▶ Bringing back Program Manager

▶ Getting rid of menus that fade

▶ Seeing every item on the menu

▶ Finding the Briefcase

▶ Locating Windows Explorer

. . . .

Some of your old favorites from earlier versions of Windows NT are either gone or not as prominent in Windows 2000 Professional. For example, Windows NT 3.51 and Windows 3.11 both used Program Manager, which Windows has shunned since Windows NT 4. Sure, Windows 2000 provides replacements that work very well, but some people still like their dial phones and standard transmissions.

Luckily for the antique collectors, Windows 2000 still comes with hidden versions of Program Manager and File Manager.

Also, Windows 2000 Professional adds some dazzling visual effects that you may find less than thrilling. This chapter shows you how to turn off the glitter and recover some old Windows favorites too.

Where Did My Program Manager Go?

Windows NT 4 dumped Program Manager (used in Windows NT 3.51 and Windows 3.11) in favor of the Start menu, which pops up when you click on the Start button. And after you scratch your head (and play with the Start thing for about 15 minutes), the similarities between the Start menu and Program Manager start to appear.

For example, Program Manager lets you organize your programs in separate Program Group windows. The Windows 2000 Start menu organizes programs in separate folders branching out from the menu's Programs listing.

But if you prefer the old-style Program Manager for starting programs — or you want to use Program Manager until you grow more accustomed to Windows 2000 — here's how to rev the ol' program back up:

1. **Click on the Start button and choose Run from the menu.**

   A box pops up, asking you to type the name of a program you want to run.

2. **Type** PROGMAN **into the Open box and click on the OK button.**

   After you click on the OK button, Program Manager appears, as shown in Figure 17-1.

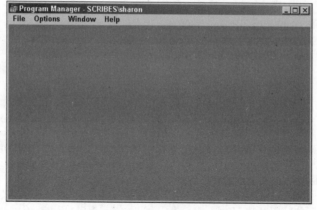

Figure 17-1: The Program Manager in Windows 2000 can look embarrassingly different from the one used in Windows NT.

Be prepared for a few adjustments, however. First, Program Manager is wearing Windows 2000 clothing. In fact, it may not have any windows or icons at all, as shown in Figure 17-1. Minimized Program Groups stack themselves along the screen's bottom like cigars in a box, and the Tiling and Cascading features don't work very well.

✔ If your Program Manager doesn't have any windows or icons, you have to add them yourself: Open Program Manager's File menu, choose New, click on Personal Program Group, and click on the OK button. Type a description for your new Program Group window into the Description box and click on OK. Voilà! This amazingly painstaking process makes the Program Group take form. You still have to add program icons to the windows, as described next.

TIP

✔ To put a program's icon on Program Manager, just drag the icon there from the My Computer or Explorer program. Windows 2000 automatically turns the icon into a shortcut — sans the traditional shortcut arrow, however — that can launch the program.

✔ With the new Program Manager, dragging and dropping icons onto Program Groups, which are minimized along Program Manager's bottom, is harder. The minimized group icons are much closer together than they used to be, so you can't always tell where your dropped icon will fall.

✔ Face it — is Program Manager really worth all this fuss? It's time to move on and start fiddling with My Computer and Explorer, which we cover in Chapter 13.

I Hate Those Fading Menus

Every time you turn around, some new "effect" has been added to Windows. We can only conclude that there are a bunch of people at Microsoft whose only job it is to make things look weird. In Windows 2000, one of their weirdnesses is the fading menu. In other words, when you open a Windows 2000 menu, instead of unfolding onto the desktop, it sort of *appears*. If you find this disconcerting, you can change the fading menu back to a scrolling menu, using these steps:

1. **Right-click on a blank spot on the Desktop and select Properties from the menu that pops up (or fades in).**

2. **Click the tab labeled Effects.**

3. **On the Effects page, change the Fade effect to Scroll effect in the Visual Effects area.**

   Or clear the check box entirely for an effect that's hardly special at all. The menus appear but they don't fade in and they don't scroll out.

4. **Click OK when you're done.**

I Wanna See Everything on My Menus

Speaking of weird, another new effect in Windows 2000 is the "personalized" menu. This smarty-pants feature keeps track of how often you're using different menu items (in Internet Explorer, too) and shows only the popular ones when you first click. Figure 17-2 shows a personalized menu and Figure 17-3 shows a menu that displays everything.

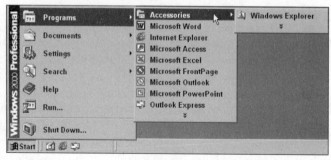

Figure 17-2: Personalized menus start out showing you just the items you've recently used.

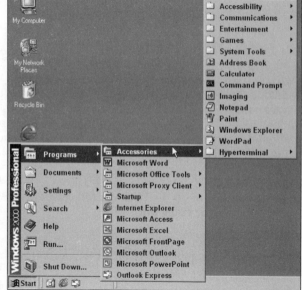

Figure 17-3: Without personalization, everything shows all the time.

To see everything on a personalized menu, just click the double arrowheads.

To change from personalized to de-personalized menus, right-click on a blank spot on the taskbar and select Properties from the menu. Down at the bottom of the General page, find the box with labeled Use Personalized Manus. Click in the box to remove the check mark and then click the OK button.

Did I Misplace My Briefcase?

In Windows NT 4 (as well as Windows 95 and Windows 98) the Briefcase icon is a permanent fixture on the Desktop. The Windows 2000 designers apparently figured out that it wasn't the most popular feature in town, so they gave it a hiding place.

To roll out a Briefcase, just right-click on a blank spot on the Desktop and select New and then Briefcase from the popup menu. Presto, you have a nice, new, unscuffed Briefcase on the Desktop.

Locating Windows Explorer

In earlier versions of Windows, the Explorer was either right on the Desktop or in the first stack of the Start menu. Now for the usual inexplicable reasons, it's several layers down on the Accessories menu.

To get to the Windows Explorer, click the Start menu then choose Programs and then Accessories and finally Windows Explorer.

To make a shortcut to the Explorer for your Desktop or to put on the Quick Launch bar, click the Start menu, then select Programs, and then Accessories, and finally right-click Windows Explorer — only this time, don't release the mouse button! Move the mouse to a blank spot on the Desktop and then release it. Doing so automatically creates a shortcut to Windows Explorer.

To put the shortcut on the Quick Launch portion of the taskbar, just click on the shortcut and drag it to the Quick Launch bar. Then release the mouse button and it's there — ready to use.

Chapter 18

What Can I Do in Four Steps or Less?

● ●

In This Chapter

▶ Copying a file to a floppy disk

▶ Finding the Start button and the Start menu

▶ Finding a lost file, folder, or program

▶ Adding programs to the Start menu

▶ Arranging open windows

▶ Opening a new compact-disc box

▶ Changing the screen's wallpaper

▶ Installing a new program

● ●

*T*his is it — quick and easy answers to the Windows 2000 Professional questions everybody's asking. Feel free to highlight or put sticky notes next to your favorite answers.

How Do I Copy a File to a Floppy Disk (And Vice Versa)?

Want to copy a file from your hard disk to a floppy disk? It's easy! Just do the following:

1. **Double-click on the My Computer icon and open the folder where your file is currently living.**

2. **Using the right mouse button, click on the file's icon and stand back.**

    A menu pops out.

3. **Point at the Send To command.**

   Another menu shoots out.

4. **Finally, click on the name of the floppy disk you'd like to send the file to — drive A or drive B, for example.**

Oh, and don't forget to put a floppy disk into the drive — if you have such a drive. Unfortunately, some networked computers don't come with floppy drives.

This method doesn't work for copying files from floppies to a hard disk; the hard disk doesn't appear on the Send To menu. To move your coveted file to the hard disk, drag the file's icon from the floppy-drive window to the folder on the hard disk. For more information, head to Chapter 13.

How Do I Copy a File to a Different Folder or Drive on a Network (And Vice Versa)?

This one's easy: Just drag the file's icon over to the folder or hard disk. If you can see an icon for a folder or hard disk on your screen, you can drag your file's icon there — and copy the file over there in the process.

Can't remember how to move or copy a file? Then drag the icon from place to place while holding down your right mouse button. Release the button when the icon is in place and choose either Move Here or Copy Here from the convenient menu that pops up.

How Do I Make a Copy of a Floppy Disk?

No floppy drive on your computer? You'll have to track down somebody who has one, or track down your network's administrator. Then follow these steps:

1. **Double-click on the My Computer icon.**

   And, of course, make sure you put your floppy disk in the disk drive.

2. **With your right mouse button, click on the icon for that floppy drive.**

3. **Choose Copy Disk from the menu that appears.**

4. **Follow the instructions on-screen.**

How Do I Find the Start Button and Start Menu?

Normally, you find the Start button lurking on the end of the *taskbar* — a long, ribbonlike string that covers an edge of the screen. Can't even find the taskbar? Then press Ctrl+Esc. That key combination almost always brings up the Start menu — the menu that pops up when you click on the Start button.

How Do I Start a Program?

Click on the taskbar's Start button and point your mouse at the word Programs on the pop-up menu. When you point at the various folders that pop up, the folders open, revealing more options.

Spot the program you're after? Click on its name, and Windows 2000 Professional brings the program to life. If you don't spot the program, head for the "How Do I Find a File, Folder, or Program?" section coming up next.

More taskbar information lurks in Chapter 12.

You can also start programs from My Computer or Explorer: Double-click on a folder to open it; double-click on a program to load it. Double-clicking on a file usually loads the program that created the file, as well as opens the file itself.

How Do I Find a File, Folder, or Program?

Need to find a wayward file, folder, or program? No problem! Just follow these steps:

1. **Click on the Start button and then point at the Search command.**

2. **Click on the For Files or Folders option.**

3. **Type the name of your program, file, or folder — or at least as much of it as you can remember.**

4. **Click on the Search Now button.**

The Search program lists all files, folders, and programs on drive C that contain the letters you typed. If you spot your file, folder, or program, double-click on it to bring it to life. If you don't spot what you're after, head to Chapter 8 for a more detailed explanation of the Search program.

How Can I Add Files, Folders, and Programs to the Start Menu?

The congenial Windows 2000 allows several ways to add files, folders, and programs to the Start menu, but here's one of the easiest:

1. **Double-click on the My Computer icon and find the icon for your file, folder, or program.**

2. **Point at the desired icon and, while holding down the mouse button, point at the Start button.**

3. **Let go of the mouse button.**

That's all there is to it. Click on the Start button, and you see your newly added file, folder, or program at the top of the menu.

Hit Chapter 12 for more Start button tips.

How Can I Add a Program to the Quick Launch Bar?

Adding a program to the Quick Launch bar is just as easy as adding a program to the Start menu. Then what's the difference, you may ask? Well, the Quick Launch bar is the ideal choice for those of you who are really in a hurry, since all that's required to start the programs that live there is a single click of the mouse. Follow these steps to add a program to the Quick Launch bar:

1. **Double-click on the My Computer icon and find the icon for your favorite program.**

2. **Point at the desired icon and, while holding down the mouse button, drag it to the Quick Launch portion of the taskbar.**

If the Quick Launch bar isn't displayed on your computer, right-click on an empty area of the taskbar, click Toolbars, and click Quick Launch to make it appear.

How Do I Keep My Icons Neatly Arranged?

When first installed, Windows 2000 lines up all your icons neatly in their folders. But if you start changing a folder's size or moving icons around, they quickly lose their orderly arrangement and start overlapping.

The solution follows:

1. **Click on a blank part of the folder with your right mouse button.**

2. **Point at Arrange Icons on the menu.**

3. **Click on Auto Arrange.**

   Now, Windows 2000 automatically keeps your icons arranged in neat rows.

The downside? Lazy Windows 2000 makes you repeat this command on *every* window or folder you want to keep automatically arranged. Sigh. (Don't sigh too long, however. The next section shows how to make *all* your windows and folders stay automatically arranged.)

How Do I Organize Open Windows So That They're All Visible?

Too many overlapping windows scattered across your screen? Then use one of the Tile commands so that Windows 2000 gives each window an equal amount of space on your Desktop.

1. **Using the right mouse button, click on a blank part of the taskbar.**

   Clicking near the clock usually works well.

2. **Choose Tile Windows Horizontally or Tile Windows Vertically.**

   Tile Windows Vertically lines up the windows in columns; Tile Windows Horizontally lines them up in rows. Try whichever scheme looks best. Or turn to Chapter 7 for more information.

How Can I Stop Having So Many Open Windows?

If you're opening folders inside of folders inside of folders, soon you have a zillion open windows all bumping rudely into one another. If you want to reuse windows instead of wastefully opening each folder in its own window, do the following:

1. **Click the View menu on any open window and select Folder Options.**

2. **In the Browse Folders section, click the button next to Open Each Folder In The Same Window; then click OK.**

How Can I Reduce All Open Windows to Taskbar Buttons?

 There are times where you might like to be able to see your Desktop rather than gazing at piles and piles of open windows. To reduce all open windows to buttons on the taskbar, click the Desktop icon on the taskbar. To re-open a window, click the mouse on its icon on the taskbar.

 If the Quick Launch bar isn't displayed on your computer, right-click on an empty area of the taskbar, click Toolbars, and click Quick Launch to make it appear.

 If you've found your Desktop and you want to restore all windows and dialog boxes to their previous state (that is, windows open and dialog boxes displayed), click the Desktop button again.

How Can I Make All My Windows Look the Same?

If you want all your windows to display their contents as large icons or one of the other choices on the View menu, you can set things up to achieve complete uniformity. Just follow these steps:

1. **Open a folder and set it as you want it — using the choices from the View menu.**

2. **Select Folder Options from the Tools menu of the same folder.**

3. **Click the View tab and click Like Current Folder.**

   A box appears asking you to confirm that you want all your folders to look like the current one.

4. **Click Yes and then click OK to close the Folder Options box.**

How Can I Make All My Windows Look Different — and Stay That Way?

Sometimes you find that after you set your windows up *just so,* Windows 2000 gets forgetful, and you find your careful setup gone from some windows. To remind Windows 2000 that you know what you want, do the following:

1. **Click the Start button, choose Settings, and then Control Panel.**

2. **Double-click on the Folder Options icon in the Control Panel.**

3. **Click the View tab and check the box labeled Remember Each Folder's View Settings.**

4. **Click OK.**

   Now each window will stay the way you put it.

How Do I Get Rid of Those Annoying Popup Descriptions?

Although they're intended to be helpful, after a while you may find the little popup descriptions of folder and Desktop items just plain annoying. Here are the steps you need to follow if you want to turn those silly windows off:

1. **Click the Start button, choose Settings, and then Control Panel.**

2. **Double-click the Folder Options icon in the Control Panel.**

3. **Click the View tab and scroll down until you find the checkbox labeled Show Pop-Up Descriptions For Folder And Desktop Items.**

   If you haven't found the box yet, keep scrolling; it's the last one in the list.

4. **Uncheck this box and click OK.**

   From here on in, you're on your own — unless you decide to turn the pop-up descriptions back on, of course.

How Do I Make the ClipBook Viewer Available All the Time?

If you find that you use the ClipBook Viewer a lot, you may want to make it more accessible so you don't have to keep rummaging around for it. Here's what you need to do to add a ClipBook Viewer shortcut to your Desktop:

1. **Double-click on My Computer and find the icon for the ClipBook Viewer.**

   You can find the icon for the ClipBook Viewer file, which is named clipbrd, inside the System32 folder, which is inside the WinNT folder.

2. **Right-click on the ClipBook Viewer icon and select Create Shortcut from the pop-up menu.**

3. **Right-click on the icon for the new shortcut, drag it to your Desktop, and select Move Here.**

   If you want, you can select Copy Here instead, but either way, you end up with an easy way to fire up the ClipBook Viewer.

How Do I Open a New, Plastic-Wrapped Compact Disc Box?

Use your teeth, being careful not to scratch your gums. Sometimes a thumbnail works well, or even a letter opener. Small amounts of nitroglycerine are effective, but the outcome can be unpredictable. It's a miracle of technology, but the plastic wrap is actually tougher than the plastic case itself.

How Do I Change My Screen's Wallpaper?

To change the background design of your screen, do the following:

1. **Using the right mouse button, click on a blank area of your Desktop.**

   A menu pops up out of nowhere.

2. **Next, choose Properties from the pop-up menu.**

3. **Peruse the list of names in the second column, under the Wallpaper section.**

Click on one of the names for a quick preview.

4. If you find a design you like, click OK. If not, click Cancel.

More wallpaper instructions are hanging around in Chapter 11.

 Wallpaper files can be *tiled* across the screen to cover up everything or *centered* in the middle of the screen to hang like a painting. (That's what those Tile and Center commands do — the ones you see in the menu that appears when you click on the taskbar with your right mouse button.)

How Do I Change the Name of a File or Folder?

To change the name of a file or folder, follow these steps:

1. Click on the icon of the file or folder you'd like to rename.

That click highlights the icon, making it change color.

2. Wait a second or two and then click directly on the file or folder's current name.

3. Start typing the new name.

The new name automatically replaces the old name.

4. Press Enter when you're through.

Windows 2000 won't let you change every icon's name, however. For example, you're stuck with the names *Recycle Bin* and *3½ Floppy (A:)*, along with a few others.

How Much Room Do I Have on My Hard Disk?

To check out how much room is available at the inn, do the following:

1. Double-click on the My Computer icon.

2. Click on your hard disk's icon with your right mouse button.

3. Choose Properties from the menu.

A box appears, listing your hard disk's size and free space (and showing you a pretty graph, too).

To keep a wary eye on the amount of room left on a hard disk, open My Computer, open the View menu, and choose Status Bar. My Computer starts displaying the currently selected disk's capacity and amount of free space along the bottom of the window.

How Do I Install a New Program?

Here's the easy way, if everything works the way it's supposed to:

1. **Double-click on the My Computer icon and double-click on the Control Panel.**
2. **When the Control Panel hits the screen, double-click on the Add/Remove Programs icon.**
3. **When the next window pops up, click on the Install button and follow the on-screen instructions.**

Flip to Chapter 11 for more-detailed instructions.

If you're on a big network, however, the Network Administrator probably won't let you install Descent II for lunch-hour, six-person free-for-alls. (Even if you can sneak it aboard, the joysticks will give you all away anyway.)

How Do I Tune in a Radio Station?

Thanks to the Internet and the direct Webcasts that many radio stations offer now, you can even use Windows 2000 to tune in the radio while you're work-ing at your computer. Here are the steps you need to follow:

1. **Double-click on the My Computer icon.**
2. **Click the View menu, choose Toolbars, and choose Radio.**

   You now notice that an extra toolbar appears on the My Computer window, right below the standard buttons and the Address Bar.
3. **Click the Radio Stations button and choose Radio Station Guide.**

   Windows 2000 now connects to the Internet and retrieves a list of Web-enabled radio stations from the Microsoft Network. If you enter your zip code in the box on the radio station search page and click Go, you can even have the list of radio stations personalized for your area.
4. **Locate the button for the radio station you want to listen to and click it.**

   Get ready to click the Stop button in case you're interrupted.

Part V
Getting Help

The 5th Wave — By Rich Tennant

"Amazingly enough, Plug and Play installed it without a problem."

In this part . . .

Windows 2000 can do hundreds of tasks in dozens of ways. That means that approximately one million things can fail at any given time.

Some problems are easy to fix. For example, a misplaced click on the taskbar makes all your programs disappear. Yet one more click in the right place puts them all back.

Other problems are far more complex, requiring teams of computer surgeons to diagnose, remedy, and bill accordingly.

This part lets you separate the big problems from the little ones. You'll know whether you can fix it yourself with a few clicks and a kick. If your situation is worse, you'll know when it's time to call in the surgeons.

Chapter 19

Fixing Windows That Don't Work

. . . .

In This Chapter

▶ Getting your mouse to work right

▶ Escaping from Menu Land

▶ Installing a driver for a new computer gizmo

▶ Clicking on the wrong button

▶ Thawing a "frozen" computer

▶ Handling a printer that's not working correctly

. . . .

Sometimes you just have a sense that something's wrong: The computer makes quiet grumbling noises, or Windows 2000 Professional starts running more slowly than Congress. Other times, something's obviously wrong: Pressing any key just gives you a beeping noise, menus keep shooting at you, or Windows 2000 Professional greets you with a cheery error message when you first turn it on.

Many of the biggest-looking problems are solved by the smallest-looking solutions. Hopefully, this chapter points you to the right one.

My Mouse Doesn't Work Right

Sometimes, the mouse doesn't work at all; other times, the mouse pointer hops across the screen like a flea. Here are a few things to look for:

✔ If no mouse arrow appears on the screen when you start Windows 2000, make sure that the mouse's tail is plugged snugly into the computer's rump. Then log off and log back on to Windows 2000.

✔ If the mouse arrow is on-screen but won't move, Windows 2000 may be mistaking your brand of mouse for a different brand. Press Ctrl+Esc to open the Start menu, and use the arrow keys to choose Control Panel (it's hiding under the Settings area). Use the arrow keys to select the Mouse icon, and press Enter. When the Mouse menu appears, press Ctrl+Tab until you highlight the Hardware tab. Press tab again to reach the Troubleshooting button and then click Enter. Press F6 to move to the Mouse Troubleshooter pane; then click Tab and Enter to see if the troubleshooter can solve your problem.

If none of this stuff works, take your hand off the mouse and raise it in the air to flag down your Network Administrator.

✔ If the mouse pointer jumps around, there may be a conflict on its interrupt. You may have to pull out the mouse manual and see how to change the mouse's *interrupt setting* to fix this one. Or, better yet, leave this one to the Network Administrator. It can get ugly.

✔ A mouse pointer can jump around on-screen if the mouse is dirty. To clean it, first turn the mouse upside down and clean off any visible dirt stuck to the bottom. Then remove the retaining ring (turn the little device holding the mouse ball in place — many mice have an arrow showing which way the device moves — until the mouse ball pops out). Wipe off any crud and blow any dust out of the hole. Pull any stray hairs off the little rollers and stick the ball back inside the mouse. If you wear wool sweaters or have cats, you may have to clean the ball every month or so.

✔ If the mouse was working fine and now the buttons seem to be reversed, you probably hit the left-handed button configuration setting in the Control Panel. Double-click on the Control Panel's Mouse icon and make sure that the configuration is set up correctly, whether you're right- or left-handed.

My Menus Act Weird

If your keystrokes don't appear in your work but instead make a bunch of menus shoot out from the top of the window, you're stuck in Menu Land. Somehow, you've pressed and released Alt, an innocent-looking key that's easy to hit accidentally.

When you press and release Alt, Windows 2000 turns its attention away from your work and toward the menus along the top of the window.

To get back to work, press and release Alt one more time. Alternatively, press Esc. One or the other is your ticket out of Menu Land.

I'm Supposed to Install a New Driver

When you buy a new toy for the computer and plug it in, Windows 2000 should immediately detect its presence and (after notifying you of its intentions) install the new toy with dispatch. However, on some rare occasions, Windows 2000 may be completely flummoxed, in which case you may have to supply a piece of software called a *driver*.

A driver is a sort of translator that tells Windows 2000 how to boss around the new toy. If you buy a new sound card, compact disc player, printer, mouse, monitor, or almost any other computer toy, it will come with a floppy disk or a CD-ROM that contains the necessary driver. Fortunately, you don't often need to use those discs, but if you do, Windows 2000 will tell you.

✔ Companies constantly update their drivers, fixing problems or making them better. If the computer device is misbehaving, a newer driver may calm it down. You can find new drivers from the producing company's Web page, or by calling the company's technical support lines and asking them to mail you their newest driver.

✔ A few computer toys won't work with Windows 2000 Professional. Just about anything you buy new will work fine — though it never hurts to ask at the store.

I Clicked on the Wrong Button (But I Haven't Lifted My Finger Yet)

Clicking the mouse takes two steps: a push and a release. If you start to click on the wrong button on-screen and haven't lifted your finger yet, slowly slide the mouse pointer off the button on-screen. *Then* take your finger off the mouse.

The screen button pops back up, and Windows 2000 pretends nothing happened. Thankfully.

My Computer Has Frozen Up Solid

Every once in a while, Windows 2000 just drops the ball and wanders off somewhere. You're left looking at a computer that just looks back. Panicked clicks don't do anything. Pressing every key on the keyboard doesn't do anything — or worse yet, the computer starts to beep at every key press.

When nothing on-screen moves except the mouse pointer, the computer has frozen up solid. Try the following approaches, in the following order, to correct the problem:

Approach 1: Press Esc twice.

That approach usually doesn't work, but give it a shot anyway.

Approach 2: Press Ctrl, Alt, and Delete all at the same time.

The official-looking Windows 2000 Security box pushes its big shoulders onto the screen, listing six official-looking buttons. Click on the button named Task Manager. A window appears, listing the currently running programs. Click on the name of the program that's causing the mess — you'll often see "Not Responding" or "Misbehaving" or something to that effect listed after the program's name — and click on the End Task button. You lose any unsaved work in your program, of course, but you should be used to that.

Approach 3: Press Ctrl, Alt, and Delete all at the same time and choose Shut Down.

If none of these methods fixes the problem, try pressing Ctrl+Alt+Delete again and clicking the Shut Down button instead of the Task Manager button. This is a fairly drastic step, although you're unlikely to lose anything irreplaceable.

If you somehow stumbled onto the Ctrl+Alt+Delete combination by accident, press Esc at the unresponsive-application message to return to Windows 2000.

Don't push the computer's Reset button and don't turn the computer off and on again, no matter how tempted you may be. Instead, flag down the Network Administrator — who will probably turn the computer off and on again anyway, but then it'll be his fault if something gets munged.

The Printer Isn't Working Right

If the printer isn't working right, start with the simplest solution: Make sure that the printer is plugged into the wall and turned on (which may involve a trip down the hall if you're using a networked printer). Surprisingly, this step fixes about half the problems you may ever have with printers. Next, make sure that the printer cable is snugly nestled in the ports on both the printer and the computer that it's attached to — assuming the printer cable is attached to any computer at all. If the printer cable is not attached to a specific computer, it should still have a cable that attaches it to a network hub. Make sure that both ends of that cable are firmly attached. Then check to make sure that the printer has enough paper — and that the paper isn't jammed in the mechanism.

The Windows 2000 Help program is surprisingly helpful with this one: Open the Start menu, and click on Help. When the Help window appears, double-click on the word Troubleshooting in the right-hand pane (under Start Here), then scroll down the list of troubleshooters and click Print. Windows 2000 Professional leads you through a program designed to figure out why the printer's goofing off.

If you still can't get the darned thing to work, you need to call in the Network Administrator. Don't be in too much of a hurry, though. If the network printer has gone down, the disgruntled administrator has probably already heard from several dozen people before you.

Chapter 20

The Terror of the ERROR! ERROR! ERROR!

• •

In This Chapter

▶ A:\ is not accessible. The device is not ready

▶ Disk drive (or destination drive) is full

▶ You must type a filename

▶ Access is denied

▶ The system could not log you on

• •

*M*ost people don't have any trouble understanding error messages. A car's pleasant beeping tone means that you left your keys in the ignition. A terrible scratching sound from the stereo means that the cat has jumped on that aging turntable.

Things are different with Windows 2000 Professional, however. A Senate subcommittee could've written its error messages, if only Windows' error messages weren't so brief. When Windows 2000 tosses an error message your way, it usually gives you just a single sentence and rarely describes what you did to cause the error. And even worse, Windows 2000 hardly ever says how to make the error go away for good.

Here are some of the words you find in the most common error messages that Windows 2000 Professional throws in your face. This chapter explains what Windows 2000 Professional is trying to say, why it's saying it, and just what the heck it expects you to do about it.

A:\ Is Not Accessible. The Device Is Not Ready

Meaning: Windows 2000 can't find a floppy disk in drive A.

Probable cause: No floppy disk is in there.

Solution: Slide a disk inside and wish that all errors were this easy to fix.

Disk Drive or Destination Drive Is Full

Meaning: Windows 2000 Professional has run out of room to store something on a floppy disk or on the hard disk.

Probable cause: Windows 2000 Professional tried saving something to a disk but ran out of space.

Solution: Clear more room on that disk before saving your work. Delete any junk files on the hard disk. BAK (backup) files and TMP (temporary) files often qualify as junk files that you can safely delete, but only if their dates show them to be old and forgotten. Also, delete any old programs you don't use anymore, like those games you snuck onto the computer for playing during lunch hour.

Also, if you're trying to copy something to the hard disk, be sure to empty the Recycle Bin first: Click on the Recycle Bin icon with your right mouse button and choose Empty Recycle Bin from the menu.

A Filename Cannot Contain Any of the Following Characters: \ /:*?"<>|

Meaning: Windows 2000 Professional refuses to accept your choice of filename.

Probable cause: You tried to name a file by using one or more of the forbidden characters.

Solution: Turn to the section about renaming a file in Chapter 13 and make sure that you're not naming a file something you shouldn't. Chances are that you slipped in a question mark or slash.

Click the Program You Want to Use to Open . . .

Meaning: Windows 2000 can't show you what's in the file you just double-clicked.

Probable cause: Windows 2000 doesn't recognize what kind of file it is.

Solution: If you know what program the file belongs to, click on the program name in the Open With box.

The following trick doesn't always work, but it's worth a try: Drag and drop the mysterious file into an open Notepad window. Sometimes, Notepad can display a file's contents. After you finish viewing the file — if you can see it at all — be sure to exit Notepad *without* saving the file. Doing so preserves the file in its natural state.

The File [Name] Is a Program. If You Remove It, You Will No Longer Be Able to Run This Program . . .

Meaning: You're trying to delete a file containing a program.

Probable cause: You're clearing off some hard disk space to make room for incoming programs.

Solution: First, be very careful — grab a Network Administrator by the pocket protector if you're not sure what you're doing. Then make sure that you know what program you're deleting before you delete that file. Then don't delete the file unless you're sure that you no longer need that program. Finally, make sure that you have the program's box and installation disks sitting on the shelf so you can reinstall the program if you decide you need it after all.

You Must Type a Filename

Meaning: Windows 2000 Professional insists that you type a filename into the box beneath a file's icon.

Probable cause: You chose (accidentally or otherwise) the Rename command from a menu or clicked on an icon's title in *just the right* way. Then you deleted the file's previous name, leaving just a blank box.

Solution: Type a new filename consisting of mostly numbers and letters, and you'll be fine. Or if you're frantically trying to get out of this weird situation and don't give a darn about changing filenames, press Esc, and the Rename box dissipates.

Cannot Copy File: Access Is Denied. Make Sure the Disk Is Not Full or Write-Protected and That the File Is Not Currently in Use

Meaning: You're trying to copy a file to a place that Windows 2000 doesn't allow.

Probable cause: You're trying to copy a file to a place that can't hold new files — a compact disc, for example, or a write-protected floppy disk. (We cover those items in Chapter 2.)

Solution: Don't try to copy files to compact discs. This process works only with writable CD-ROM drives, and the Network Administrators usually hog those for themselves. For tips on un-write-protecting a floppy disk, hit Chapter 2.

Access Denied

Meaning: You can't get there from here.

Probable cause: You don't have permission to use the file or folder you just selected.

Solution: If you're trying to grab a file or folder on your network — and you're supposed to be able to grab it — the situation is probably just a permission mix-up that your administrator can fix in no time at all.

But if you can't reach a site on the Internet, your network may not be allowing it. In that case, the Access Denied message will probably mention something about a "proxy server" or "firewall." That means your network's administrator isn't allowing access. You can appeal that decision, but be prepared to explain why getting to the Wrestlemania Web site is necessary to your job.

Error Opening Printer

Meaning: The network can't find the printer you want.

Probable cause: The printer is out of service for some reason.

Solution: Try another printer. If you don't have another printer, walk over and see whether the one you want is plugged in. If the printer looks okay, then you need to find the Network Administrator.

The Other Computer Did Not Respond

Meaning: No one answered your Chat call.

Probable cause: Either you typed in a computer name that doesn't exist, or the other computer isn't active on the network.

Solution: Check the name of the computer. Wait and try again. Go down the hall and *talk* to the person you're calling.

The System Could Not Log You On

Meaning: You can't log onto this machine.

Probable cause: Most likely scenario is that you made a mistake typing in your password, but there can be (sigh) other causes.

Solution: Re-enter your password — slowly this time. Remember, passwords are case-sensitive. To a computer, *bozo* is not the same as *Bozo*. Check to be sure that your username is correct. If you still can't get in after repeated tries, it's time to get help from the administrator.

Chapter 21

Helpful Handouts from the Windows 2000 Help Program

*J*ust about everybody's written a bizarre computer command like Alt+F4 onto a stick-on note and slapped it on the side of the monitor.

Windows 2000 comes with its *own* set of stick-on notes built right in. You can pop them up on-screen and leave them there for easy access. In a way, they're *better* than real stick-on notes because they can never slip away and vanish only to reappear stuck to your shoe one night.

This chapter covers the Windows 2000 built-in help system. When you raise your hand in just the right way, Windows 2000 walks over and offers you some help.

The Quickest Way to Find Answers

Don't bother plowing through this whole chapter if you don't need to: Here are the quickest ways to make Windows 2000 dish out helpful information when you're stumped.

Press F1

TIP

When you're confused in Windows 2000, press the F1 key. That key *always* stands for "Help!" Most of the time, Windows 2000 checks to see what program you're using and fetches some helpful information about that particular program or your current situation. In fact, pressing F1 usually brings up a huge Help program, described later in this chapter.

Click the right mouse button on the confusing part

Windows 2000 tosses a lot of forms in your face. When a particular form, setting, box, or menu item has your creativity stifled, click on it with your right (the opposite of left) mouse button. A What's This? box appears, as shown in Figure 21-1, letting you know that Windows 2000 can offer help about that particular area. Use your *left* mouse button to click inside the What's This? box, and Windows 2000 tosses extra information onto the screen, explaining the confusing area you clicked on.

Figure 21-1:
Click here to see more information about a confusing area.

What's This?

Hover the mouse pointer over the confusing icon

Face it: Icons can be confusing, especially when they're arranged in endless little rows like pastries in a bakery shop. In Windows 2000's WordPad, for example, which icon helps you find text — the icon of the magnifying glass or the one of the binoculars?

To find out quickly, just let your mouse pointer hover over the confusing icon. In a moment or two, a little box pops up from nowhere, listing the icon's name — and often a short reason for the icon's existence.

This trick doesn't work with all icons, but it works with plenty of 'em, so make it your first line of defense.

Click on the little question mark

Look in the program's upper-right corner. Do you spot a little question mark lurking up there? Then click on it. Your pointer turns into a question mark.

Now, here's the helpful part: Click your newly shaped pointer on any confusing area of the program: boxes, windows, buttons, and icons. A helpful explanation appears, describing what those things are supposed to do. Click on that little question mark again to turn off the feature.

You don't find that helpful question mark everywhere, but keep an eye out for one when a program's obtuseness is starting to get on your nerves.

Choose Help from the main menu

If pressing F1 doesn't get you anywhere, look for the word Help in the menu bar along the top of the confusing program. Click on Help, and a menu drops down, usually listing two choices: Help Topics and About — or variations similar to those. Click on Help Topics to make the Windows 2000 Help program leap to the screen.

Clicking on About merely brings a version number to the screen, which can be dangerously irritating when you're looking for something a little more helpful.

Click on the leaping arrows

Sometimes the Windows 2000 Help program scores big: It tells you *exactly* how to solve your particular problem. Unfortunately, however, the Help program says you need to take some *other* step to solve your problem. Don't get grumpy, though: Look for a little "leaping arrow," like the one shown in Figure 21-2.

Click on the little leaping arrow, and Windows 2000 automatically takes you to that other program you need to use. Yep, it's refreshingly helpful.

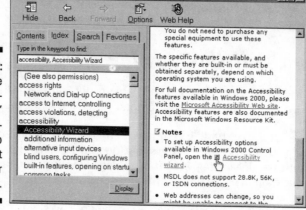

Figure 21-2: Click on the little "leaping arrow" to automatically go to the right place for help.

Pestering Windows 2000's Built-in Help Program

Almost every Windows 2000-based program has the word Help in its top menu bar. But if you're not in a specific program and you're just trying to find out how to do something in Windows 2000, click the Start button and then select Help and the built-in computer guru rushes to your aid with the majorly BIG Windows 2000 Help program shown in Figure 21-3.

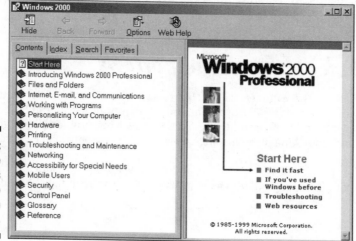

Figure 21-3: The Windows 2000 Help program rushes in.

The Windows 2000 Help file is very friendly but somewhat ungainly — dealing with it may make you feel like you're trying to waltz with a walrus.

So it's important to pick your approach to Help based on what you already know about what you're looking for.

I know just what I want

If you know what you want to do, click the Index tab in the Windows 2000 Help window. Start typing in the term you're looking for. As shown in Figure 21-4, the display moves to the topics matching that combination of letters.

Highlight the topic you want to read about and click Display.

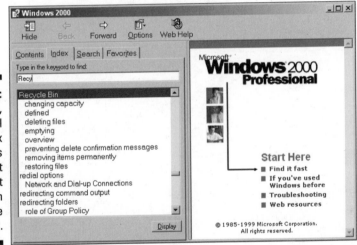

Figure 21-4:
As you type, the helpful Index displays whatever it has that begins with those letters.

Windows 2000 searches alphabetically and, unfortunately, isn't very smart. So if you're looking for help on margins, for example, don't type *adding margins* or *changing margins*. Instead, type **margins** so that Windows 2000 jumps to the words beginning with *M*.

If you have trouble finding help for your specific problem, use the Search command, described in the next section. Instead of forcing you to type the right words in the right order, the Search command roots through every word in the Help file and brings back every match.

I know what I want to do, I just don't know what it's called

Lots of times you know what it is you want to do, you just don't know what it's called in Windows-speak. When that happens, click the Start Menu and select Help. Then click the Search tab.

Let's say you just want to hide that thing at the bottom of the screen — whatever it's called. Just type in **hide** and click List Topics. As shown in Figure 21-5, every piece of the Help file that has the word "hide" in it appears in the list. Scroll through the topics until you find some likely candidate. Highlight it and click Display.

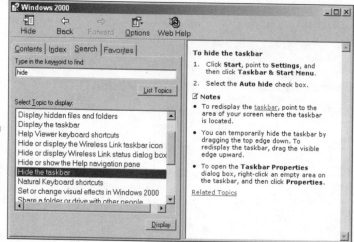

Figure 21-5: Double-click on a topic to see more specific help areas.

✔ Using a very general search term produces a lot of results, so the more specific you can be, the easier it is to find what you want.

✔ On the other hand, being too specific may not turn up what you're looking for, so be prepared to try a couple of different search terms.

I know exactly what it was, but it's not in the same place in Windows 2000

If you've spent some time in Windows NT 4 or in Windows 98, you've already invested precious energy in figuring out where things are — and now in Windows 2000, you have to start all over.

Not quite. The people who did all the moving also left a trail of breadcrumbs to where things are now. Open the Windows Help program by clicking the Start button and then choosing Help. In the right-hand pane, click on the link If You've Used Windows Before (see Figure 21-6).

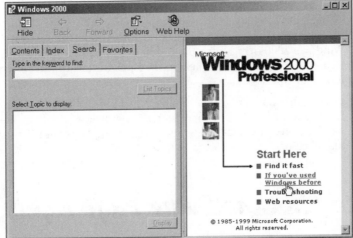

Figure 21-6:
Click here to find out where things are now.

Click on any of the terms in the list shown in Figure 21-7 and you're magically transported to a Help page telling you where the errant Windows NT 4 or Windows 98 feature is now.

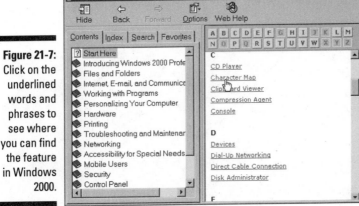

Figure 21-7:
Click on the underlined words and phrases to see where you can find the feature in Windows 2000.

> ✔ The quickest way to find help in any Windows 2000-based program is always to press F1. Windows 2000 automatically jumps to the table of contents page for the help information it has for the current program.

> ✔ Windows 2000 packs a lot of information into its help boxes; some of the words usually scroll off the bottom of the window. To see them, click on the scroll bar (described in Chapter 6) or press PgDn.

> ✔ Underlined phrases and words appear throughout the Windows 2000 help system. Whenever you click on something that's underlined, Windows 2000 brings up a definition or jumps to a spot that has information about that subject. Click on the Back button to return to where you jumped from.

> ✔ If you find a particularly helpful reference in the help system, shrink the Help program's window to an icon on the taskbar: Click on the button with the tiny bar, near the window's upper-right corner. Then you can just click on the icon to see that page again.

Trying to Find the Same Page Again

The Windows 2000 help system is better than ever, and finding help for a particular trouble is relatively painless. But how do you return to that page a few minutes — or even a few days — later?

When you find that perfect page, click on the Favorites tab in the Windows 2000 Help window. Click Add and the helpful page is added to the list of Topics on the page. Now you can return to the page any time.

Part VI
The Part of Tens

The 5th Wave   By Rich Tennant

"ALRIGHT, WHICH ONE OF YOU CLOWNS IS RESPONSIBLE FOR THURSDAY'S DOWN TIME?"

In this part . . .

*E*verybody likes to read Top Tens in magazines —
especially in the grocery store checkout aisle when
you're stuck behind someone who's just pulled a rubber
band off a thick stack of double coupons.

Unlike the reading material at the grocery store, the chapters in this part of the book don't list ten new aerobic
bounces or ten ways to stop your kids from making explosives with kitchen cleansers. Instead, you find lists of
ways to make Windows 2000 be more efficient — or at
least not as hostile. You find a few tips, tricks, and explanations of eccentric icons.

Some lists have more than ten items; others have fewer.
But who's counting, besides the guy wading through all
those coupons?

Chapter 22

Ten New Windows 2000 Features for Windows NT 4 Users to Check Out

*L*ike a new car model, Windows 2000 adds several improvements over the old Windows NT 4 version. Some of the changes are cosmetic, like the fancy new lime-green, 3-D mouse pointers. Other changes are more useful, like the Quick Launch bar and the new settings for the Start menu.

Consider this chapter a pamphlet explaining some of the best new features Windows 2000 has to offer over its replacement, Windows NT 4.

Getting Rid of the Double-Click

Everyone who uses Windows is used to the venerable convention of single-clicking an item to select it and double-clicking to open it. Everyone who uses the World Wide Web is used to the convention of pointing at an object to select it and clicking once to open it.

With the interface changes added to Windows 2000, you can adopt the point-to-select, click-once-to-open convention — and you don't have to use the Active Desktop (see Chapter 11) to do it. Just follow these steps:

1. **Click the Tools menu in any window and select Folder Options.**

2. **Click the General tab and look for the Click Items As Follows section at the bottom of the page (see Figure 22-1).**

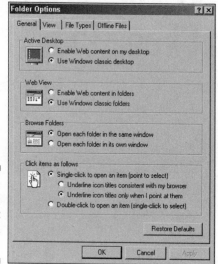

3. **In the Click items section, select the Single-click option.**

   You can also decide whether you want your icons to be underlined all the time (so they look like links on a Web page) or only underlined when you point to them.

4. **Click on OK when you finish.**

Using the Quick Launch Bar

With Windows 2000, Microsoft added the Quick Launch bar to the taskbar. Quick Launch is just a special reserved spot for shortcuts. It comes already configured with shortcuts to the Desktop, Internet Explorer, and Outlook Express.

A single click on any icon on the Quick Launch bar opens the program (even if you're using the double-click option).

Got a program you use *all* the time? Just drag a program shortcut to the Quick Launch bar and drop it there. When you want to get rid of the shortcut, right-click on it and select Delete from the pop-up menu.

Looking Inside My Network Places

My Network Places

A newcomer to the Desktop is My Network Places, but don't be deceived. It's really just a renamed Network Neighborhood. If you know how to poke around the Neighborhood, you won't have any trouble with My Network Places. (Otherwise, check out Chapter 9.)

Looking Inside My Documents and My Pictures

My Documents

My Documents is a new folder on the Desktop (and My Pictures hides inside). Many Windows 2000 programs try to save files in the My Documents folder. Pictures from a digital camera and graphics you create or download from the Internet go to the My Pictures folder by default. So if you misplace a document or a picture, try these two folders first — before launching a full-fledged search.

If you'd prefer not to have the My Documents folder cluttering up your Desktop, you can hide it. Double-click the My Computer icon. Click the Tools menu and select Folder Options. Click the View tab and scroll down to the bottom of the Advanced Settings window. There you can remove the check from in front of Show My Documents On The Desktop. To get the My Documents folder back onto your Desktop, just come back to this spot and replace the check mark.

New Start Menu Settings

From the beginning you've been able to drag programs on and off the Start menu but it's always been a delicate business — sometimes requiring multiple tries and sometimes yielding unexpected results. Now, you can make lots of changes with a simple check mark.

Right-click on a blank spot on the taskbar and select Properties from the popup menu. Click the Advanced tab to open the box shown in Figure 22-2.

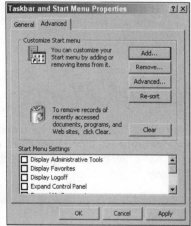

Figure 22-2:
Using the
Start menu
settings.

If you're not sure what the results will be from a particular choice, check it and then click the Apply button. Then, leaving the Taskbar and Start Menu Properties box open, click the Start button and see the effect on how the menu looks.

Don't like it? Go back to the Taskbar and Start Menu Properties box, remove the check mark and try another.

Fancy Menus

Menus abound in all versions of Windows, but Windows 2000 gives you the option of fiddling with their looks — at least some of them.

Want your menus to fade in and out or scroll out like the credits in a movie from the '50s? Right-click on a blank spot on the Desktop and select Properties from the pop-up menu. Click the Effects tab.

In the Visual Effects section, check the option labeled Use Transition Effects For Menus And Tooltips. Choose Fade Effect or Scroll Effect. Click OK.

Another option that's turned on by default is the "personalized" menu. This just means that Windows 2000 takes notes on how often you use different entries on your Start menu and the Favorites menu in Internet Explorer. Figure 22-3 shows some menus that have been personalized — showing just the most recently used entries. You can see all the entries by either keeping the mouse still until the bottom of the menu spills out (a matter of a few seconds) or by clicking the double arrowheads at the bottom of the menu.

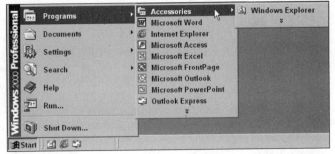

Figure 22-3:
Menus that
have been
personal-
ized.

Personalized menus have their advantages — especially when you have long, long menus — because they can save time. But if you absolutely hate 'em, you can disable the feature by taking the following steps:

1. **Right-click on a blank spot on the taskbar and select Properties from the pop-up menu.**

2. **Click the General tab.**

3. **Remove the check mark from the box next to Use Personalized Menus. Click OK.**

Webby Desktops

Want your Desktop to look like a page from the World Wide Web? Easy enough. Just right-click on a blank spot on the Desktop and select Active Desktop and then Show Web Content.

If you don't see much in the way of change, right-click again, select Active Desktop again to see the new items added to the pop-up menu:

- **Customize My Desktop:** Lets you add Internet elements to your Desktop.

- **Add New Desktop Item:** Lets you type in an Internet (or intranet) location to show in a window on your Desktop.

- **Synchronize:** Updates active Desktop items with their counterparts on the Internet.

You can play around with this stuff endlessly — except when that report is due in an hour, and Mr. Crumpet is pacing in the hallways.

Personalized Help

You can uncover a whole lotta Help in Windows 2000 — so much that it may take a while to find the answer to a question. And once you find the answer, you want to be able to find it again without starting from scratch.

When you find the page in Help that you want to be able to find again, click the Favorites tab. Then click the Add button and the current Help page is added to your Favorites list. Next time you need to refer to this topic, just open Help and click that Favorites tab one more time. Highlight the topic and click Display. The Help topic reappears in the right-hand pane of the window.

Chapter 23

Ten Windows 2000 Shortfalls (And How to Work around Them)

*W*indows 2000 would be great if only. . . [insert your pet peeve here]. If you find yourself thinking (or saying) this frequently, this chapter is for you. This chapter not only lists the most aggravating things about Windows 2000 but also explains how to fix them.

My Documents Folder Is Too Dorky

If you just can't stand the sight of the My Documents folder and you'd like to remove its icon from your Desktop, we can sympathize. Here are the steps you need to follow:

1. **Click the Start button and choose Settings and then Control Panel.**

2. **Double-click the Folder Options icon in the Control Panel.**

3. **Click the View tab, scroll down the list of items until you see the Show My Documents On The Desktop checkbox, and click it to remove the check mark.**

Now the icon for the My Documents folder will no longer trouble you; the folder still exists (Windows 2000 won't let you delete this one), but you'll have to go digging for it if you ever want to find it — or a file that it contains.

The Taskbar Is Missing

The taskbar is a handy Windows 2000 program that's always running — if you can just find it. Unfortunately, it sometimes vanishes from the screen. Here are a few ways to bring it back:

✔ Try holding down the Ctrl key and pressing Esc. Sometimes this key combination makes the taskbar appear, but sometimes it only brings up the Start menu.

✔ Try pointing at the very edges of your screen, stopping for a second or two at each of the four sides. If you point at the correct side, some specially configured taskbars will stop goofing around and come back to the screen.

✔ If you can see only a slim edge of the taskbar — the rest of it hangs off the edge of the screen, for example — point at the edge you *can* see. When the mouse pointer turns into a two-headed arrow, hold down your mouse button and move the mouse toward the screen's center to drag the taskbar back into view.

✔ If you want to make sure that the taskbar shows nearly all the time (unless you intentionally hide it), click Start, choose Settings, choose Taskbar & Start Menu, and make sure that the Auto Hide box is not checked.

The Taskbar Takes Up Too Much Room

Would you like to put your taskbar on a reducing diet so that it doesn't take up so much of your screen? Try one of the following:

✔ Point at the upper edge of the taskbar. When the mouse pointer turns into a two-headed arrow, hold down your mouse button and move the arrow away from the screen's center to thin out the taskbar.

✔ If you want to make the taskbar disappear completely, try this: click Start, choose Settings, and choose Taskbar & Start Menu. Check the Auto Hide box and the overweight taskbar hides when you move away the mouse pointer. (Move the mouse pointer back to where the taskbar is hiding to make it crawl back out of its hole.) And be sure to check out the preceding section if you find that you've lost track of the taskbar altogether.

I Want the Double-Click Back

Windows 2000 lets you use either a single-click or a double-click to open items in folders and on the Desktop, depending on how certain options are set. If you've inherited a Windows 2000 computer from somebody who decided that the single-click was preferable and you'd really, really like to get that ol' double-click back, here's what you need to do:

1. **Click the Start button and choose Settings and then Control Panel.**

2. **Double-click the Folder Options icon in the Control Panel.**

3. **Scan down to the Click Items As Follows area and check to see that Double-Click To Open An Item is selected.**

   With this option in place, a single-click selects an item and a double-click opens it. This is the way that Windows has functioned since the very beginning, which may explain why single-clicking to select something and double-clicking to open it feels so familiar — and so right.

I Wanna Keep Working Even If the Network's Down

If the statement above applies to you, then you must be a real die-hard, but suit yourself. Whatever your reasons for wanting to work without your connection to the network (offline), Windows 2000 is equipped to satisfy this need. Do these things to keep plugging away, regardless of what the network's up to:

1. **Click the Start button and choose Settings and then Control Panel.**

2. **Double-click the Folder Options icon in the Control Panel.**

3. **Click the Offline Files tab and choose whatever options you like.**

Here are the options you can choose:

- **Enable Offline Files:** This is the box that absolutely must be checked if you want to work with network files offline. Use either My Computer or My Network Places to select the specific network files you'd like to have available.

- **Synchronize all offline files before logging off:** This box is checked by default because it's intended to ensure that the offline files you're working with are the latest and greatest version. If this box is not checked, your offline files should be complete, but they may not be the most recent version, so you're taking a chance.

- **Enable reminders:** All this box does when checked is specify that reminder balloons appear over the system tray when computers go offline.

- **Place shortcut to Offline Files folder on the desktop:** If checked, this box does exactly what its name implies; it puts a shortcut to the folder where your offline files live right on your Desktop where it's easy to find.

I Want My Folders to Look Like They Used To

You've probably noticed by now that Windows 2000 has jazzed up various elements of the Windows interface. One thing that's happened is that you can display folder contents as Web pages. This is nice if you'd like to customize the appearance of folders by modifying or creating Web pages in HTML, but who has the time for that? If you'd rather turn back the clock and see your Desktop looking like it did in previous versions of Windows, follow these steps:

1. **Click the Start button and choose Settings and then Control Panel.**

2. **Double-click the Folder Options icon in the Control Panel.**

   Click the General tab, if it's not showing already.

3. **Scan down the General tab until you find the Web View area and make sure that the Use Windows Classic Folders option is checked.**

   Ahhh, that's better! Now your Desktop looks and works like the classic Windows Desktop once again.

Even if you've selected the Use Windows Classic Desktop option as described, the contents of My Computer and the Control Panel will always be displayed as Web pages.

The Desktop Icons Are Too Big (Or Too Small)

If your Desktop icons look gigantic (or puny), here's a trick to adjust their size to suit your tastes. Follow these steps:

1. **Click the Start button and choose Settings and then Control Panel.**

2. **Double-click the Display icon in the Control Panel.**

3. **Click the Effects tab and scan it until you locate the Visual Effects list. Check or uncheck the Use Large Icons checkbox according to the nature of your problem (icons too big or small).**

   If the problem is that your Desktop icons are too big and the Use Large Icons checkbox is checked, uncheck it and your icons magically shrink as soon as you apply the new settings.

   On the other hand, if the problem is that your Desktop icons are too small, check the Use Large Icons checkbox and you'll find your screen easier to read as soon as you apply the new settings.

I Have a Folder I Don't Want to Share

If you have a folder that's chock-full of private or otherwise sensitive files, you probably don't want to let other users on the network examine its contents at will. Luckily, Windows 2000 gives you the option to share or not share folder(s) alike. Do these things to ensure that your top-secret folder isn't going to fall victim to prying eyes:

1. **Open My Computer and locate the folder whose contents you want to keep to yourself.**

2. **Right-click on the folder's icon and choose Properties from the menu that pops up.**

   This summons the Folder Properties window shown in Figure 23-1.

3. **Click the Sharing tab and click the circle next to Do Not Share This Folder (if it's not already clicked).**

   Do Not Share is the default security setting for Folder Properties, so unless you've specifically acted to share this folder (by opening the Folder Properties window, clicking the circle next to Share This Folder, and so on), you're probably already OK on the sharing front — whether you know it or not.

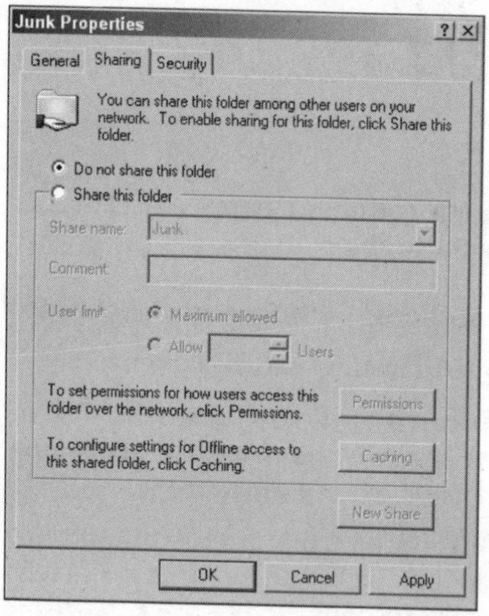

Figure 23-1:
Making
sure that
no one else
has access
to your
precious
documents.

My Computer Shows the Wrong Stuff on My Floppy Disk

The My Computer program sometimes gets confused and doesn't always list the files currently sitting on a disk drive. To prod My Computer into taking a second look, open the View menu and choose the Refresh command. Or press the F5 key — whichever method is easier to remember.

I Need Some Help Reading the Screen

Reading the Windows 2000 screen isn't always as easy as it might be; if you have any kind of visual impairment or you've just added too many icons to your desktop, the built-in Magnifier can help you out.

To fire up the Magnifier, click Start, choose Programs, choose Accessories, choose Accessibility, and choose Magnifier. This produces the Magnifier Settings box and a magnified strip at the top of the screen as shown in Figure 23-2.

As you move the mouse pointer around, the magnified area always shows where you're pointing. The default Magnification level is 2X, but you can select all the way up to 9X in the Magnification Level box.

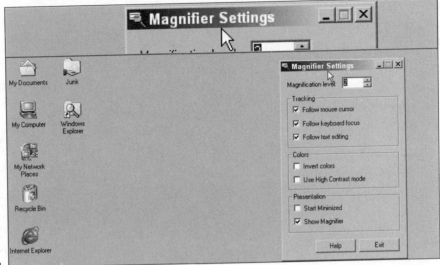

Figure 23-2:
Get an
enlarged
view of the
screen
using
Magnifier.

By default, all three of the boxes in the Tracking section (Follow Mouse Cursor, Follow Keyboard Focus, and Follow Text Editing) are checked; if you uncheck these, navigation may get tricky, so we'd recommend leaving these as they are.

The Colors section of the Magnifier Settings box allows you to get fancy if you want, but beware — fancy is not always better. Try checking Invert Colors if you think that will make your screen more legible, or experiment with Use High Contrast Mode. We find that neither of these options helps us a whole lot, but depending on your reasons for using the Magnifier, you may not agree.

You may very well want to adjust the size of the window you're magnifying in order to see everything as you wish. To do this, position the mouse over the border between the normal-sized window and the magnified one, and wait until the mouse cursor turns into a double-headed arrow. Once that happens, click and hold the mouse button while you size the windows according to your needs.

Chapter 24

Ten Windows 2000 Icons and What They Do

· ·

*W*indows 2000 uses different icons to stand for different types of files. That means it's packed with enough icons to befuddle the most experienced iconographer.

Table 24-1 shows pictures of the most common icons you come across in the Windows Explorer and My Computer programs and what the icons are supposed to represent.

Most of them represent *data files* — files created by programs — but we've tossed in a few icons that stand for hardware at the beginning to help you get your bearings.

Table 24-1 Icons in Windows Explorer and My Computer Windows

What It Looks Like	What It Stands For
	3½-inch floppy drive
	Hard disk
	Shared hard disk that's accessible on a network (Any icon with that little hand has been shared and can be used by other people on the network)
	Mapped drive: A folder or drive on another computer that gets a drive letter so your own computer can treat it like one of its own drives
	Shared network file or folder created in My Network Places

(continued)

Table 24-1 *(continued)*

What It Looks Like	*What It Stands For*
	CD-ROM drive
	Folder: A computerized storage area for files
	DOS-based program
	Word-processor file created by WordPad
	Batch file: A collection of DOS commands for the computer to run automatically
	Sound: A recorded sound saved as a WAV file
	Music: A MIDI file containing specially formatted instructions that tell synthesizers or sound cards what sounds to create
	Old-style fonts that are stored in a certain size
	Newer, TrueType fonts that can be easily shrunk or enlarged
	A TrueType Open font that can also be made larger or smaller
	Help files: Contain instructions stored in a special format for the Windows 2000 Help program
	A text file containing technical information, usually special settings for a program

What It Looks Like	*What It Stands For*
	Text; usually created by Notepad
	Bitmap file: Graphics created by Windows 2000 Paint or another graphics program
	GIF: Graphics Interchange Format — frequently used for putting pictures on the Internet
	JPG: Joint Photographic Expert Group, another graphics file format; stores pictures in very small files — looks just like GIF, doesn't it?
	PCX, another graphics file; doesn't stand for anything; TIF (Tagged Image File Format) files look the same
	Scrap: A piece of a document that's been dragged from one program and left on the Desktop for further action (works with WordPad)
	A file that Windows 2000 doesn't think it recognizes

✔ To open one of these files and start working with its contents, double-click on it. If all goes right, Windows 2000 looks at the file's name, grabs the appropriate program, and brings both the file and the program to the screen.

✔ Unfortunately, Windows 2000 judges a book by its cover: It doesn't look *inside* a file to see what information the file contains. Instead, Windows 2000 merely looks at the file's name, particularly the last three letters of the file's name (the extension). If Windows 2000 recognizes those three letters, it assumes that it recognizes the file, and it tosses the file to what it *thinks* is the right program.

The result? Sometimes Windows 2000 uses a familiar icon to represent a file, but because Windows 2000 tosses the file to the wrong program when you double-click on the icon, the file refuses to open.

✔ You'll see a few other icons popping up here and there that don't appear in this chart for several reasons. First, newly installed Windows 2000 programs often come with their own arsenal of icons. Also, My Computer shows some icons that are listed in the Control Panel, so head for Chapter 11's Control Panel chart for the lowdown on those icons.

Glossary

Windows 2000 comes with its own Glossary program. Open the Start menu, choose Help, click on the Contents tab, click on the Glossary icon, and then click on the next Glossary icon.

Plus, the Windows 2000 Help program lets you look up words on the fly: If you spot an unfamiliar word in the Help program — and it's underlined — click on the word, and Windows 2000 defines it for you. (The Help program gets its due in Chapter 21.)

But if Windows 2000 refuses to give you a helping hand, here's a list of some of the more common words you'll encounter.

32-bit: Computers push their information through "pipes." The first IBM PC used eight pipes. The next version, the 286, used 16 pipes. A 386 computer can use 32 pipes, but most programs just shoot their stuff through 16 pipes. For extra speed and power, Windows 2000 uses all 32 pipes at the same time.

account *or* **user account:** When Windows 2000 runs on a *network,* it lets groups of people access files and folders. To keep track of who's using what, Windows 2000 assigns each user an account: a collection of information defining who that person is and what he or she is allowed to access, as well as more frivolous information, like wallpaper preferences. See ***log on/log off.***

Active Directory: A new way of managing folders that administrators get all excited about. Most people won't be able to tell the difference except that searching for things on the network is faster and somewhat easier than in Windows NT.

active window: The last window you clicked on — the one that's currently highlighted — is considered active. Any keys you press affect this window.

address: Name by which the Internet identifies you. The format is *username@hostname,* where username is your user name, logon name, or account number, and hostname is the name of the computer or Internet provider you use. The host name may be a few words strung together with periods.

administrator: The person or people in charge of making the computers work correctly. Administrators set up networks, set up and delete user accounts, and perform other dreadfully thankless tasks. They're also called Network Administrators, System Administrators, or epithets we're not allowed to put in the book.

Apply: Click on an Apply button, and Windows 2000 immediately applies and saves any changes you've made from the current list of options.

background: All the screen area behind the active window. Can also mean a process that is going on someplace other than in the active window.

bitmap: A graphic consisting of bunches of little dots on-screen. The graphic is saved as a bitmap file, which ends with the letters BMP. The Windows 2000 Paint program can create and edit BMP files.

border: The edges of a window; you can move the border in or out to change the window's size.

case-sensitive: A program that knows the difference between uppercase and lowercase letters. For example, a case-sensitive program considers *Pickle* and *pickle* to be two different things.

click: To push and release a button on the mouse.

client: Some computers mainly grab information and process it; other computers mainly spit out information for the first type of computers to process. The grabbers are the clients, which usually run Windows 2000 Professional, Windows 98, or Windows 95. The spitters are the servers, which usually run Windows 2000 Server. See *server.*

Clipboard: A part of Windows 2000 that keeps track of information you've cut or copied from a program or file. It stores that information so you can paste it into other programs.

cursor: The little blinking line that shows where the next letter you type will appear.

default: Choosing the default option enables you to avoid making a decision. The *default option* is the one that the computer chooses for you when you give up and just press Enter. Default options are usually highlighted and ready to run.

Desktop: The area on your screen where you move windows and icons around. Most people cover the Desktop with *wallpaper* — a pretty picture.

dialog box: A window that opens to ask you boring questions or request input. Windows 2000 and Windows-based programs in general are knee-deep in dialog boxes.

directory: A distinct location on a hard disk for storing files. Storing related files in a directory makes them easier to find. Windows 2000 no longer uses the word directory; it prefers the word *folder.* See *folder.*

document: A file containing information such as text, sound, or graphics. Documents are created or changed from within programs. See *program.*

domain: The basic unit of a Windows 2000 client/server network. In its simplest form, the domain consists of a server and a couple of workstations that share a common user database and security policy. Not the same as an Internet domain. See ***domain name.***

domain name: A unique name that identifies an Internet site. A given machine may have more than one domain name, but a given domain name points to only one machine. It's also possible for a domain name to exist but not be connected to an actual machine. This is often done so that a group or business can have an Internet e-mail address without having to establish a real Internet site. In these cases, an Internet service provider's machine must handle the mail on behalf of the listed domain name.

DOS: Short for Disk Operating System. An older operating system for running programs. Windows 2000 can run programs designed for DOS as well as programs designed for Windows. See ***operating system.***

double-click: Pushing and releasing the left mouse button twice in rapid succession. (Double-clicking the *right* mouse button doesn't do anything special.) See ***click*** and ***drag.***

drag: A four-step mouse process that moves an object across your Desktop. First, point at the object — an icon, a highlighted paragraph, or something similar. Second, press and hold your left mouse button. Third, point the mouse arrow at the location to which you'd like to move that object. Fourth, release the mouse button. The object is "dragged" to its new location.

drop: Step four of the *drag* technique (see ***drag***). Dropping is merely letting go of the mouse button and letting your object fall onto something else, be it a new window, folder, or area on your Desktop.

DRV: A file ending in DRV usually lets Windows talk to computer gizmos such as video cards, sound cards, CD-ROM drives, and other stuff. (DRV is short for *driver.*)

FAT: An acronym for File Allocation Table, the file system type used by DOS and Windows and one of the file system types recognized by Windows 2000.

file: A collection of information in a format designed for computer use.

firewall: A protective filter for messages and logons. An organization connected directly to the Internet uses a firewall to prevent unauthorized access into their network.

folder: An area for storing files to keep them organized. (Formerly called a *directory.*) Folders can contain other folders, for further organization. See ***subfolder.***

highlighted: A selected item. A different color usually appears over a highlighted object to show that it's been singled out for further action.

icon: The little picture that represents an object — a program, file, or command — making that object's function easier to figure out.

INI: Short for *initialization*. INI usually hangs on the ends of files that contain special system settings. They're for the computer to mess with, not users.

Internet: A global network of computers connected by telephone. Currently, people use Web browsing software to connect to the World Wide Web, where they find information ranging from Duracell battery advertisements to up-to-the-minute charts listing the latest locations of earthquakes. Windows 2000 comes with Internet Explorer software for connecting to the Internet's World Wide Web. (See Chapter 16.)

intranet: A network using the same "language" as the World Wide Web but restricted for use inside a company. Employees may use Internet Explorer to read a corporate newsletter, for example. See *network*.

IRC (Internet Relay Chat): A system that enables Internet users to talk with each other in real time over the Internet.

log on/log off: By typing a password into a computer, you (the user) can access your user account and start working on Windows 2000. Then by logging off, you can temporarily shut down your user account. The point? Logging on and off a computer with a password keeps a system more secure — nobody can use another person's user account to do something sneaky. See *account or user account.*

maximize: The act of making a window fill the entire screen. You can maximize a window by double-clicking on its title bar — that long strip across its very top. Or you can click on its Maximize button — that button with the big square inside, located near the window's upper-right corner. See *minimize.*

memory: The stuff computers use to store on-the-fly calculations while running. The more memory that's stuffed inside your computer, the better it runs. (Windows 2000 needs at *least* 16MB of memory.) See Chapter 2 for more memory madness.

minimize: The act of shrinking a window down to a tiny icon to temporarily get it out of the way. To minimize a window, click on the Minimize button — that button with the little horizontal bar on it, located near the window's upper-right corner. See *maximize.*

multitasking: Running several different programs simultaneously.

network: Connecting computers with cables so that people can share information without getting up. Also used to refer to the collection of computers that are linked together.

newsgroup: On the Internet, a distributed bulletin-board system about a particular topic. Usenet News (also known as Netnews) is a system that distributes thousands of newsgroups to all parts of the Internet.

NTFS (New Technology File System): The preferred file system for Windows 2000. Supports long filenames, a variety of permissions for sharing files, and a transaction log that allows Windows 2000 to finish any incomplete file-related tasks if the operating system is interrupted.

operating system: Software that controls how a computer does its most basic stuff: storing files, talking to printers, and performing other gut-level operations. DOS, Windows 95, Windows 98, and Windows 2000 are all operating systems.

password: The secret code you type into a computer while logging on to access your user account (provided you can remember your username). See *username* and *account or user account.*

path: A sentence of computerese that tells a computer the precise name and location of a file.

Peer-to-peer: A type of network in which computers can communicate without an intermediary device. On a peer-to-peer network, a computer can be both a client and a server.

Plug and Play: A set of rules developed by Intel and now widely adopted. When everyone obeys the rules, the computer automatically detects and installs new hardware such as modems and printers.

program: Something that lets you work on the computer: Spreadsheets, word processors, and games are *programs*. See *document.*

protocol: A set of rules that determines how computers talk to each other. Computers on a network all have to agree on the protocol they're using, or communication breaks down completely. See *network.*

RAM: Random-Access Memory. See *memory.*

remote access service: Allows users to dial in from remote locations and access networks for files, e-mail, printing, and databases.

scrap: When you highlight some text or graphics from a program, drag the chunk to the Desktop, and drop it, you create an official Windows 2000 *scrap* — a file containing a copy of that information. You can save the scrap or drag it into other programs. See *drag.*

server: The backbone of a network. A comparatively large computer set up to deliver large amounts of information to other computers on the network. See *client, Windows 2000 Professional,* and *Windows 2000 Server.*

shortcut: A Windows 2000 icon that serves as a push-button for doing something — loading a file, starting a program, or playing a sound, for example. A shortcut icon has a little arrow in its bottom corner so you can tell it apart from the icon that *really* stands for the file or program.

shortcut button: A button in a Help menu that takes you directly to an area that can solve your problem.

shortcut key: As opposed to a shortcut (see *shortcut*), a shortcut key is an underlined letter in a program's menu that lets you work with the keyboard instead of the mouse. For example, if you see the word Help on a menu bar, the underlined H means you can get help by pressing Alt+H.

Shut Down: The process of telling Windows 2000 to save all its settings and files so that you can turn off your computer. You must choose the Shut Down option, found on the Start menu, before turning off your computer.

Start button: See *Start menu.*

Start menu: A menu of options that appears when you click on the Start button (located on the taskbar). From the Start menu, you can load programs and files, change settings, find programs, find help, and shut down your computer so you can turn it off.

subfolder: A folder within a folder, used to further organize files. (Also called a *subdirectory*.) For example, a Junkfood folder may contain subfolders for Chips, Peanuts, and Pretzels. (A Celery subfolder would be empty.) See *folder*.

taskbar: The bar in Windows 2000 that lists all currently running programs and open folders. The Start button lives on one end of the taskbar.

TCP/IP (Transmission Control Protocol/Internet Protocol): The *protocol* that networks use to communicate with each other on the Internet.

URL (Uniform Resource Locator): The standard way to give the address of any resource on the Internet that is part of the World Wide Web. This is an example of a URL: `www.dummies.com/index.htm`. The most common way to use a URL is to type it into a Web browser program such as Microsoft Internet Explorer.

username: The name you type into a computer while logging on to access your user account. (Then you type your password and hope you remembered both correctly.) See *password* and *account or user account.*

VGA: A popular standard for displaying information on monitors in certain colors and resolutions. VGA has been replaced by SVGA — Super VGA — that can display even more colors and even finer resolution.

virtual: A trendy word to describe computer simulations. Commonly used to describe things that *look* real but aren't really there. For example, when Windows 2000 uses *virtual memory,* it's using part of the hard disk for memory, not the actual memory chips.

wallpaper: Graphics spread across the background of your computer screen. The Windows 2000 Control Panel lets you choose among different wallpaper files.

window: An on-screen box that contains information for you to look at or work with. Programs run in *windows* on your screen.

Windows 2000 Professional: Windows 2000 comes in two versions. This is the client version, although it works fine for networking about ten computers. See *client, server,* and *Windows 2000 Server.*

Windows 2000 Server: Windows 2000 comes in two versions. This server version is also a network operating system. See *client, server,* and *Windows 2000 Professional.*

Index

• E •

• J •

• K •

• U •

Notes

Notes

Notes

Notes

Discover Dummies Online!

The Dummies Web Site is your fun and friendly online resource for the latest information about *For Dummies* books and your favorite topics. The Web site is the place to communicate with us, exchange ideas with other *For Dummies* readers, chat with authors, and have fun!

Ten Fun and Useful Things You Can Do at www.dummies.com

1. Win free *For Dummies* books and more!
2. Register your book and be entered in a prize drawing.
3. Meet your favorite authors through the Hungry Minds Author Chat Series.
4. Exchange helpful information with other *For Dummies* readers.
5. Discover other great *For Dummies* books you must have!
6. Purchase Dummieswear exclusively from our Web site.
7. Buy *For Dummies* books online.
8. Talk to us. Make comments, ask questions, get answers!
9. Download free software.
10. Find additional useful resources from authors.

Link directly to these ten fun and useful things at **http://www.dummies.com/10useful**

For other technology titles from Hungry Minds, go to
www.hungryminds.com

Not on the Web yet? It's easy to get started with *Dummies 101®: The Internet For Windows® 98* or *The Internet For Dummies®* at local retailers everywhere.

Find other *For Dummies* books on these topics:
Business • Career • Databases • Food & Beverage • Games • Gardening
Graphics • Hardware • Health & Fitness • Internet and the World Wide Web
Networking • Office Suites • Operating Systems • Personal Finance • Pets
Programming • Recreation • Sports • Spreadsheets • Teacher Resources
Test Prep • Word Processing

FOR DUMMIES
BOOK REGISTRATION

We want to hear from you!

Visit **dummies.com** to register this book and tell us how you liked it!

✔ Get entered in our monthly prize giveaway.

✔ Give us feedback about this book — tell us what you like best, what you like least, or maybe what you'd like to ask the author and us to change!

✔ Let us know any other *For Dummies* topics that interest you.

Your feedback helps us determine what books to publish, tells us what coverage to add as we revise our books, and lets us know whether we're meeting your needs as a *For Dummies* reader. You're our most valuable resource, and what you have to say is important to us!

Not on the Web yet? It's easy to get started with *Dummies 101®: The Internet For Windows® 98* or *The Internet For Dummies®* at local retailers everywhere.

Or let us know what you think by sending us a letter at the following address:

For Dummies Book Registration
Dummies Press
10475 Crosspoint Blvd.
Indianapolis, IN 46256

BESTSELLING
BOOK SERIES